Practice Makes Practice

Practice Makes Practice

A Critical Study of Learning to Teach,
Revised Edition

Deborah P. Britzman

State University of New York Press

Published by
State University of New York Press, Albany

For information, address the State University of New York Press,
90 State Street, Suite 700, Albany, NY 12207

Production by Michael Haggett
Marketing by Fran Keneston

Library of Congress Cataloging-in-Publication Data

Britzman, Deborah P., 1952–
    Practice makes practice : a critical study of learning to teach / Deborah P.
Britzman. — Rev. ed.
        p. cm. — (SUNY series teacher empowerment and school reform)
    Includes bibliographical references and index.
    ISBN 0-7914-5849-0 (alk. paper) — ISBN 0-7914-5850-4 (pbk. : alk. paper)
    1. High school teachers—Training of—United States.   2. Student teaching—
United States.   I. Title.   II. Teacher empowerment and school reform.

LB1715.B73 2003
373.1102—dc21   2002044798

10 9 8 7 6 5 4 3 2 1

For my mother Alice J. Lerman

Contents

Foreword

Centering on the lived experiences of student teachers, this book sends out rays of surprising light towards the enterprise of teacher education today. Doing so, it transfigures what is often conceived of as a nesting of commonplaces. We are made witness to the drama, indeed the *agon*, of human beings constructing their identities as teachers in situations marked by tension between what seems given or inalterable and what may be perceived as possibility.

Deborah Britzman is a critical ethnographer and a scholar of discourse and literature. At once, she is a person who is herself in process. Through a wonderfully accessible language of her own, she makes herself present in these pages as observer, critic, questioner, listener, and co-learner with the student teachers she describes. Because she herself is so atuned to the polyphony in the schools and the surrounding culture, to what Mikhail Bakhtin called the "heteroglossia" that has so much to do with our becoming, she is able to avoid the authoritative voice. She engages her readers in an ongoing dialogue about how *we* choose to be together and, in our emergent communities, resist passivity and injustice as we learn what it is to teach.

This is the kind of open text that will not permit closure, even on the part of those of us who come to it. We cannot read many pages and assert that we *know* what it signifies to make meaning and to relate to the world around, to what we "read" as real. It follows that we cannot summon up comfortable answers to questions having to do with the contest between what the technological society demands of its teachers and the personal visions of those teachers, their often repressed notions of what is desirable and what ought to be. Nor can we easily resolve the conflicts that arise when teachers confront what they recognize as privileged knowledge based on relations of power in the silent awareness that there are alternative ways of knowing and seeing that might allow for what this author calls "internally persuasive discourse." Engaging with her interpretations of teachers trying to break with subject/object separations, trying to reposition themselves with regard to what belittles and constrains, we find our own horizons being modified. The accounts of people's changing relationships to one another, to language and to power, may lead to new events in our own understanding. There is no final solution; there is no packageable remedy. There is only more and more critical reading of the texts of action, the texts of practice, the texts of learning to learn.

We are provoked, by means of such reading, to recover some of what we have known about George Counts and John Dewey and their efforts to break with the formalist and conforming traditions in teacher education. Then we are brought forward to confront the critical accounts of curriculum, canon, and controls associated with such people as Henry Giroux, Linda McNeil, Jean Clandinin, Madeleine Grumet, and other proponents of perspectivism, multiplicity, and creative resistance. There follow, with peculiar appropriateness, the narratives of student teaching: Jamie Owl's and Jack August's stories.

Knowing well how difficult it is to represent others' accounts of their lived experiences (and the connection between those accounts and what is actually lived), Deborah Britzman presents narratives of unusual complexity and depth. There is a sense of the unspoken underlying what is spoken; there is, in both cases, a difficult coming to terms with biography and previous education, with the pursuit of meanings, with theory and authoritative discourse and the odd isolation of the teaching role. Jamie and Jack are distinctive personalities; there is the quality of good fiction in parts of their stories. What readers may find most challenging, however, is the way in which both of them render problematic conventional notions having to do with the teacher as autonomous, the teacher as knowledge-bearer, the teacher as responsible for covering the material, the teacher as the embodiment of assurance and stability. Suddenly we see the student teacher as contextualized and in relation to a variety of significant others: children, supervising teachers, university professors, school administrators, community people, and figures in the foreground and background, many of them emerging from the lived past. We see the student teacher against the screens of the "reform" reports, the corporate talk, the political language; and we become conscious of the great differences among the student teachers and the range of difference when it comes to definitions of teaching and learning as they are presented, and as they are variously grasped.

At the end of what cannot but be an adventure into meaning, readers may find themselves posing questions about teacher education that seem fresh and new. They may be questions about the relation between pedagogy and experience, about the grounding of pedagogical responses in discursive practices, about critical thinking and participatory learning, about expertise and individuality. Climactically, they may become questions about the meaning of dialogic understanding; they may become questions about open possibilities. This book will make the life of the educator harder and more tonic;

it will urge the reader to confront the contradictory and the tension. But it will also disclose the unexpected. Education will be viewed as if, after all, it can be otherwise.

Maxine Greene
Teachers College
Columbia University

Acknowledgments

I am grateful to Priscilla Ross, Director at the State University of New York Press for suggesting that *Practice Makes Practice* become a revised edition. While it can seem as if a great deal has changed for those entering teacher education, in revising this study I came to believe that the persistent dilemmas and existential angst of learning to teach continue to require our attention and acknowledgment. Indeed, over the years, readers have remained interested in understanding experience in education from its flaws, accidents, and misconceptions; they seem to take solace in the view that learning to teach is not so much a problem of success or failure as it is one of constructing understanding and psychological significance. Learning to teach is a time when newcomers glimpse the magnitude of uncertainty in education. Narrating this difficult encounter as a problem of language is perhaps what this present study does best.

Chapter Seven originally appeared in earlier form in the *International Journal of Qualitative Studies in Education* (1995) 8 (3), 229–38.

Introduction to Revised Edition

That the education of teachers has become one of the great anxieties of the Twentieth Century follows on the heels of mandating education as compulsory and universal and so qualifying education to be a mass experience. Our present study begins within the fissures of this social fact to explore the persistent dilemmas made and found by those learning to teach. We will see how the circumstances of education as a mass experience haunts both the history of teacher education and the experiences of those who live there. And these ghosts are not new; readers have met them before as children. Two tensions should be held in mind. First, because teachers were once students in compulsory education, their sense of the teacher's world is strangely established before they begin learning to teach. We enter teacher education with our school biography. Teaching is one of the few professions where newcomers feel the force of their own history of learning as if it telegraphs relevancy to their work. Second, over-familiarity animates the fantasy that no one can teach anyone to become a teacher; each must learn his or her own way. Theoretical knowledge of teaching is not easily valued and school biography matters too much.

Mass experience, however, is not the same thing as mass production so the problem is not that everyone must go to school. After all, we are not making widgets but investigating how learning a profession occurs. We are interested in how this particular mass experience makes for some common anxieties and how these anxieties structure the language of teacher education. While schooling composes intimate histories of learning of varying kinds and types there is also a great population divide: those who have made it through and those who, for whatever reason, have been left behind. Our skeletal depiction suggests that more often than not, to know education is to be able to measure it as success or failure and so reduce educational experience to an authoritative order of compliance and noncompliance. As we will see over the course of this present study, understanding the experience of having to be educated and then trying to learn how to educate others is far more complex, ambiguous, and paradoxical than supposed in the reigning binary split of success and failure and the rigid notions of authority and control that follow. Learning is never so cut and dried, even if the structure of schooling is organized to belie the belatedness of learning. Indeed, for the learner and the teacher, what counts as success and failure is subject to wild vacillations and, so, to revision. Mistakes, misrepresentations, confusion, conflicts, and little gifts of error are all crucial to the stuff of understanding and constructing knowledge, as are the small and large adjustments and insights we make from these events. And the oddest conditions and circumstances of *not learning*, it will turn out, will be extremely significant to the matter of who we think we are as we become subjected to and subjects in education.

The mass experience of schooling composes another dimension: a second chance for those who return, not as required by law, but as inspired by way of trying to learn the contours and loopholes of a profession. If one tries to undo one's own school biography through becoming the teacher one wished for as a child one is still likely to meet an old, disappointed version of the self. To enter the profession of teaching means one must work thought these wishes in order to recognize students who are not and need not mirror the teacher's educational regrets or achievements. And because we grow up in school, part of this second chance involves separating authority from our fantasies of it. The new preoccupation is with how others learn, what learning means for them, and what one's efforts as a teacher have to do with that. Then, when the directions of education, knowledge, authority, and power become entangled with the scenery of self and other learning, the script of the teacher's school biography becomes relational. New thoughts are crafted from one's efforts in trying to think about becoming a teacher and feeling one's way through the organization of school structure and its imperatives, even as one tries to represent these. New identities spring from the fact that teachers need students as much as students need them. But this raises new problems of dependency and vulnerability for life in classrooms.

The difficulty then, comes from at least two directions. Teachers bring to their work their own idiomatic school biography, the conflicted history of their own deep investments in and ambivalence about what a teacher is and does, and likewise they anticipate their dreams of students, their hopes for colleagues, and their fantasies for recognition and learning. With each new teacher a student meets, the student also encounters her or his own history of learning. The teacher's work brings new and conflictive demands that well exceed the resources of her or his school biography. If the original pulls of judging learning from the confines of success and failure become frayed by the contingencies of educating others, an unexpected pressure emerges: figuring the significance of the contradictory realities of and competing perspectives on learning to teach and becoming a teacher. As we will see, there is a disjunction between these two experiences. One of the great surprises is just how conflictive the work of teaching feels, but also there is an anxiety that seems to emanate from the very structure of school organization: without being consciously taught the newly arrived teacher has to grapple with the belief that before the students can learn, the teacher must control the class. Conflict threatens to overturn the teacher's authority before it is even established. And here we confront a key paradox in learning to teach: there can be no learning without conflict, but the conflict that animates learning threatens to derail the precarious efforts of trying to learn. Our present study attempts to narrate this incomplete history.

Suddenly, teachers are confronted with a difficult existential truth about education rarely discussed and, more often than not, actively avoided: trying to teach is deeply unsettling and conflictive because experience itself—what is called in this present study, "practice"—is a paradox, an unanticipated social relation, and a problem of interpretation. Practice here falls somewhere between a dress rehearsal and a daily performance. It is sometimes a real event, or only its anticipation. But it also reaches into thinking about what has happened or what did not happen. Practice raises and accumulates myriad doubts and makes intimate the question of the teacher's authority. From these doubts come cycles of self-blame and an overblown sense of control that runs from the ridiculous to the sublime. Teachers feel an inordinate responsibility to single-handedly make students learn while they wonder how students are affecting and influencing them. They hope there is a direct relation between teaching and learning. More often than not, this wish feels spoiled. The practice of teaching, because it is concocted from relations with others and occurs in structures that are not of one's own making is, first and foremost, an uncertain experience that one must learn to interpret and make significant. The surprising force of uncertainty in education and the myriad ways in which it is repressed, denied and inexplicably returned is one grand theme of this present study. Representing this uncertainty from the available discourses of education and confronting the army of doubts that follow is another theme. I characterize this residue of representation as, "a struggle for voice," because the tensions of experience are lost and found in language and touch the deepest recesses of the self.

These bare observations can do justice neither to the surprising range of mistakes and misunderstandings learning and having to convey it to others leave scattered along the way nor to the pressures of having to act before one understands the consequences of the choices made. Nor can this happenstance make sense of the accrued and at times persecuting memories made from the condensations of simply having to be in school while one waits to grow up and then returns there as an adult. If, at times, education feels like a holding pen, a place of preparation, a timeless presence, a spectacular promise or betrayal, and a hot house of experience; if education can feel like that and become associated with all these things, this is only to say that it is difficult to extricate ourselves from the story of how we narrate the autobiography of experience in education. Indeed, if we are now used to speaking of experience as something we learn from, as an indicator that gauges the currency of our actions and its consequences or as a stamp of authority, if we speak now of experience as that great cure for inexperience and for having to learn in order to now avoid repeating one's history of mistakes, this habit is cultivated most exquisitely in the very place we call schooling. There, we first encounter that mantra, "we learn from experience," as if this can settle the matter. And yet it is in school where learning is demanded to matter in very particular ways, where schooling and education may be felt as synonymous, and where learning is thought to anchor experience, practicality, and relevance to the artifice of the school curriculum and now, to the testing industry. And this mantra returns with exaggerated and at times tyrannical force to the field of teacher education: practice makes perfect. The large issue our study considers runs contrary to this exhausting demand.

If this depiction of idealized experience seems too naive, it cannot be easily dissuaded. In the idealized story of learning to teach, classroom experience guarantees the teacher's continuity and progress. And while, of course, familiarity with the teacher's work does matter, it is not a direct line to insight. For the newcomer, more is at stake because he or she already feels the teacher's work as uncannily familiar and utterly strange. In the daily work of learning to teach, experience in education feels discontinuous, disjointed, fragmented, and alienating. Much about the experience of learning to teach is negative: learning what to avoid, what not to do, and what not to become even as one finds oneself performing these disclaimed actions. Oftentimes, student teachers feel split between identification with the teacher's role and disassociation from the teacher's function as authority. It is from this contradiction of wanting to become a teacher but not necessarily wanting to step into the role of a cruel authority figure that one crafts what will become in retrospect, a teacher's identity. These processes of projection, identification, and disassociation, partly render teaching its emotional flavor. The other part, of course, is that becoming a teacher in a classroom is a personal matter. And it can feel as if experience itself is a crisis.

We are approaching a second a second theme of this present study: how experience is structured, the ways it is used, and how practice requires second thoughts. These second thoughts are called throughout this study, "theory." And yet this view that theory can and should matter to how one thinks about the tensions in one's word is highly debated in teacher education. One of the great complaints we will meet in this study is that university-based teacher education is too theoretical and abstract to be of use in the real world of classrooms. How it is that practice and a school classroom become affixed to reality while theory and university courses become relegated to ideals is a part of what this complaint covers over. The issue, however, is more complex. It spans the very different cultures of the university and compulsory education. And teacher education has one foot in each world. If schools depend upon the great divide between success and failure, then teacher education fills this gap with classroom practice as the royal road to success. This also means that university theory comes to be dreaded as the dead-end.

So far, we have been considering a small world of teacher education. Beyond the confines of the school walls and the educational biographies mustered there, we can also observe a great deal of pressure to define the politics of education. This, too, affects the social imaginary, or the dreams, structures, and narrative styles of newcomers. The politics of education allow us to conceive how the preparation of teachers and their continuing education is recognized and contested.[1] On the one side, education is considered a human right and so is associated with the possibilities for social justice, social change, and self and cultural transformation. This is because educational attainment and sophistication with literacy are related to one's life chances and to the capacity to participate in civic life. When joined to the imperatives of social transformation, those entering teacher education are often seen and see themselves as social change agents, as critical, and as ready to change school culture and its curriculum. The newly arrived, in this view, bring not just fresh ideas, experimentation, and revitalization to those already there, but also important critiques of education and its transmission models. On the other side, education is considered in more conservative terms. Education is used to promote national unity and uniformity, protect respect for authority, and serve as a common mechanism for the preservation of traditions and their continuity. When joined to conservative agendas, teacher education is likely to emphasize the acquisition of stable knowledge, skill-based teaching, and curriculum practices that are accountable to the teaching of the basics. Whether known as the culture wars or the reading wars, matters of instruction turn the conservative agenda. Those already in school, then, are viewed as teaching the newcomers the "ropes" as beginners make that transition from the student's world to the teacher's work. Regardless of the emphasis, both critical and conservative views on the education of teachers tend to see the transition from student to teacher as seamless.

When *Practice Makes Practice* was first published, this was the great dualism: education and, so, teachers as well, were either in the service of critical pedagogy or the state apparatus. And yet, splitting the world of education into progressive or regressive tendencies, just as splitting education into success and failure, does not do justice to the surprising forces of uncertainty, discontentment, helplessness, and disorganization that are also education. Nor does this dichotomy make a place for pleasure, laughter, and the absurdities that also enliven our educational stagings. Changing education, whether it is the transformation of people and changing their minds, or the introduction of new knowledge and perspectives to the curriculum, is more difficult than we imagined.[2] It is just as difficult to anticipate how one is also changed by having to be educated and then trying to educate others and how knowledge is transformed by classroom life. If our afterthoughts lend needed significance to this uncertainty, the immediacy of classroom life threatens to unravel efforts to be thoughtful.

From whatever vantage, then, the screen of education invites public and private projections of dreams for knowledge to make life good, even if we cannot agree as to what makes life worth living. Indeed, there is a terrific social pressure on education to matter—to do its work well—even if we cannot agree on what specifically this can mean. But when education is perceived of as not working—again, there may be terrific arguments over what is broken and what needs fixing—the efforts of teachers and their education is suspected as contributing to the breakdown of meaning and so to the fissures of authority in education. This pressure, what an early critic of education saw as the consequences of the public caught between "a tolerance for the ideas of education [and] a resolute and cold disbelief in its programs, means, and promises,"extends from teachers about to retire to those just beginning to try out the profession.[3] It is also an historic pressure within the field of teacher education and its apprenticeship model: theoretically, it is a good idea, practically, it seems unworkable. Yet it is also difficult to figure out what public incredulity toward the profession can mean, particularly because the public was also subject to the very education it now criticizes. Perhaps the best we can say is that what makes the field of education so contentious and unique, compared to other professions, is that everyone can feel like an expert.

There is, however, no single road to becoming a teacher or to critiquing its currency. Nor is there a single story of learning to teach. There are, however, some shared persistent dilemmas, contradictory realities, and common narratives that the newly arrived personally confront and internalize as their own. From this confrontation, we can assume some familiar themes made from that strange and volatile combination of school biography, school structure, and the desires of wanting to become a teacher but not yet knowing in advance what precisely this entails. These themes are called, in this present study, "cultural myths." They all revolve around and organize ideal notions of the autonomous and competitive individual and provide a narrative of standards that render irrelevant arguments for other ways of becoming a teacher.

Cultural myths narrate a heroic story of a self-made profession that can rise above beleaguered education. In doing so, they banish from consideration the isolation of teachers, the dependency and vulnerability teaching accrues, and the problems of knowledge teachers are supposed to possess. And it is no coincidence that these myths flourish in secondary education where the newly arrived may not be much older than the students they try to teach, where adolescents express their desire to make up their own minds despite the teacher's efforts, and where teachers are supposed to be experts in their subjects. In secondary education, where our present study occurs, cultural myths serve as a kind of defense mechanism for teachers. Each myth distorts the social sense and institutional context of learning to teach, the constructed qualities of knowledge, and the ambivalence made from relations of power. Three cultural myths are discussed: everything depends upon the teacher, teachers are self made, and teachers are experts. They situate the teacher's individuality as the problem and proffer a static solution of authority, control, mastery, and certainty as the proper position. They seem to explain competency as the absence of conflict.

EDUCATION AND CRISIS

There are other ways to consider our modern dilemma of teacher education. An early attempt was made with William James's *Talks to Teachers on Psychology*, written between 1891–1898.[4] A hint of his approach can be found in the subtitle to these lectures: "and to students on some of life's ideals." For we find in this subtitle the hopes for an audience and the dreams of education. James appended to his talks a series of lectures just for students. One lecture titled, "What makes life significant?" joined education with a search for meaning, what James also saw as the problem of constituting psychological significance, where meaning becomes something that matters to how one's life is lived and narrated. James was concerned with the individual's psychology, and he saw this psychology as an allegory for larger social processes, including what we can think of as a psychology of teaching. In this particular lecture, James considered the problem of tolerance, or what it can mean to encounter something not understood or unintelligible to the viewer without the viewer's recourse to foreclosing the conflict this can entail. How do we make our responses to not understanding "less chaotic?"[5] James found his answer in the course of ideals, the key one being what he called "non-interference" or the teacher's allowance for the unanticipated ways we do participate in and learn from life. Such an idyllic ideal is difficult in a place called school, for after all, having to learn does feel like one is being interfered with and the teacher's anticipation is the grounds for making learning objectives, lesson plans, and evaluation, all familiar features of the teacher's work.

James's allowance of non-interference bumps up against a particular feature of education discussed most forcefully, more than thirty years later, by Anna Freud in her lectures to parents and teachers: education is composed from all types of interference.[6] Like those who came before her, for instance Rousseau and Kant, Miss Freud dates education from the beginning of life. She is not very far from the philosopher Immanuel Kant's much earlier Eighteenth Century insistence in his lectures on pedagogy: "Man is the only being who needs education" and Rousseau's moral pedagogy: "We are born capable of learning but able to do nothing, knowing nothing."[7] Anna Freud, however, is also opening another perspective: education begins in individuals, it is not just something done to them. For Kant and Rousseau that first education is largely negative but it is also both the source of progress and the reservoir of inhibition. But whereas for Kant, the problem of education resides in the teacher's decision as to which ideals are necessary to teach, for Anna Freud, the problem begins in the very relation—both possible and given—between teacher and student and parent and child. These relations are qualified by the push and pull of dependency and autonomy, immaturity and maturity, and mutual interference and influence. Essentially, individuals must interfere with one another because having to learn and having to teach is felt as interference, as a battle of wills, and as a confluence of influence. Paradoxically, significance, or better, education, is made from this conflict. And this conflict, which feels like a crisis of the self, is the heart of this present study of learning to teach.

In the middle of the Twentieth Century, social theorists were describing education as a crisis. When the critical theorist Theodor Adorno considered the historical devastations of World War II, insisting that even language is a catastrophe, he asked the question, what is the responsibility of educators after Auschwitz?[8] While William James raised the question of what makes life significant in education, Adorno turned this question on its head: how does thinking become a significant responsibility? Adorno was charged with examining secondary history teachers in postwar Germany. While these beginning teachers could recall the names and dates of historical events, they did not view these events as transforming their present and the reach of their educational responsibilities. How does it happen that catastrophic history is so easily forgotten, or reduced to an answer to a question on a test? Unlike contemporary discussions of historical amnesia, Adorno believed that knowledge itself, in a place called education, became irrelevant. This, for him, was the crisis of education.

Adorno's contemporary, Hannah Arendt, used the term crisis in the ordinary sense: as a conflict of continuity and difference.[9] Like those before her, she, too, describes education from "the fact of natality," that we are born into the world, and that we require the care of others. It is a fact that includes the tensions of welcoming new generations into the world with the hopes of those already there. Education was, for Arendt, an ordinary crisis but one made severe and grotesque through benign neglect of the vulnerability that education also represents. For there, part of the work of the teacher consists in creating the conditions for the young to learn traditions and histories that are not of their own making but that they are expected to continue. Yet this burden can be overbearing, leaving little room for the new generation to create their own sense of life's becoming. Arendt views the problem thusly: "For education belongs among the most elementary and necessary activities of human society, which never remains as it is but continuously renews itself through birth through the arrival of new human beings. These newcomers, moreover are not finished but in a state of becoming."[10] We will see this conflict played out in the world of teacher education, even if all too often the profession forgets that student teachers are in a state of becoming and instead, and to the detriment of the newly arrived, considers them as a social measuring device for the currency and effectiveness of their education.

By the end of the Twentieth Century and continuing with Adorno's and Arendt's preoccupation, the term crisis continued to be centered in discussions of education. Maxine Greene would write of "the matter of mystification" in teacher education, and describe the problem as one of "challenging what is taken for granted and transmitted as taken-for-granted: ideas of hierarchy, of deserved deficits, of delayed gratification, and of mechanical time schemes in tension with inner time."[11] The crisis here is one of quietism for both teachers and students, a fear of ideas, and a fear of questioning knowledge. From a different vantage, Shoshona Felman argued that there can be no education without crisis for two reasons.[12] First, because education is a part of our world it registers, it is affected by crisis and the crisis that it is. Second, Felman insists that meaningful learning begins in the scramble to make sense of the force of knowledge. Significant learning, she suggests, is first felt as a threat and a surprise. This is particularly the case at the end of the Twentieth Century, a century that ushered in new and terrifying words for events like "genocide," "holocaust," and "ethnic cleansing." To think about the relation between crisis and teaching is for Felman part of an obligation for teaching itself. And so she asked a question that called into account the relation between learning and not learning: "In a post-traumatic century, a century that has survived unthinkable historical catastrophes, is there anything that we have learned or that we should learn about education that we did not know before?"[13] In doing that, learning and crises become interminable and the work of the teacher, to return to James's earlier view, is to help students enter from the ruins of crisis, a renewed sense of and tolerance for significance and meaning. We have come full circle. If learning to teach wavers on this precipice of meaning—of making sense of both personal and historical crisis—this is very difficult work, far more complex than the measures we have made. Indeed, the very measures for success and failure in learning shut out the existential crisis that allows the newly arrived their chance in becoming.

Narrative and Voice

Here, then, are the grand terms of this study: crisis, the antimony of experience, the dread of vulnerability and uncertainty, and the existential problems of dependency, autonomy, and, creativity in learning to teach. I offer these different pressures as illustrative of a struggle for voice, but they are emblematic, more generally, of a problem of narrative. To learn to teach is also to tell a story of what learning to teach "does" to and for student teachers. In this effort, the narrative impulse bumps up against the work of not quite knowing if the story can do justice to the emotional experience of learning itself. My orientation to narrative draws its force from literary models. There, all we have is language. Think of the way Tolstoy begins his novel, *Anna Karenina*: "All happy families are alike; each unhappy family is unhappy in its own way."[14] And consider the work this sets for the reader. Listening to those who are learning to teach is like reading a novel, and the reader does not only read between the lines, but also within the lines of thought. Perhaps there should be a warning: the story of learning to teach may not be the one that is expected. In residing with the hesitations of experience our study follows those inevitable stumblings of a profession and how those who live in that world make sense of their detours of experience.

Readers will soon enter very particular worlds of two student teachers, Jamie Owl and Jack August and their chronology of despair and hope in trying to learn to teach in public secondary high schools. They will also meet those who surround them, professionals the research literature calls, without irony, "significant others." These others express their discontentment with how it is the university prepares student teachers for their schools. At times, they may describe student teachers as "accidents waiting to happen." Many narrate their disappointment with newcomers and in doing so must also recall their own fragile biography of learning to teach. Some will blame theory and judge university course work in education as pretentious, useless, and idealistic. For others, the problem is with the student teacher who seems to be a wrong-headed idealist or cannot control a tendency to over-identify with the plight of her or his students and, consequently, under-identify with the authority of the school. Still others will try to be affected by the newly arrived, take them in as confidantes of their secrets, or even try to warn them of the emotional risks to avoid. They will counsel them to just finish student teaching. And they will promise that after student teaching is over, they can become real teachers. These significant others desire student teachers to identify with the teacher's world but some believe that it is not often helpful to dwell in the unsuccessful lesson, the missed opportunity, or the regrets that occur along the way of not knowing what to do. Still others will pretend to leave the student teacher alone, believing in the theory that one learns to teach through trial by fire, or sink or swim. Many will see classroom teaching as the ultimate test of being able to tolerate a teacher's reality, while for others, including those leaning to teach, practice teaching will be relegated to the artificial and idealized world of the student teacher. If to listen to the significant others is to be struck by their complaint that teacher education does not prepare students for school reality, even if they are at a loss as to how anyone prepares for the radical uncertainty that is daily life in schools, to listen to those learning to teach means to confront uncertainty, constraints, and the desires for invention. Student teaching, for the student teacher, is constraining. One feels like a guest in someone else's classroom and if one learns what not to do when one becomes a real teacher, this also seems to sustain the misperception that no one can teach anyone how to teach, each must learn it herself.

All of these characters will play out, sometimes awkwardly and some-times exquisitely, sometimes consciously, other times accidently, the drama of learning to teach. Whether they are aware of it or not, they will also act out the history of tensions and conflicts in teacher education. This return of a forgotten history, is, perhaps, one of the surprises of this present study; whether one knows a history or does not, one can still live out its dilemmas, contra-dictions, and its underlying logic. In the course of this study, I have called such a dynamic the problem of discourse, by which I mean our reliance and dependence upon narrative conventions, modes of reasoning, categories of thought, styles of meaning making, and implicit and taken-for-granted values on comportment, responsibility, and blame. If this concept of discourse begins in a certain formality, one can even find discourse lurking in that common remorse uttered when things go wrong, "It is all my fault." While there is always more than one discourse in any institution, one discourse on learning to teach predominates and readers will see its problems over the course of this study. It is a discourse that sustains a particularly isolating and competitive view of the individual: a discourse that confines asking for help, or having feelings of helplessness, vulnerability, ambivalence, and dependency to a sign of individual weakness.

My approach to interpreting narratives of learning to teach is critical. This means that I am interested in the contradictory realities, indeed, the conflicts and crisis that structure the work and narratives of learning to teach. I am also interested in the emotional contradictions of trying to become a teacher and so a critical analysis is also given over to the difficulties of learn-ing from experience, the hesitations of reflections, and the unspoken frustra-tions that are also a part of learning to teach. Readers will not read an idealized story, although they will see how idealizing learning to teach is part of our dilemma. Nor will there be any grand remedies or cures for the un-happiness and discontentment that are also a part of teaching, just as there will not be a cure for the elation made on a good day. On the other hand, there may be some relief in learning that it is rather ordinary to feel so unsure of what to do in a place called school; that ordinary crises are the beginning of what we can even notice retrospectively as experience, and that classroom practice is not the punctuation mark of our teaching efforts. If our student teachers seem to exaggerate these strange facts, it is only because beginners also must learn to make significance from uncertainty and because learning is awkward. The little tragedy in learning to teach is that mistakes are rarely tolerated; one learns to sink or swim and mistakes this harshness as a necessary test.

ETHNOGRAPHIC HINDSIGHT

Practice Makes Practice is an ethnographic study of learning to teach in high school. The individual struggles of particular people become an allegory for the crisis of learning a profession and the more general condition of education as such. I begin with the view that teaching is an interpretive relation as well as expressing something about the language of education. This book is also a thought experiment that began from a simple question drawn from the literature of educational sociology: what does learning to teach do to student teachers? Readers will meet this question in chapter one. My first encounter with such a question took my breath away. This was because teaching was not supposed to do anything to the teacher; it was what the teacher did to others, or at least that was my naive sense, drawn from years of compulsory education and then the very different experience of studying in the University. For me, it was in the university that I began to try to pry apart learning from compliance, conformity, and, mastery. Once I entered teacher education as a student, it dawned upon me that learning to teach was doing something to who I was becoming. At the time, I could barely say what it was, except to note some new preoccupations: what does a teacher look like? How does one become happy back in a classroom? What should I know to do this work? Is there a character in the teacher? How will my students affect me? And, why is trying to teach so perplexing and so emotional?

Hindsight is a strange affair: one can look backward and feel confirmed in the present, or make remorse for lost opportunities that then overtake and diminish new accomplishments. One can demonstrate how one has learned from experience or regret missed encounters and replay old misunderstandings and the ways we do misrecognize our intentions and actions. It is not that hindsight works like an eraser of history, although it does reconfigure what one hoped would be long ago settled. That old complaint seems to punctuate one's history of learning: if only I had known what I now know, things would have been different, or easier, or better. It can be, however, more than a complaint, for the knowledge that can be made in hindsight can take on abstract significance, making from the past new ways to conceptualize the constellation of our present. In the return that is hindsight, then, we are referencing a conceptual affair; it organizes experience, stretches and distorts some edges of experience over those of others, and even allows one to decide that what seemed to matter so much is now irrelevant, or worse, beside the point. Clearly hindsight is a play of meanings, a strategy of signification, a possible resource for both learning and not learning. And, whatever hindsight is, and a hint of its meaning can be located in the ways it is used, it is not a culmination of experience. Rather, hindsight can be thought of as a deconstruction of experience, that is to say, a work of thought, second thoughts, actually, and, at its best, allows imagination its surprising depth and breadth.

Surely experience has something to do with hindsight. After all, events seem the material necessary to even wonder if things could be otherwise. However, if we begin with the idea that experience is an experience with signs, with language, and so with conflictive forms of meaning, if we think of experience as the aftereffect of expressing our understanding of what happens, we are still in the realm of trying to understand our perceptions of events, and so, our epistemological commitments and what these mean for interpretation. That places experience somewhere between the poles of discourse and desire, and, so, experience as lived rather than as picked up or acquired. Something different from mere circumstance, yet also containing the circumstantial, the conditions not of our own making yet still requiring something of a response, experience in education is a foundational discourse, one that will go on to structure the values we bestow onto theory and practice, reading and doing, thinking and acting, knowing and ignoring. And when brought to the problem of learning to teach, experience will be that great arbiter of success even as it also involves the failure to make experience form and so gel significance for one's daily work. Indeed, it will seem as though the more one teaches, the more experience seems lost. Experience, then, feels as if it comes too soon for understanding, not soon enough for help, filled with obstacles that frustrate and so devoid of that primal experience: the experience of satisfaction. But all of this is hindsight. At the time one begins teaching as a student teacher, one has great hopes for experience, indeed, sees it almost as a cure for ignorance, for the fate of being a beginner, indeed, for having to learn as one teaches others.

In *Practice Makes Practice*, hindsight has paradoxical qualities because experience does as well. For example, teachers who greet the newly arrived student teachers drew upon their past understandings of their educational biography as a measure for another's successes. They may try to save the newly arrived from their old mistakes, or tell them in advance that their theories will be useless when they encounter a greater reality: the classroom. Experience will turn learning into a hierarchy, and make a new appearance: it will be the things one picks up along the way such as helpful hints, a teaching style, and a program of classroom management that works without the university. Experience will be akin to a map. But it will also mark the breadcrumbs one leaves behind to find one's way back. It will implicate events before they can be encountered, be mistaken for anticipation, and will be like an investment one makes to guarantee the future. Student teachers wish for this kind of experience and this wish will defend against their sense of uncertainty in education. And the sentence will go like this: "After the experience of experience I will finally know what to do."

If this hindsight seems to allow us to find something inadequate in the past and feel remorse, it seems to also be its own corrective to a mistake that has already occurred. This mistake will be called "uncertainty" and even though everyone who surrounds the student teacher feels its threat, there will be the overwhelming sense that uncertainty and doubt should be avoided at all costs. So should subjectivity, that human idiom that cannot quite be justified, even if it must be used. Readers will certainly encounter remorsefulness, for there remains something difficult about trying to learn to teach and trying to teach others to learn. And part of this difficulty, what this study illustrates, is that feelings of remorse, self-blame, and vulnerability are in essence what was once called, in the early Seventies, "the hidden curriculum" of learning to teach. Alas, feelings of remorse are not good teachers, unless one wants to learn better how to complain. This is because remorse spreads its awkward tentacles into what has passed, tries to reach toward our wishes for the future, and slows down our momentum in the present. And yet, hindsight is perhaps one of the interesting resources for teacher education; after all, everyone involved has their years of compulsory schooling to draw from and if these biographical markers only become eventful when one tries to convey their worth to others, if the many years of being a student make the experience of education, at times, uneventful, and if part of what happens when we learn to teach is that we are constructing a vision of education that we wished we had already experienced, then hindsight may hone such vacillation and return us to the question of practice. What used to be called "practice teaching" and now goes under various names such as "student teaching," "teaching apprenticeship," and "classroom practicum" can become thought of differently, not quite as rehearsal for the real thing, but as the stage where aspects of the teacher's work, world, paradoxes, and dilemmas become a resource. All this is possible, provided that the language of teacher education open itself to the conflicts and crisis that make education ordinary.

SECOND THOUGHTS

When writing the first edition of *Practice Makes Practice*, I did not think about learning to teach as "a new edition of old conflicts."[15] This was Freud's phrasing, and he used it to describe the psychoanalytic tool and phenomenon of the transference, or the ways we lend old meanings to new events, the ways we give ourselves over to new authority, the ways we enact old dilemmas by projecting them onto new ones, and the ways we find new beloved objects in the world. These are the qualities of identification and the needed displacements that initially, but with some measure of ambivalence, offer us a means to relate to others. And so, it is in our investigations into the world as well as our resistance to the knowledge we may find and make there that compose the transference. In looking backward, now with psychoanalytic hindsight, Freud's description is quite apt; after all, schooling is so familiar, teachers were once students and of course they were once children. Their history of learning can be unconsciously repeated, now transferred onto the position of teacher. If, as I suggested earlier in this introduction, it is possible for those in the profession to repeat the history of conflicts within their profession without being conscious of that history, the other side of the coin is that we unconsciously repeat the history we have already lived and are, at some level, conscious of. Just walking into a school perhaps only smelling a whiff of lunch from the school cafeteria can animate old unresolved conflicts, take one back to that childhood cafeteria, return one to old feelings as if they had never left. Anna Freud linked transference to teaching when she wrote about the teacher's rescue fantasies, when the teacher's actions are those of trying to save her old self in the guise of helping the new student, of saying, albeit unconsciously, in one's pedagogical efforts "this is how I should have been treated!" and of attempting to undo what has already happened. These rescue fantasies affect which students will be noticed and which will be ignored, indeed, which students might be loved and which ones hated. Then, we confront the shadow of one's teaching style, the elsewhere of pedagogy, the intimate enactment of unconscious conflicts, that do return in learning to teach. These are the psychical consequences of teaching and learning. Perhaps these conflicts become coarsened in student teaching for there, the student teacher confronts the uncertainty of teaching and learning, made even more so by accompanying feelings of helplessness and dependency.

Has Teacher Education Changed?

Practice Makes Practice resides in a particular time of teacher education. I began writing it in the early 1980s and its first edition appeared in 1991. At first glance, a great deal has changed for current readers, for those learning to teach, and for education *writ large*. At the time of the study, the internet, and so the information highway, was about to be constructed. Computers were about to enter compulsory schooling and the most common technologies in use were the pencil, the copy machine, carbon paper, and the classroom television, educational films, and the overhead projector. The testing industry only had its toe in the classroom door. While there were standardized tests in use across the grades, evaluations of teachers and students were idiomatic and specific to the local district. It was a time when the three large US television networks devised a new narrative broadcast, TV movies of the week. Viewers could choose from personal illness, social catastrophe, gigantic technological crashes, and historical enactments of nationhood which all found their way, the day after, into classroom discussions. There were unexpected student comments that in no way answered the teacher's original question but that brought the movie into the math class, there were conversations in school cafeterias and teachers' lunch rooms, and there were videos of the last night's telecast replayed in school media laboratories. Clip by clip, commercial by commercial, the outside world slowly made its way into the schools. The networks mattered and a TV movie of the week could stop the daily march of curriculum material, indeed, could stop school routine as well.

The decade of the Eighties was also the beginning of what is now known as the AIDS pandemic, a global health crisis that was also what Paula Treichler called early on, "a crisis of signification."[16] And if concepts like safer sex, AIDS education, and condom distribution were not yet common parlance at the time of *Practice Makes Practice*, all that prevents thoughtful educational responses to the event of AIDS was certainly operative: homophobia, racism, sexism, and many other forms of degrading bodies, communities, and nations. But there were also spaces where important world events were considered, where students and teachers began with the view that history is indeed an argument of perspectives, an archive of contention and even of silences. It was not so much that the decade of the Eighties was one of quietism, for after all, there were, at the time, many ways to speak one's mind, to convolute and therefore go beyond the expectation of censoring ideas, to gesture toward possibilities, to create new identities. If, then, my new introduction to *Practice Makes Practices* is sounding a bit like Charles Dickens' sweeping opening sentence of a *Tale of Two Cities*, where it was then the best and worst of times, where time itself held its own contradictory possibilities and constraints, this is also because while many of the conditions and technologies of culture have changed, the very novelistic structure of learning to teach has not. It is still organized by apprenticeship in school classrooms, there are university courses to take, and those learning to teach still struggle with the contradictory realities of teaching and learning.

Practice Makes Practice resides in a particular time of educational research and curriculum inquiry as well. Two conceptual shifts began. Culture, as a noisy and unruly context, became a primary locus of study and a wave of school culture, in particular, made popular a cultural studies approach to educational ethnography. Readers were offered more intimate, perhaps more unsettling, narratives of unfolding education. There was also the subjective study of education, where the materials for theory were made from autobiography, memory, and a renewed consideration of the educational archive, what Maxine Greene aptly named as "that slow moving river of educational theory."[17] As for a sense of time, it was called the postmodern and for some was unwelcome, an uninvited guest. Theories of poststructuralism renewed important discussions on the nature of our knowledge, the question of subjectivity, and the very design of language, experience, and yes, even culture. It was a time of social construction, of discourse, and even, of desire.

In the decade of the Eighties, the concept of "voice" was particularly useful, even as the field of education studies argued over its underlying problems. And a key argument was that voice was tied to feelings of authenticity where it should be thought of as a particular discourse of self improvement, subjection, and discipline. At the time of this study, two views of voice vied for our attention and analysis. *Practice Makes Practice* resides in that argument over self and social representation and tries to clarify it.

One view of voice came from opposition politics, or identity politics. It posited that groups of people were voiceless and these groups included children, women, people of color, and gays and lesbians, for example. These groups were just beginning to represent themselves in social policy, curriculum deliberations, and institutional matters. It was never the case that these groups of people had nothing to say. Rather, the question of voice had to do, in this depiction, with questions of power and so, of empowerment. Power was defined as a possession one kept or lost. So, too, with voice. When voice became synonymous with representation, voice was seen as a quality one either possessed or lost. Thus in the Eighties, a great deal of education research was devoted to questions of silencing, being silenced, or not speaking. Aspects of this orientation work within *Practice Makes Practice*; the student teachers are worried about not being represented, being silenced by those already experienced, and also they worried about the silences in the curriculum, along with the hidden curriculum. They felt that power is a possession just beyond their reach and so they could hardly wait to become real teachers and so be able, they thought, to determine their conditions. This wish for the future without conflict became tied to the first version of voice.

The second way "voice" was used, and one that dominates this study, is metaphorical. That is to say, voice is linked to trying to represent something of the self but in doing so, bumping up against the language, or the prevailing discourses in education and the larger social. Voice still was used to signify something unique in the individual, such as finding one's real voice, but it also meant encountering even more contradictory realities on the way to self definition. In this second view, we always make more than one voice and in the case of learning to teach, student teachers try to construct a "teaching voice," from available discourses. This version suggests a struggle for voice: finding the words, feeling heard, understanding one's practical constraints, learning from negative experiences, speaking one's mind, and constructing a new identity from speaking differently the language of education. In *Practice Makes Practice*, many of the participants had great difficulty making a voice from these sorts of experiences, and then, experiencing what voices they managed to make. It was this double sense of voice, as both borrowed and made, as tradition and change, and as continuity and discontinuity that came as such a surprise. And at some level, while all of the participants understood voice as an artifice of the conditions and institutional pressures made from teaching, there was tremendous emotional pressure to prove oneself worthy, to forget feelings of helplessness and not being in control, and to pretend that one had already learned and so could just get on with teaching. When this occurred, voice became like a pre-existing position one expressed, not an existential dilemma that allowed for new learning dispositions.

These two views of voice may well be two sides of the same coin: individuals feel encumbered in the institution of education and not recognized for who they hope to become (as opposed to who they might actually be). And this pressure for identity and identification seems to come from the outside, even as its force is felt from within. We might ask privately, who is making me feel this way, but we might also acknowledge that if our feelings are statements of needs, having feelings in education is often discouraged. Finding a voice, however, is not. On the other side, the concept of voice tries to settle how social experience is expressed as it passes through conventional means of expression. Voice is, after all, a problem of language, and it is this problem of language that allows experience to be noticed, valued, dismissed, or even regretted. Voice still answers the question of how one expresses understanding as borrowed from readily available ideas. It is perhaps the most personal discourse. Yet, how does voice become authoritative and internally persuasive? And, what happens when the authoritarian ways of conceptualizing experience bump up against the wishes one has for an experience? This is the second aspect of voice, but as we will see, it is propped up by the constraints of our first static notion: voice is repressed and waiting to be liberated!

To mediate this dilemma of voice—is it inside or outside, made or found, constructed or essentially there?—I borrow from W. E. B. Dubois's (who borrowed it from Freud's) notion of "double consciousness." This is an uncanny feeling of being caught by, even fragmented from, institutional pressures. It is a sense of being watched, and viewing the self through the eyes of others. But it is also the wishes one makes for existence and learning. If we all seem to know what a "teacher's voice" sounds like, and here, we require parody, irony, and bald humor, we may not be so sure of all that props up the teacher's voice: some fundamental fragmentation in teacher education that structures what we take as the experience of learning to teach. This fragmentation, described in chapter two, concerns the problem of knowledge: the compartmentalization of knowledge in curriculum, the separation of knowledge from pedagogy, the separation of knowledge from perspectives, and the fragmentation of practice from theory and so of experience from thinking.[18] The teacher's voice is these conflicts: institutional imperatives and constraints, curricular pressures, and the social, historical, personal, and economic contexts of learning. The conceptual category of voice, then, is that conflict between internal and external reality and narrating these conflictive events. If, at times, voice is felt as a valued possession, it can also be that voice in the head that will not stop berating.

SOME KEY ASSUMPTIONS ABOUT LEARNING TO TEACH

What can it mean to think about learning to become a teacher from the perspectives of those who experience this work, those who surround and supervise them, those who research the field of teacher education, and then consider these populations as encountering, repeating, and rethinking some of the historic arguments over what makes a teacher? What theoretical tensions are reconfigured from such an admixture? Alongside these question lay a series of presuppositions about learning to teach. First, learning to teach is a search for meaning and a hope that experience in teaching can make meaning into insight. At times, meaning and experience are collapsed. Traditionally, it is thought that experience makes meaning. In the course of this study, I try to keep them separated in order to account for what happens when experience cannot deliver its promise: competence, clarity, and confidence. I suggest that it is language that makes experience. Second, if it is this search for meaning that underscores and conducts the work of learning to teach, then learning to teach is both a problem of significance and an interpretive activity. The idealistic view is that meaning is awaiting in the classroom, and significance, too, is what others give to punctuate experience. More ordinarily, the problem of significance begins with the understanding that a great deal of the story of learning to teach concerns learning what not to become, and this negative experience drains significance of its potential.

Third, when we learn to teach, we are also trying to make from this uncertainty narratives of education: our own and those of others. It is not just that we must put into words how we think about our learning, although this activity is what teachers ask of their students and theoretically should be able to ask themselves. The existential tension is that just as we try to make from our learning a narrative of what we think has happened, we are also learning the happenstance of narrative. We try out a series of story lines that may or may not be acceptable, useful, or intelligible to us and to those who surround us. Yet these narratives of learning are not just overlaid upon a preexisting experience; they are constitutive of experience itself. One of the surprises of narrative is that it crafts the thing it must presuppose. This means that narrative is always on the cusp of myth even as it tries to allay contradictions and dramatic conflict. And, fourth, while there is no single story of learning to teach, even if there exist some idealistic cliches, such as "practice makes perfect," or, "experience is the best teacher," or even the joke of "those who can do, those who can't teach," then a great part of this narrative work is composed from what I have called throughout this study, "a struggle for voice."

The struggle of voice, and voice itself, however, is made from a contradictory complex of realities in teaching and learning. Three intermixing aspects of the struggle for voice are worth exploring: biography, emotions and institutional structure. The struggle resides between the biography of a structure called schooling and a biography of a learner. And the struggle for voice is not an unidirectional one. That is, it is not just that student teachers worry over how others see them, how others listen to them, and how, at times, they feel as if they must censor their thoughts, hold back their suggestions, avoid controversies, and even delay their creativity until they become "a real teacher" as opposed to an apprentice in the classroom. All of this occurs and it does feel as if one has to repress an identity in the making. That the teacher's identity emerges from a conflict in and with authority, imagination, and flurries of autobiography that seem to return when least expected, is of course what makes the teacher's identity so uncertain and surprising. After all, student teachers are still under the auspices of their university education and their cooperating classroom teachers; they are beholden to the condition of being a student while learning to teach others. But they are also beholden to their own years of being a student and the images of education they made and continually make from that. And while it may seem like a stretch to compare learning to teach with growing up, much of the dependency and desire to be seen as already knowledgeable without having to learn characterize the relation between student teachers and their others.

If those who surround them waver in enthusiasm or seem tired by the dolens of classroom routine, over-familiarity with inherited and created constraints, and the glacial rate of learning, if those surrounding our student teachers are wary of their idealism, their need to experiment with curriculum, and even with their hopefulness that they will reach the unreachable or forgotten student, if those who surround them know at some level that part of what one learns when one learns to teach is a certain disappointment and even a shock at the difficulty of educating others, of learning authority, of trying to explain concepts that seem clear to the teacher but puzzling to the student; if all of these background experiences feel like so many obstacles to the student teacher, these obstacles, too, become part of their struggle for voice. The surprise is that one's voice, whether we call it the voice of experience or the voice of the beginner, seems to come from the outside in, even if it is intimately felt from the inside out.

This sense of intimacy, a personal moment in becoming a teacher, an internal drama really, is our second dynamic in the struggle for voice. One of the great surprises in learning to teach is how deeply emotional an experience it is and how quickly one's emotions become fantasies of rescue and revenge. How easily one can move from elation and hope to embarrassment and blame, from feeling all is in control to becoming undone, all within a moment's notice. How easily one can become lonely in a crowded room or suddenly wish for solitude and to be left alone. In the emotional life of a teacher, how easy it is to hate and love students, colleagues, and the self, to wish a student would just disappear or that an ungrateful student would, out of the blue, become appreciative of the teacher's efforts and send a letter of gratitude. How, even if no other adult is in the classroom, one feels watched and judged, or that one wishes someone would magically appear and help because that other knows exactly what to do to fix a mess. And long after events have occurred, nagging thoughts remain to repeat what the event left unresolved. There is a hope that teaching techniques will stabilize the efforts of teaching, guide classroom control, and so techniques will become experience that can eventually compose a sort of warning system in the technology of teaching: mistakes can be preempted, things can go smoothly, and everyone will learn what the teacher proffers. Yet continually, one bumps up against these wishes as they suddenly dissolve into so many disappointments, missed opportunities, failed attempts. And there is a sense that all of these thoughts and affects should remain hidden, lest the teacher appears too emotional, uncertain, or vulnerable.

The emotional world of the teacher casts a shadow on what becomes of experience and being there in the classroom. It is difficult to make a mistake and even more difficult to make from this mistake a work of learning. Here is where we find the internal struggle for voice: it is in the making of emotional significance from the ruins of experience. How does one put into words the roller-coaster of emotional response when things do not go well, when time is up before one is ready, when the least expected circumstance becomes the curriculum or takes it over? How does one narrate the creepy detours of teacher development without recourse to adapting to preexisting models of education and so become stultified or disassociate from the implications of one's decisions? For example, who would have ever thought that giving permission for someone to go to the bathroom would make or break one's authority? Yet granting permission, signing hall passes, ignoring or addressing someone's behavior, all of these snap judgements take place in the theater of the classroom; there are witnesses and one never knows in advance how the testimony will turn out, be used, or revise the event.

Preexisting models of education are the third term in the struggle for voice. By this I mean the structure of education as an institution and the experience of this structure. We meet the parade of grades, of subject areas, of dividing students and preexisting notions of what counts as intelligence and stupidity; we meet a certain history of teacher education, its values, its certification requirements, its curriculum. We meet an apprenticeship arrangement of teacher education that seems to separate university course work from classroom practice. It is a division that will return in theory and practice debates: which comes first, but also where does theory come from? How can practice lose its force? And, should practice and theory be in agreement? We meet a profession that can feel so misunderstood and unrecognized that those just entering are almost embarrassed to mention their aspirations. No one wants to look like a teacher, even if we can never quite agree what a teacher looks like. These models take on even more pressure when we meet two of the facts of compulsory education. First it is the law. Children and adolescents must go to school. Second, all teachers grew up in compulsory education. Unlike any other profession, one enters teacher education with an over-familiarity of the work of students and teachers.

The struggle for voice contains and expresses institutional structures, biography, and emotions. It is also experienced as an internal conflict, for over the years of being a student in a compulsory setting, one learns experiences never meant to be educative: compliance, conformity, and dependency. It is also experienced as a social relation to others. Give the teacher what she or he wants, avoid difficult conversations, don't ask too many questions or someone will think you are stupid, assume the teacher always knows what she or he is doing, questions have answers, don't stand out, and mistakes are personal flaws to be overcome. Such an odd combination of resentment, inhibition, and prohibition return once one assumes the teacher's role. Yet this role is not quite an identity, even if the long forgotten knowledge of being a student is suddenly animated, returns as strangely unhelpful but also as estranging and compelling. The struggle for voice is a conflict between old and new events, with what will be discarded and what will remain as the self becomes something other than itself. The struggle for voice is a struggle for narrative, not authenticity or adaptation into a preexisting identity. And if education feels as if it is predetermined, a fate one must bear, and a constraint on the self, the struggle for voice suggests something far more interesting, creative, and emotionally alive: the work of narration, making significance from the accidental qualities of life events. This is the view of Julia Kristeva, and her understanding of narrative as "the ability to put biography into words" but not just any words and not a story devoid of its conflicts. Rather, what narrative can do is "expose and put into practice an incessant tendency toward conflict: a revolt."[19] This mode of narration puts into words the actions of living and while the struggle for voice resides in that revolt, narrative attempts to make from this action significance. It is, then, the grounds for thinking and so, for making something new from the ruins of experience.

A Note On Knowledge

While something significant happens to the self learning to teach, something happens to knowledge as well. At times, the curriculum becomes a thing to deliver and then learning is reduced to a thing that can be observed. Knowledge, then, loses its constructiveness, banished to the cliché "a teachable moment." This is not something to wonder over, nor is it the fuel of curiosity or the imagination. Nor is it even meant to cast the teacher and learner in awe. Instead, the features of knowledge become a means to an end; teaching about the knowledge is the preoccupation and the myth that there is a direct relation between the teacher's efforts and the student's learning is sustained. When knowledge is reduced to a speech act, an answer, say, it becomes the proving ground of competence. In the course of this present study, knowledge does not work in these ways and at first this can be felt as a great betrayal. But it is emblematic of the ways meaning breaks down so easily; knowledge, too, it turns out, is a problem of interpretation.

So readers will meet the conflicted narratives made from teacher education. And it is here that the research will take the narrative turn. The reason we engage with narratives of learning is to create a different conversation on the problem of experience in education. It is also to study the difficulties others make from that. At the time of the original publication of *Practice Makes Practice,* there were not many studies that focused on the daily rhythms of learning to teach. Nor were there many studies that happened to narrate the problem of uncertainty in teaching and learning. My hope is that this approach continues to be relevant to readers in education.

1

Contradictory Realities in
Learning to Teach

One of the most provocative questions in the research on teaching was raised over fifty years ago by Willard Waller in what is now known as the first sociology of teaching.[1] There, Waller asked, "What does teaching do to teachers?" This question opens the underside of teaching, the private struggles we engage as we construct not only our teaching practices and all the relationships this entails, but our teaching voices and identities. We are invited to explore the felt experiences of our teaching lives because such a question allows us, as Walter Benjamin put it, "to brush history against the grain"[2] in order to uncover the dynamics, tensions, exclusions, and inclusions engendered by the activity of teaching.

When we stop and look at teachers in this way—to see teachers as being shaped by their work as well as shaping their work—we are able to shift the discourse of teacher education from an instrumentalist belief in controlling and manipulating variables—an orientation based upon the suppression of subjectivity—to a dialogic discourse. A dialogic discourse can take into account the discursive practices and their social relationships that realize pedagogy and the lived experiences of teachers. Such a commitment requires implicitly the teacher's presence and our own capacity to listen to the teacher's voice. For in considering what teaching does to teachers, our concern is with *how* the activity of teaching expresses something about the subjectivities of teachers and determines ways teachers come to construct their teaching identities. This present study is concerned with such problems.

Waller's question is extended to the arena of student teaching for it is there that one first confronts the multiple meanings, constraints, and

25

possibilities of the teacher's identity in the process of constructing one's own. In its broadest sense, this study asks the question: What does learning to teach do and mean to student teachers and those involved in the practice of teaching? In its more specific sense, this study explores how our teaching selves are constituted in the context of learning to teach, and how the selves we produce constrain and open the possibilities of creative pedagogies. In focusing on the ways teachers construct themselves as they are being constructed by others, this study does not provide the reader with grand solutions about the best way to learn to teach. Instead, my intention is to raise thorny questions about the inherited discourses of student teaching and to theorize the contradictory realities that beckon and disturb those who live in this field.

Theorizing about these questions reorients us to the work of teachers, and requires an understanding not simply of the structures of schools or the skills necessary to teach there, but the construction of one's identity as a teacher. To pursue this, we must develop a "double consciousness" of persons and of places, relating those involved in the practice of teaching to the history, mythology, and discourses of the institutions framing their work. We must cultivate an appreciation for the *process* of education that can critically take into account what Maxine Greene has termed, "the immediacy of the felt encounter,"[3] and become concerned with whose immediacy is felt and what possibilities are encountered. To value such a process, learning to teach must be rendered problematic. The complexity of relationships—both given and possible—that work through pedagogy must be understood as intimately shaping the subjective world and the discursive practices of the teacher.

Enacted in every pedagogy are the tensions between knowing and being, thought and action, theory and practice, knowledge and experience, the technical and the existential, the objective and the subjective. Traditionally expressed as dichotomies, these relationships are not nearly so neat or binary. Rather, such relationships are better expressed as dialogic in that they are shaped as they shape each other in the process of coming to know. Produced because of social interaction, subject to negotiation, consent, and circumstance, inscribed with power and desire, and always in the process of becoming, these dialogic relations determine the very texture of teaching and the possibilities it opens. They fashion as well the ways teachers understand their practices and the subjectivity that bestows this practice with identity. Indeed, negotiating among what may seem to be conflicting visions, disparaging considerations, and contesting interpretations about social practice and the teacher's identity is part of the hidden work of learning to teach. This unmapped territory, then, must be charted in ways that can permit a double consciousness of how systemic constraints become lived as individual dilemmas.

The story of learning to teach begins actually much earlier than the time one first decides to become a teacher. The mass experience of public education has made teaching one of the most familiar professions in this culture. Implicitly, schooling fashions the meanings, realities, and experiences of students; thus those learning to teach draw from their subjective experiences constructed from actually being there. They bring to teacher education their educational biography and some well-worn and commonsensical images of the teacher's work. In part, this accounts for the persistency of particular worldviews, orientations, dispositions, and cultural myths that dominate our thinking and, in unintended ways, select the practices that are available in educational life.

The overfamiliarity of the teaching profession is a significant contradiction affecting those learning to teach. We have all played a role opposite teachers for a large part of our school lives. It is taken for granted that we all know what a teacher is and does. This knowledge is based upon years of observation. It must be remembered that by the time a person enters teacher education, she or he has spent approximately thirteen thousand hours observing teachers.[4] As Dan Lortie notes,[5] this observation time is not passive but is charged by the relations of power operating in compulsory contexts. Observation skills acquired through schooling allow students to "survive" in classrooms: students not only learn to interact with the formal curriculum of teaching and learning, but act as well within a hidden curriculum. In fact, those who are most "successful" actively read the text of the teacher—her or his moods, behaviors, values, judgments, discourse strategies, and classroom expectations.

It is little wonder that many students leave compulsory education believing that "anyone can teach," for it is so easy to "read" the teacher and anticipate her or his practices. Indeed, for many students, pedagogy is not rooted in the production of knowledge but rather in its public image. For those who leave this world to enter teacher education, their first culture shock may well occur with the realization of the overwhelming complexity of the teacher's work and the myriad ways this complexity is masked and misunderstood. But what occurs as well is the startling idea that the taking up of an identity means suppressing aspects of the self. So at first glance, becoming a teacher may mean becoming someone you are not. It is this dual struggle that works to construct the student teacher as the site of conflict.

To view the work of teachers as "easy" implies a particular understanding of their practice. Robert Everhart, in his ethnographic study of junior high school males, describes how the experience of observing teachers, within the context of school structure, shapes what these students come to understand about the work of teachers:

From the student point of view there was little else involved in what teachers did in the classroom other than represented in this simple "factory model" of learning; that is, the teachers pouring in the facts and the students pouring them back in the form of papers and tests. . . . The student picture of teachers provided little room for emotion, with the exception of that associated with student violation of school standards. The teacher's world, in the student's eyes, was straightforward and linear, hardly complex at all.[6]

Issues of pedagogy do not enter into a student's view of the teacher's work. Rather, the teacher's skills are reduced to custodial moments: the ability to enforce school rules, impart textbook knowledge, grade student papers, and manage classroom discipline appear to be the sum total of the teacher's work. Hidden is the pedagogy teachers enact: the ways teachers render content and experience as pedagogical, consciously construct and innovate teaching methods, solicit and negotiate student concerns, and attempt to balance the exigencies of curriculum with both the students' and their own visions of what it means to know.

Rarely disclosed by teachers themselves and absent from the student's account are the more private aspects of pedagogy: coping with competing definitions of success and failure, and one's own sense of vulnerability and credibility. Residing in the "heads" and "hearts" of teachers, and emerging from their personal and institutional biography, this "personal practical knowledge," or knowledge made from the stuff of lived experience,[7] is so intimately a part of teachers' enactments that its appearance as skills becomes taken for granted. Taken for granted as well are how their discursive practices come to express something about the structure of institutional life, and the ways in which power and authority are experienced there.

Stereotypical images of teachers abound. If some are said to "look like teachers," they are thought to resemble the subject content they teach. Teachers are said to look "bookish," "brainy," "like a narc," "a big head," "mean," or, in the case of women, "like an old maid." Trapped within these images, teachers come to resemble things or conditions; their identity assumes an essentialist quality and, as such, socially constructed meanings become known as innate and natural.

Likewise, the backhanded compliment of "Funny, you don't look like a teacher," attempts to disassociate the individual from a social caricature.[8] Many of these stereotypes, commonly associated with women teachers, are profoundly sexist and reveal a disdain for the teaching profession's female roots.[9] In the dominant society, so-called favorable images that characterize the teacher as selfless also mirror the stereotypes associated with women. Like the "good" woman, the "good" teacher is positioned as self-sacrificing, kind, overworked, underpaid, and holding an unlimited reservoir of patience. Waller observed:

We may say that [the] favorable stereotype represents the community ideal of what a teacher ought to be and that the unfavorable one
represents the common opinion of what a teacher actually is.[10]

The persistency of such stereotypes, however, does more than caricature
the opinions and hopes of a community. Such images tend to subvert a
critical discourse about the lived contradictions of teaching and the actual
struggles of teachers and students. Stereotypes engender a static and hence
repressed notion of identity as something already out there, a stability that
can be assumed. Here, identity is expressed as a final destination rather than
a place of departure. For example, the image of the "good" teacher is implicitly antiworker in that any attempt to unionize, agitate for better working
conditions, or seek more of a voice in the governance of schools is viewed as
an individualistic example of being "selfish," "greedy," "into power," or "unprofessional."[11] In the case of women teachers, who are merely seen to carry their
"natural" abilities into the marketplace, they are apt to be characterized as
either martyrs or idiots.[12] Male teachers are expected to assert a machismo
identity in their classrooms, and depending upon their proximity to this
image, become characterized either as wimps or as tough guys.[13]

These images displace the collective concerns of real teachers with measures of individual behavior based upon adherence to patriarchal conventions,
notions of a unitary non-contradictory identity, and images of professionalism
that preclude the struggles of gender, class, race, and generation. In either case,
the multiple identities of the teacher—both given and possible—become lost in
a cycle of cultural determinism.[14] Such a cycle depends upon the process whereby
the identity of a teacher becomes overpopulated with cultural myths.

To explore the cultural myths that summon teachers and their work
requires an excursion into superficial knowledge, how it becomes produced
and lived. Superficial knowledge is first of all ensconded in the situations of
visceral knowing; it is made from the stuff of tacit understandings and the
discursive practices that are produced and then produce and organize how
educational life is interpreted and lived. Superficial knowledge makes available particular practices as it orients understanding. Sherry Turkle, in her
ethnographic study of the French popularization of psychoanalytic culture,
termed the problem of superficial knowledge as "decipher[ing] some elements
of an emergent modern mythology."[15] While we all live in myths, some myths
instigate repressive notions of pedagogy and identity, while others open us to
the dialogic. This latter image of teachers—as negotiators, mediators, and
authors of who they are becoming—is the place where identity becomes
infused with possibilities.

As suggested above, superficial images of the work of teachers become the
material for cultural myths about teaching and may bear upon the expectations,

desires, and investments one brings to and constructs during the process of becoming a teacher. Cultural myths offer a set of ideal images, definitions, and justifications that are taken up as measures for thought, affect, and practice. These images instantiate the characteristics of modern myth: value-laden, it is masked by a naturalized appearance that seems complete and speaks for itself. A myth makes available particular discursive practices that position situations as given without the quality of contingency; its form asserts a stable meaning despite unstable contexts by offering reasons in the guise of motives.[16] As Roland Barthes observes, a myth, as a language for codifying what a culture values, serves contradictory functions: "it points out and it notifies, it makes us understand something and it imposes it on us."[17] Teachers' classroom appearance, sustained by school structure and serving as the basis for cultural myths, represses teachers' subjectivity: they are subsumed by predictability and hence immune to changing circumstances and incapable of interventions. The overfamiliarity of the teacher's role, the taken-for-grantedness of school structure, and the power of one's institutional biography are open to the suggestions cultural myths offer about the work and identity of teachers. In the case of learning to teach, cultural myths partly structure the individual's taken-for-granted views of power, authority, knowledge, and identity. They work to cloak the more vulnerable condition of learning to teach and the myriad negotiations it requires.

One such myth, explored throughout this study, is rooted in the very structure of student teaching. The myth that experience makes the teacher, and hence that experience is telling in and of itself, valorizes student teaching as the authentic moment in teacher education and the real ground of knowledge production. There, normative notions collapse the distinction between acquiring pedagogical skills and becoming a teacher by objectifying experience as a map. In this discourse, everything is already organized and complete; all that is left to do is to follow preordained paths. The problem is that when experience is perceived as a map, it is taken to order perception and guarantee essential truths. For example, conventional wisdom such as "we learn by experience," or "experience is the best teacher," legitimatizes the regime of a particular discourse on experience. And while such slogans are taken up as common sense, what is expressed in actuality is a discourse of common sense.[18] As a discourse, common sense depends upon what is already known—the obvious—and hence resists explanations about the complications we live. Missing in this valorization of experience is an interrogation into how the dynamics of social expression—the discourses that bear upon the conceptual ordering we give to construct experience as meaningful—produce accompanying discursive practices that constitute experience as already filled with essential and unitary meanings. Such a myth presents experience as given and implicitly requires the student teacher to accept preordained meanings as natural and self-evident.

Despite the persistency of cultural myths that position the teacher as expert, as self made, as sole bearer of power, and as a product of experience, those learning to teach feel a rupture between the ethic and the experience, because learning to teach constitutes a time of biographical crisis as it simultaneously invokes one's autobiography. That is, learning to teach is not a mere matter of applying decontextualized skills or of mirroring predetermined images; it is time when one's past, present, and future are set in dynamic tension. Learning to teach—like teaching itself—is always the process of becoming: a time of formation and transformation, of scrutiny into what one is doing, and who one can become.

The image of teaching advocated here is dialogic: teaching must be situated in relationship to one's biography, present circumstances, deep commitments, affective investments, social context, and conflicting discourses about what it means to learn to become a teacher. With this dialogic understanding, teaching can be reconceptualized as a struggle for voice and discursive practices amid a cacophony of past and present voices, lived experiences, and available practices. The tensions among what has preceded, what is confronted, and what one desires shape the contradictory realities of learning to teach.

Learning to teach is a social process of negotiation rather than an individual problem of behavior. This dynamic is essential to any humanizing explanation of the work of teachers. Teaching concerns coming to terms with one's intentions and values, as well as one's views of knowing, being, and acting in a setting characterized by contradictory realities, negotiation, and dependency and struggle. Yet the normative discourse of learning to teach presents it as an individual dilemma that precludes the recognition of the contradictory realities of school life. The contradiction here is that while learning to teach is individually experienced and hence may be viewed as individually determined, in actuality it is socially negotiated. However, as will be discussed throughout this study, the press for individual control over the teaching process obscures its social origins; individual notions of power privatize contradictions and thereby thwart those learning to teach from theorizing about and effectively intervening in such contradictory realities. Moreover, the vulnerable condition of being a social subject becomes "taboo" discourse when learning to teach is viewed as a private dilemma of acquiring predetermined dispositions and skills, and of taking up preexisting identities.

This study takes up the above concerns. Its organization follows my own chronology of coming to understand the contradictory realities of learning to teach. The first two chapters of this study are meant to orient the reader to my theoretical investments. The concepts I use to work through the meanings of practice, pedagogy, and becoming, and the discourses that express their particular meanings are theorized in the first two chapters. Chapters 3 and 4 narrate the stories of two different student teachers as they set about learning to teach in high school settings. As will be explained in each of these chapters, I have ordered their narratives chronologically because I learned of their episodes week by week and because this sense of time unfolding qualified their sense of the immediate and their visions of the future. Chapter 3 magnifies the world of Jamie Owl, a student teacher in English studies, while chapter 4 looks at Jack August, a student teacher in social studies education. Chapter 5 pulls the ethnographic zoom lens back and considers the contradictory views of professional educators: secondary teachers, school administrators, and teacher educators. Chapter 6 is concerned with the multiple voices and heteroglossic tensions working through the discursive practices of teacher education, and the last chapter returns to the textual dilemmas of narrating conflict in an ethnography of learning to teach.

THE STUDY OF LIVED EXPERIENCE

This book is an ethnographic study of the contradictory realities of learning to teach in secondary education and how these realities fashion the subjectivities of student teachers. An ethnography is the study of lived experience and hence examines how we come to construct and organize what has already been experienced. Lived experience "hints at a process whereby we attribute meaning to what happens to us."[19] The purpose of such a research style, as Linda Brodkey argues, "is to examine how in the course of dramatizing their own lives, individuals also fabricate material culture."[20] As an ethnography, this narration is constructed from the perspectives and experiences of its central subjects: student teachers, classroom teachers, university professors and supervisors, school administrators, and myself, the researcher. Each represented perspective has different investments in positioning the ways in which one learns to become a teacher. Such investments complicate the stories of learning to teach. What makes this reality so contradictory is the fact that teaching and learning have multiple and conflicting meanings that shift with our lived lives, with the theories produced and encountered, with the deep convictions and desires brought to and created in education, with the practices we negotiate, and with the identities we construct.

This is not the problem. Rather, when such multiplicity is suppressed, so too is our power to imagine how things could be otherwise. Here I am referring to the dilemmas of carving out one's own teaching territory within preordained borders, of desiring to be different while negotiating institutional mandates for uniformity, and of struggling to construct one's teaching voice from the stuff of student experience. How do student teachers and the significant others with whom they interact make sense of their inherited and socially constructed circumstances? Part of what I attempt to theorize is the complicated process of theorizing, how "the small imaginings of local knowledge"[21] and cultural myths about teaching are discursively produced and lived, and how the conditions of learning to teach inscribe the subjectivities, voices, and practices of its subjects.

Two questions—part descriptive and part interpretive—initially shaped this study: What is it like to learn to teach? And what does it mean to those involved? These questions are ethnographic because they required my presence in the world of student teachers for the purpose of understanding student teachers and the practitioners who surrounded them as they understood themselves. But I did not enter this world as innocent or as an empty vessel waiting to be filled with the knowledge of student teachers. Indeed, throughout my career, I have been a student teacher, a cooperating teacher, and a teacher educator. These positions have shaped my present understanding. My project, then, is not merely to describe what happens to those learning to teach from their perspectives alone. Unlike traditional educational ethnographers who enter the familiar world of school and linguistically render this familiar experience as strange, my project is to take the familiar story of learning to teach and render it problematic through cultural critique and by asserting multiple voices.

The above questions become critical when they are juxtaposed with questions about the context and structure of student teaching. The context of student teaching is not a neutral zone where one "receives" either the rudimentary foundations of a teaching style, or the unitary position on the nature of the teacher's work and the identity one must assume. Neither is the structure of teaching innocent of ideology and the normative discourse of what it means to know and learn. Rather the context of teaching is political, it is an ideological context that privileges the interests, values, and practices necessary to maintain the status quo, and ironically, the powerlessness of teachers.

Because learning to teach means coming to terms with particular orientations toward knowledge, power, and identity, and because it is experienced in a context characterized by an unequal distribution of power that acts to constrict people's lives, I am also interested in how people become entangled in oppressive structures. My concern is to theorize not just about what student teachers do but what it is that structures their investments, interpretations, and practices. In this way, I share Roger Simon and Donald Dippo's concern that a critical ethnographic work theorizes:

How people are implicated in the regulation and alteration of the terms of how they live together and how they define what is possible and desirable for themselves and others. . . . It is an interest organized by a standpoint which implicates us in moral questions about desirable forms of social relations and ways of living. Thus the interest that defines critical ethnographic work is both pedagogical and political. It is linked to our assessment of our own society as inequitably structured and dominated by a hegemonic culture that suppresses a consideration and understanding of why things are the way they are and what must be done for things to be otherwise.[22]

This is not to suggest, in approaching the social arrangements of teaching from a political perspective, that the conditions one confronts are immutable. Rather, the critical questions I raise concern the complex relationship between learning to teach and our capacity to transform the experience of education through a deep commitment to social justice, personal thoughtfullness, and an openness to difference, contradictions, risks, and change. Juxtaposed with the descriptive and interpretive questions previously raised, then, are two critical questions: How do student teachers see themselves as resisting cultural hegemony? How can student teachers come to take up discursive practices that both challenge the taken-for-granted passivity presently dominating learning and teaching, and fashion activist and participatory styles of knowing and being?

An attentiveness to language and the personal voices of the participants in this study allows us entry into their practical world. Language shapes and is shaped by meaning. Voice, in this context, suggests the individual's struggle to create and fashion meaning, assert standpoints, and negotiate with others. Voice permits participation in the social world. Through the alterity of the speaker, voice affirms one's relationship to the world and to others. Here I am using alterity to refer to the dialogue between the self and others, to the idea that one can only know the self through relationships with others. Consequently, voice suggests the inflections and intonations of who we are. It is the means whereby we reaccentuate language with personal meanings. And while we may speak the same language, it is with a polyphony of voices.

The study of voice, however, makes for a cautious study in three regards. First, we do not have one voice but many. Our voice is always contingent upon shifting relationships among the words we speak, the practices we construct, and the community within which we interact. As practices, perspectives, and communities shift, so too does the voice we use to name them. Second, our capacity to make language work for us is problematic. There is never a simple correspondence between the words we use and the things to which we refer. Language can mask and illuminate, and also affirm and challenge, how we understand our social conditions. It has the potential either to reproduce given realities as immutable and ubiquitous, or to produce critiques that have the potential to construct new realities.[23] Third, interpreting the voice of others leads to the development of yet a different voice. My dilemma as a researcher is to reconstruct and critically re-present the voices of others, and, in so doing, care for their integrity, humanity, and struggles.

Uma Narayan, in discussing the difficulties of understanding others, describes two necessary stances the listener must assume: methodological humility and methodological caution. Methodological humility requires the listener "sincerely conduct herself under the assumption that, as an outsider, she may be missing something, and that what appears to be a mistake on the part of the insider may make sense if she had a fuller understanding of the context." Similarly, methodological caution requires the listener "carry out her attempted criticism of the insider's perceptions in such a way that it does not attempt to, or even seem to amount to an attempt to denigrate or dismiss entirely the validity of the insider's point of view."[24]

To assume a critical voice then, does not mean to destroy or devalue the struggles of others. Instead, a critical voice attempts the delicate and discursive work of rearticulating the tensions between and within words and practices, or constraints and possibilities, as it questions the consequences of the taken-for-granted knowledge shaping responses to everyday life and the meanings fashioned from them. A critical voice is concerned not just with representing the voices of oneself and others, but with narrating, considering, and evaluating them.

Re-presenting the voices of others means more than recording their words. An interpretive effort is necessary because words always express relationships, span contexts larger than the immediate situation from which they arise, and hold tensions between what is intended and what is signified. In repositioning the voices of others, we can begin to tease out what Raymond Williams terms "the structure of feeling," or the particular sense of life constructed by those who live it.[25] In detailing the ordinary days that compose the struggle to teach, part of my goal is to represent—for the reader's interpretation—the structure of feeling engendered by learning to teach. Yet a further lacuna of representation must also be acknowledged. And this is the danger, as Linda Brodkey so aptly warns, "of confusing the narrative of lived experience with experience."[26] They can never be synonymous. Nor is an identical correspondence a desirable or possible goal. The retelling of another's story is always a partial telling, bound not only by one's perspective but also by the exigencies of what can and cannot be told. The narratives of lived experience—the story, or what is told, and the discourse, or what it is that structures how a story is told—are always selective, partial, and in tension. The contradiction is that while the ethnographic narrative pushes the reader to accept the story of student teaching as a unitary whole, characterized by a beginning, a middle, and an end, the theoretical perspectives I employ work to disrupt the myth of the seamless narrative and the omnipresent narrator.[27] Thus the structure of feeling supposed by my narration should be read as radically contingent.

My focus is on the situation of the student teacher because the student teacher's delicate position in the classroom allows insight into the struggle for voice in both teaching and learning. Marginally situated in two worlds, the student teacher as part student and part teacher has the dual struggle of educating others while being educated. Consequently, student teachers appropriate different voices in the attempt to speak for themselves yet all the while act in a largely inherited and constraining context. This struggle characterizes the tensions between being and becoming a teacher as student teachers draw from their past and present in the process of coming to know. Often, however, it is this struggle that is absent both from the research on learning to teach and from the normative practices of mainstream programs in teacher education. Part of this text will account for these silences as it reconstructs the polyphony of voices that mediate, persuade, and produce particular forms of practice and the concurrent discourses that legitimate or challenge them.

THEORETICAL ISSUES IN THE STUDY OF PRACTICE AND VOICE

Styles of theorizing are usually of two types: a search for mechanisms or a search for meanings.[28] A search for *mechanisms* entails a functionalist account of how things work, or do not work. It is a concrete search that attempts to posit explanations for specific problems and to prescribe solutions. A search for *meaning*, a style of theorizing practiced in this text, begins with a different set of assumptions. Such a search is interpretive, constructivist, and critical, moving back and forth between the story, its telling, and the contingencies of perspectival borders.

This style of theorizing, rooted in narration, is reflexive and not reducible to discrete variables. As Linda Brodkey explains: "The outstanding epistemological advantage of interpretation is the realization that although experience cannot be recovered, it can be narrated."[29] Central to this project, then, are the assumptions that meaning is historically contingent, contextually bound, socially constructed, and always problematic. Thus any search for meanings must be situated in the practical context within which they are voiced. The place of departure for the search for meaning is with the material practices of the subject. So while personal meaning is the sense each individual makes, it can never be reducible to one essential source.

Like the practices they articulate, personal meanings are in some ways difficult to pin down. They can appear to be the property of an individual, while also connecting that individual to a social community. They can seem ostensibly objective, and unencumbered by value or feeling, yet are underscored and sometimes undone by the deep convictions that sustain particular interests. Personal meanings can seem self-evident—and then become elusive when one attempts explanations. Appearing immutable, personal meanings can crumble during times of disputation, negotiation, and symbolic interaction. And within such dynamics, personal meanings may assert the unitary meanings we desire at the expense of recognizing the contradictory constructs we live. How we understand the context and evolutions of our practices determines whether we see a specific context as socially constructed, individually determined, or naturally inherited. These constructions will then shape interpretive possibilities and the discursive practices that accompany them. Because personal meanings are contingent upon context and upon the perspectives of others, they are always shifting. Consequently the meanings one makes from practice are in a state of continual and contradictory reinterpretation as other contexts and other voices are taken into account or are ignored.

To say that personal meanings are contradictory—they simultaneously express the said and the unsaid, pose myths and construct realities, and can be seen as belonging to individuals and cultures—is not to assert a dreary relativism that all meanings are equal, accurate, just, or empowering, or that communication is either impossible or a mere matter of individual thought and determination. Just the opposite: this capacity for contradiction, or the situation of multiple and conflicting meanings that constitute the heteroglossic in language, can serve as the departure for a dialogic understanding that theorizes about how one understands the given realities of teaching as well as the realities that teaching makes possible. Central to this study, then, is the problem of how subjects produce and reproduce meanings and myths about education through their theories, practices, routines, discourses, contexts, and reflections on educational life, and how such meanings produce identities.

Finally, a style of theorizing that is concerned with interpretation and meanings must also attend to the perspective and power of the researcher. In the case of ethnography, the researcher's presence always already implicates her in her own research in at least two significant ways.[30] First, because ethnography is predicated upon not simply being there but with establishing relationships with people, the researcher, if invited, is obligated to sympathetically participate in the lives of those she studies. This sympathetic participation should reflect a delicate balance between probing the motivations, intents, investments, and practices of persons, and respecting their boundaries of privacy and vulnerability. It is a difficult participation to invite because typically such participation is not mutual. I am not the one revealing my stories, fears, and vulnerabilities. Nor is it possible, given this kind of relationship, for me to feel the kind of misrepresentation that emerges inevitably from multiple retellings of stories that are not my own.

Second, researchers have the power to reinterpret and hence authorize the experiences and voices of others in ways that may clash or not resonate with the lived experiences they seek to explore. I am referring here to a different kind of representation, made possible by the theoretical investments of the researcher. My own theoretical investments, described throughout this text, are rooted in critical traditions. No doubt other researchers, drawing upon other epistemological traditions, would differently interpret my constructions. Multiple perspectives on the same event, however, are both inevitable and desirable. The delicate work of interpretation depends upon difference. Consequently, the best I can do with such power is to take the advice of Linda Alcoff. Rather than approach my data through "a veil of ignorance," where my own interests and investments are supposedly held in some fictitious abeyance, "political theory must base itself on the initial premise that all persons, including the theorist, have a fleshy, material identity that will influence and pass judgment on political claims."[31] Indeed, as someone who has spent significant time in school and university settings, my investment in understanding the messiness of learning to teach is an investment in self-understanding and in the desire to help refashion the contexts where I live.

DISCOURSES OF EXPERIENCE

Our capacity to produce contradictory meanings determines the problematic nature of education and the language we use to describe our experience there. A problematic can be understood as, "a conceptual structure that can be identified both by the questions it raises and the questions it is incapable of raising."[32] For example, the structure of teacher education naturalizes the social organization of schooling. Typically, teaching programs are organized like schools, by grade levels and academic areas, and this deflects attention from the assumptions that built such a structure in the first place. The compartmentalized orientation of both schools and universities excludes consideration into other ways to organize knowledge and persons. To approach education and the language of experience as problematic, then, is to study its discourses and discursive practices in such a way as to reveal its commissions and its omissions.

Here, we are concerned with how student teachers express their practice: what they name and what remains unnamed. Through critique we are made able to challenge what Michel Foucault terms "regimes of discourse,"[33] or the authoritatively sanctioned and conventionally taken-for-granted ways of understanding, speaking, and acting. In this regard, Foucault's description of silences captures some of the implicit power dynamics of discourse:

> Silence itself—the things one declines to say, or is forbidden to name, the discretion that is required between different speakers—is less the absolute limit of discourse, the other side from which it is separated by a strict boundary, than an element that functions alongside the things said, with them and in relation to them within overall strategies. There is no binary division to be made between what one says and what one does not say; we must try to determine the different ways of not saying such things, how those who can and those who cannot speak of them are distributed, which type of discourse is authorized, or which form of discretion is required in either case. There is not one but many silences, and they are an integral part of the strategies that underlie and permeate discourses.[34]

Silences express power struggles because "certain accounts count,"[35] and discount others. These accounts are made from the stuff of discourse. Drawing on the work of Foucault, Thomas Popkewitz defines discourse as "set[ting] the conditions by which events are interpreted and one's self as an individual is located in a dynamic world."[36] A discourse becomes powerful when it is institutionally sanctioned. Discourse positions the subject in a dual way: in relation to what and how something is said and in relation to a community that makes particular practices possible and others unavailable. For example, every curriculum, as a form of discourse, intones particular orientations, values, and interests, and constructs visions of authority, power, and knowledge. The selected knowledge of any curriculum represents not only things to know, but a view of knowledge that implicitly defines the knower's capacities as it legitimates the persons who deem that knowledge important. This capacity to privilege particular accounts over others is based upon relations of power. Consequently, every curriculum authorizes relations of power, whether it be those of the textbook industry and demographics, established scholars, business and industry, specific traditions of knowledge, or theories of cognition and human development.

Power, however, is not an abstract thing. Power works through persons and is "instantiated in action, as a regular and routine phenomenon."[37] A person's capacity to act in ways that act upon the actions of others is not so much a matter of individual charisma, or lack of it, as it is the ability to "draw upon modes of domination structured into social systems."[38] Such a view of power can account for the ways persons learn to police their own behavior and desires, to construct desire from relations of power, and to conform to the orientations and mandates of inherited contexts. The teacher's authority to control a class, for example, is sustained by school rules and regulations, curricular organization, and an administrative structure. The male administrator's capacity to act paternalistically or chauvinistically toward women teachers is sustained by traditions of patriarchal structures. While these types of power are legitimated by traditions of school organization and social structure, their realization depends upon persons' actions and how power acts upon their actions.

Which accounts count depends upon whose voice is valued in the larger culture. Adrienne Rich provides the example of women's history: "The entire history of women's struggle for self-determination has been muffled in silence over and over."[39] Such silences sustained by institutionalized patriarchal discourse, Rich observed, sever women from their history and constitute "one of the ways in which women's work and thinking has been made to seem sporadic, errant, orphaned of any tradition of its own."[40] Its effect is to render women voiceless and then blame them for not having voice. These silences are what Tilly Olsen calls *unnatural*, "the unnatural thwarting of what struggles come into being, but cannot."[41] The work of feminists has shown that these silences, while inherited, are not immutable, the struggle for voice is implicitly a political one marked by the power struggles of resistance and domination.

Power, then, is relational (although not usually equal), and exercised within a context of resistance. This relationship informs its internal dynamics. Understanding the *context* of power, in concert with the *relationships* it articulates and effectuates, allows us to move beyond an abstract notion of individual autonomy to construct a cultural theory of meaning grounded in social circumstances and material practices. Moreover, any theory of power must also be sensitive to the capacity of persons to interpret and intervene in their world. Such a view of human agency allows us to raise the question: Could persons have acted and interpreted differently? That is, what enables or constrains particular forms of practices and the discourses that legitimate or challenge them?

Marx considered the problem of human action in its historical context in an early work, *The Eighteenth Brumaire of Louis Bonaparte*. There he analyzed the relation history has to social consciousness, and the historical forces that appear to unconsciously shape and limit our capacity for creative practices:

> [People] . . . make their own history, but do not make it just as they please; they do not make it under circumstances directly chosen by themselves, but under circumstances directly encountered, given and transmitted from the past. The tradition of all the dead generations weighs like a nightmare on the brain of the living. And just when they seem engaged in revolutionizing themselves and things, in cre-

ating something that has never yet existed, precisely in such periods of revolutionary crisis, they anxiously conjure up the spirits of the past to their service and borrow from them names, battle cries, and costumes in order to present the new scene of world history in this time-honored disguise and this borrowed language.[42]

Although Marx was describing a specific historical crisis, his observations suggest how historical forces are subjectively taken up to shape the material culture and the practices of persons. Such a concern can provide insight into the problems of social change, and in particular the paradox of constructing emancipatory social relationships from an oppressive past. In many ways, the student teacher is confronted with a similar dilemma—between tradition and change—because when student teachers step into the teacher's role they are confronted not only with the traditions associated with those of past teachers and those of past and present classroom lives, but with the personal desire to carve out one's own territory, develop one's own style, and make a difference in the education of students.

Yet the problem of acting in an inherited context, while at the same time trying to establish one's authority in a situation charged by power struggles, often finds student teachers embodying the very traditions they hoped to change. In fact, the student teacher is struggling between two kinds of "ideological practice": concrete practice, or the practical activities of persons, and symbolic practice, or the socially normative categories persons appropriate to define and organize their experiences. It is this disjuncture between one's theory of and practice in the world that characterizes ideology not so much as a set of ideas but as a constitutive and contradictory system of social practices.[43]

Returning to Marx's description for a moment, we can begin to consider how linguistic practices (a "borrowed language") become imbricated with social relationships ("traditions of dead generations") to compose the ideological practices of persons.

The concept of "borrowed languages" is richly developed in the work of Russian philosopher Mikhail Bakhtin, who connects language to the process of becoming:

The ideological becoming of a human being . . . is the process of selectively assimilating the words of others. . . . The tendency to assimilate others' discourse takes on an even deeper and more basic significance in an individual's ideological becoming. . . . Another's discourse performs here no longer as information, directions, rules, models and so forth—but strives rather to determine the very bases of our ideological interrelations with the world, the very basis of our behavior; it performs here as *authoritative discourse* and an *internally persuasive discourse.*[44]

Bakhtin explained there is always a power struggle and hence a dialogical relationship between authoritative discourse and internally persuasive discourse. This relationship determines one's ideological becoming: the orientations, investments, beliefs, and dispositions that are already inscribed in the specific discourses we take up. Bakhtin's categories of discourse presuppose particular images of knowledge, history, and agency: he poses epistemological as well as ontological purposes.

Authoritative discourse is discourse that demands allegiance, an a priori discourse that operates within a variety of social contexts and partly determines our "symbolic practices," or the normative categories that organize and disorganize our perceptions. It is "received" and static knowledge, dispensed in a style that eludes the knower, but dictates, in some ways, the knower's frames of reference and the discursive practices that sustain them. Bakhtin termed such discourse the "word of the father, adult, teacher, etc." in that these positions already have the power to authorize subjects. As Bakhtin explained: "The one perceiving and understanding this discourse is a distant descendent; there can be no arguing with him."[45] Examples of authoritative discourse in education include such contradictions as education must return to "the great books" of the academic canon and abandon the influence of the civil rights movement for a more inclusive curriculum, or that curricula must be aligned more closely to the needs of industry, technology, and national defense.[46] Authoritative discourse, then, sets the conditions for discursive practices.

Internally persuasive discourse occupies the same terrain but it is "denied all privilege."[47] Unlike the unitary meanings authorized by authoritative discourse, internally persuasive discourse pulls one away from norms and admits a variety of contradictory social discourses. As renegade knowledge, internally persuasive discourse has no institutional privilege, because its practices are in opposition to socially sanctioned views and normative meanings. It is the discourse of subversion. Internally persuasive discourse is, as Bakhtin argues, "half ours," and as we struggle to make it our own and as it clashes with other internally persuasive discourses, "this discourse is able to reveal ever newer *ways to mean.*"[48]

Discourse that is internally persuasive provisions creativity, the play of meanings. It celebrates the ambiguity of words. For Bakhtin, internally persuasive discourse is the site of departure rather than a place of arrival. A tentative discourse, subject to negotiation and shifting contexts, and able to voice possibilities unforeseen, internally persuasive discourse is a discourse of becoming. Like the word itself, this style of discourse expresses relationships between persons and things. As a many-voiced and heteroglossic discourse, it suggests something about one's subjectivity and something about the objective conditions one confronts. In education, internally persuasive discourse provisions engagement with what we know and the struggle to extend, discard, or keep it: it is characterized by those surprising questions—raised by the students and the teacher—that move from exhausted predestinations to the unanticipated. Internally persuasive discourse is opened during times of spontaneity, improvisation, interpretive risks, crises, and when one reflects upon taken-for-granted ways of knowing. In this way, internally persuasive discourse is always in dialogue with authoritative discourse.

In both kinds of discourse, however, the word is not conceived as merely mirroring the intentions of its speaker or in mimesis with the social reality it attempts to encode. In each discourse, meaning is mediated by history and context, and by the speaker and listener. This dynamic quality propels the struggles between authoritative and internally persuasive discourse and between concrete and symbolic practices. Inasmuch as the word always inheres in particular worldviews and particular epistemological commitments, or ways of knowing, the struggle to express oneself is always in tension with history and with the voices of others. It is worth quoting Bakhtin's words at length:

> All words have the "taste" of a profession, a genre, a tendency, a party, a particular work, a particular person, a generation, an age group, the day and hour. Each word tastes of the context and contexts in which it has lived its socially charged life; all words and forms are populated by intentions. . . .
>
> As a living, socio-ideological concrete thing, as heteroglot opinion, language, for the individual consciousness, lies on the borderline between oneself and the other. The word in language is half someone else's. It becomes "one's own" only when the speaker populates it with his own intention, his own accent, when he appropriates the word, adapting it to his own semantic and expressive intention. Prior to this moment of appropriation, the word does not exist in a neutral and impersonal language (it is not, after all, out of a dictionary that the speaker gets his words!), but rather it exists in other people's mouths, in other people's contexts, serving other people's intentions: it is from there that one must take the word, and make it one's own. And not all words for just anyone submit equally easily to this appropriation, to this seizure and transformation into private property: many words stubbornly resist, others remain alien, sound foreign in the mouth of the one who appropriated them and who now speaks for them; they cannot be assimilated into his [or her] context and fall out of it; it is as if they put themselves in quotation marks

against the will of the speaker. Language is not a neutral medium that passes freely and easily into the private property of the speaker's intentions; it is populated—overpopulated—with the intentions of others. Expropriating it, forcing it to submit to one's own intentions and accents, is a difficult and complicated process.[49]

Words, and their meanings then, carry the intentions and contexts of historical subjects—ideas that precede but do not preclude the speaker. Our words signify communities of discourse that realize language as social. These communities—authoritative and personal—are always in conflict. Bakhtin's description of the word as slippery, elusive, and bearing the capacity to assert another's intentions and meanings in opposition to the speaker's efforts, is of special concern in this study where teaching is reconceptualized as a struggle for voice. For in considering such a struggle, our concern is extended to the contexts and circumstances that make signifying practices possible.

The struggle for voice begins when a person attempts to communicate meaning to someone else. Finding the words, speaking for oneself and feeling heard by others, are all a part of this struggle. While tone, accent, and style qualify meaning, meaning is never realized by the individual alone. The struggle originates with the individual, is shaped through social interaction and mediated by language. Voice suggests relationships: the individual's relationship to the meaning of her or his lived experience and hence to language, and the individual's relationship to the other, since understanding is social. It may be sparked by personal intent, but voice is always negotiated within context and situations, and by the meanings of others. The struggle for voice, then, is always subjective, dynamic, interactive, and incomplete; it is never a matter of mechanical correspondence between the speaker's intentions, the language, and the listener. Admitting this struggle into the discourse of teacher education allows us to ask: For whom does the teacher speak: the curriculum, the school, the profession, the students, the teacher? How does the teacher negotiate between the polyphony of voices and the competing interests that each represent? And, what do student teachers think about when they consider their own voice?

2

The Structure of Experience
and the Experience of Structure in
Teacher Education

In 1935 George S. Counts published a short essay—"Break the Teacher Training Lockstep"—decrying conformity in teacher education.[1] Written barely ten years after the beginning of university-based teacher education and the end of the specialized and single-purposed normal school rule, Counts pointed out that changing the setting of teacher education had done little else than expand the amount of time spent in the study of teaching. Except for the salient fact that teacher education now provided an avenue to a university education previously inaccessible to large sectors of working-class women and men, this "new" teacher education was barely distinguished from its technically oriented predecessor. Arguing that the structure and knowledge base of teacher "training" is anachronistic and inadequate, Counts condemned its entire curriculum:

> The familiar curricula pattern of orientation courses, subject matter courses, theory courses, observation courses, and practice-teaching assignments is but a conglomeration of precepts and practices inherited from the more limited environment of a former day.[2]

Counts denounced as well teacher education's vocational design with its mechanistic emphasis on practicality over transformative practices. Like other educators of his generation, such as Louise Rosenblatt and Theodore Brameld, Counts believed that teachers could be significant social change agents and that teacher education should encourage a more equitable and democratic society. The prevailing directions, however, were reminiscent of W. E. B.

Dubois's depiction of vocational education as that "sordid utilitarianism,"[3] where training supplanted education. Indeed, over thirty years after Counts denounced its "lockstep" conformity, and Harold Rugg characterized teacher education as "the conforming way,"[4] Seymour Sarason and colleagues complained about its cultivated passivity: "The prospective teacher, like all other college students, spends a lot of time in a seat in a classroom or library."[5]

Implicit in these critiques is a concern about the pacification of knowers and what is to be known. When knowledge is reduced to rigid directives that demand little else from the knower than acquiescence, knowers are bereft of their capacity to intervene in the world, and knowledge is expressed as static and immutable. Conformity, however, speaks to something more than the uniformity of thought and the standardization of activity. As a measure for being, conformity diminishes prospects of becoming something other than what has been previously established. In this sense, the forces of conformity are repressive. Hannah Arendt argues that conformity "normalizes" persons because "behavior has replaced action as the foremost mode of human relationship."[6] In other words, conformity, in its adherence to the dictates of social convention, privileges routinized behavior over critical action. Its centripetal force pulls toward reproducing the status quo in behavior as it mediates our subjective capacity to intervene in the world. Education, when dominated by the discourse and discursive practices of conformity, scripts a mechanistic training. The euphemistic label "teacher training" captures the essence of this project.

The problem of conformity in teacher education stems in part from its emphasis on training. From the start, teacher education was conceived of as synonymous with vocational preparation.[7] The vocational model of teacher education poses the process of becoming a teacher as no more than an adaptation to the expectations and directives of others and the acquisition of predetermined skills—both of which are largely accomplished through imitation, recitation, and assimilation. What is privileged is an image of knowledge as "received" and an identity of the neophyte as an empty receptacle. But whereas, in this depiction, knowledge may change the knower, the knower is perceived as incapable of changing or constructing knowledge. This monological process constitutes training, not education, and lacks any theory about our creative capacity to interpret reality and bestow this experience with multiple meanings. Such a model perpetuates what Maxine Greene calls "the matter of mystification" in teacher education, or the deceitfully simplistic knowledge of the world and of human beings that teacher education reproduces.[8]

A second kind of conformity in teacher education derives from its historic dependency on the field of psychology in defining learning and development. As Thomas Popkewitz argues:

Much of school discourse after the turn of the century was organized around principles of educational psychology. The language of psychology created a way to reason about social conduct as defined tasks to be evaluated in relation to universal attributes of individuals and notions of efficiency.[9]

The work of such men as Edward Thorndike in the field of measurement and testing, Franklin Bobbitt in curriculum construction, and Joseph Rice in educational administration served to legitimate the practice of science in education as neutral, value-free, and universally applicable without regard to context.[10] Their discourse of science was grounded in the Western Enlightenment, a project that sought to determine unitary laws of nature: one truth, and an objective, reliable, and universal foundation of knowledge.[11] The effect of their work has been to shift the center of education from "the tangible presence of the teacher to the remote knowledge and values incarnate in the curriculum."[12] In their discourse, learning was depicted as the achievement of preordained goals and reduced to a behavioristic vision of stimulus and response; the problem of learning was considered a technical problem of management. Knowledge, broken down into discrete and measurable units, was arranged hierarchically, in order to convert learning to observable outcomes. Borrowing from the methodology of the natural sciences and the discourse of scientific management in industry, a technical mode of rationality came to determine the dominant approach taken in understanding and organizing teaching and learning.

In discussing the effects of technical rationality, Henry Giroux makes a series of important distinctions: its interest is in constructing law-governed regularities; knowledge is viewed as neutral and is canonized as "fact"; behavior is equated with outcomes that can be predicted and controlled; and the educator is viewed as objective.[13] Like the goals of industry, this institutionalized vision of education was one that attempted to maintain an orderly and efficient society necessary to the underlying values of social control. Such a vision is based upon repression; the individual's potential to become something other than what has been predicted is diminished.

A third kind of conformity works through the relationship between compulsory education and teacher education. The values of efficiency and order in teacher education have their roots in the development of compulsory education. Historically, the schools have functioned as an instrument of social policy. In social policy, schools became instruments of a national socialization. Their signifying values, however, were defined elsewhere; schools did not set policies, but rather attempted their implementation.[14] Such a mandate for social control was problematic.

In a study of stratification and credentialization in education, Randall Collins points out that much of the impetus to make education compulsory came from the need to control the socialization of the children of European immigrants in order to perpetuate the values and interests of the middle class and the knowledge base of traditional Anglo-Protestant culture. The myth was that education was to serve as the "melting pot" of culture. That metaphor itself was manipulative, not descriptive:

> Insofar as the school system was created to resolve the [severe multiethnic] strife by reducing cultural diversity, one can say it has met with a degree of success. It did manage to make training in Anglo-Protestant culture and political values compulsory for all children up to a certain age, and it did make it *virtually* compulsory for a continually increasing period beyond this if the student wanted to be economically successful.[15]

On the other hand, Collins indicates that as the press for credentials beyond high school became more and more a prerequisite for employment and social mobility, the knowledge base of compulsory education appeared more trivial because it had no relevancy to the majority of students' lives or to their future as workers. Here lies the tension. Ironically, the Anglo-Protestant culture that schools attempted to preserve became relevant only insofar as it could be exchanged for additional credentials. This exchange underscored the impossibility of mandating knowledge as an end unto itself. Yet the press for conformity, whether in acquiring knowledge or credentials, became a significant moment of compulsory education and hence an explicit tension in the education of teachers.

The problem of conformity in teacher education, then, begins with the fact that schools attempt to "process" not only knowledge but persons as well.[16] This is not to say that schools accomplish these values and that teachers and students universally accept and intentionally "behave" in ways that implement and perpetuate this vision. There is no simple correspondence between the values of social control and life in the classroom, because the conditions of conformity create power struggles between the situations one confronts and the ways such situations are mediated and lived. However, in identifying conformity as one tension in the education of teachers, we can explore images of teaching and learning that sustain as well as challenge this dominant ethos. Can the tensions of teacher education be experienced in such a way that its potential—as a catalyst for transforming schools and the knowledges cultivated there—becomes a possibility felt by its participants? Must teacher education be lived as an accommodation to existing school structure? Can teacher education be structured more dialogically to take into account the myriad forms of negotiation that position pedagogy and the teacher's identity?

The above questions suggest two specific approaches to understanding the tensions between being and becoming: whether the teacher is in actuality a static product of an assembly-line socialization, or whether the teacher is continually shaping and being shaped by the dynamics of social practice, social structure, and history. Whereas the former posits a repressive model of identity and pedagogy, in that both appear as unitary, noncontradictory, and already complete, the latter is dialogical because it recognizes identity and pedagogy as discursively constructed, incomplete, and subject to change. Throughout the history of teacher education, both discourses on learning to teach are available.[17] There are those who have argued that teacher education can serve the interests of democratic principles and social justice precisely because teachers have the capacity to intervene in the world. And there have been those who have argued that education should serve the interests of business, national defense, and social conformity because the goal of education, and hence the work of teachers, should be limited to cultural transmission and social reproduction. The education of teachers and the experience of teaching are lived within this contradiction.

I propose a dialogic restructuring of teacher education that begins with the recognition that multiple realities, voices, and discourses conjoin and clash in the process of coming to know. Such a restructuring, explored in the last chapter, is necessary for the goal of a more democratic schooling and for the creation of democratic pedagogies that value the struggle for voice and make available the discursive practices necessary for the struggle of social justice.

The present chapter analyzes both the theories and practices that structure experience in learning to teach, and in doing so, attends to the texture of that experience in teacher education. My focus is on the discourse of experience because learning by experience is a fundamental value in the process of becoming a teacher. Yet this value is so taken for granted that the underlying structures and assumptions that authorize it are rarely interrogated. What is the structure of experience in teacher education? How has the experience of learning to teach been represented? How do its discourses summon and disorganize our understanding of experience? How does lived experience shape our relationship to knowledge?

To explore these questions, it is necessary to consider the organization, selection and politics of knowledge in secondary teacher education, and the relationships between theory and practice in learning to teach. The first part of this chapter describes how lived experience becomes fragmented from knowledge in academic life and how this fragmentation affects teachers' understanding of knowledge, theory, power, and authority. Four types of fragmentation, each sustained by authoritative discourse are discussed: the compartmentalization of knowledge; the separation of content from pedagogy; the separation of knowledge from interests; and the separation of theory and practice. The second part of this chapter focuses on the attempts of teachers and researchers to transform the conditions of this fragmentation in order to restore the dialogic relationships among knowledge, lived experience, and theory. This direction signifies the push toward internally persuasive discourses. Two questions shape this chapter: How do the circumstances of teacher education shape our thinking about learning to teach, the work of the teacher, and the nature of knowing and learning? And how is the history of teacher education lived in the discursive practices and voices of those learning to teach?

FRAGMENTED EXPERIENCE

John Dewey, in his discussion of the meaning of experience in education, begins with the problem of continuity, or what he terms "the experiential continuum."[18] While all experience can be seen as continuous, in that what has preceded certainly shapes what follows, Dewey's concern is with the work of shaping and interpreting experience, and whether such interpretations lead to transformative knowledge about the self and the social world. Continuity, as a criterion for experience, refers to the connectedness we feel toward our social practice and activities, and whether we see ourselves as authors of, rather than as authored by, our experience. Dewey distinguishes this form of *continuity* from *routinization*, when the repetition of activity desensitizes us and undermines our critical capacity to transform it into something more than going through the motions. So while "every experience is a moving force,"[19] the point, Dewey argues, is how experience comes to be understood as knowledge and how knowledge comes to be valued as experience. That is, behind every understanding of experience is an implicit theory of knowing, as well as values and beliefs about the nature of learning. For Dewey, "every genuine experience has an active side which changes in some degree the objective conditions under which experiences are had."[20]

More recently, Maxine Greene extends this notion in her discussion of experience as a form of authorship, and connects such action to modes of reflection and forces of sociality:

To be aware of authorship is to be aware of situationality and of the relation between the ways in which one interprets one's situation and the possibilities of action and choice. This means that one's "reality," rather than being fixed and predefined, is a perpetual emergent, becoming increasingly multiplex, as more perspectives are taken, more texts are opened, more friendships are made.[21]

Experience, then, as Dewey and Greene argue, is situated in time and therefore both timely yet transitory. The difference between mere circumstance and lived experience is our capacity to bestow experience with meanings, be reflective, and take action. Without an awareness of potential and given meanings, and our own capacity to extend experience through interpretation and risk, without this active side, our capacity to participate in the shaping of experience is diminished.

Fragmented experience is the shattering of experience into discrete and arbitrary units that are somehow dissociated from all that made experience in the first place. It is experience that is less than it could be, because fragmented experience cannot be extended or transformed. This form of fragmentation separates knowledge from experience and experience from knower. Here, knowledge concerns all the ideas, discourses, and possibilities that enable one to reflect upon the meanings of experience. Yet in academic life, knowledge and experience are typically fragmented by tradition and design. There is a disjunction between the authoritative discourse required by the academy and the internally persuasive discourse that can extend the understandings and meanings one already possesses. The fragmentation of knowledge from experience, however, is so pervasive that we come to expect personal exclusion. Its roots are in the arrangement of academic knowledge, the dualism of content and pedagogy, the selection and politics of knowledge, and the tension between theory and practice.

The Compartmentalization of Knowledge

"School subjects" such as English, history, science, or math, organize more than the division of the school day, the movement of students, and the labor of teachers.[22] They also authorize the classification, arrangement, and selection of forms of knowledge. That is, school subjects represent knowledge that has been compartmentalized. This form of knowledge serves as the basis for curricular organization.

Compartmentalization defines the limits of relevancy; it brackets our definitions of context and content, and imposes measures of credibility that determine what we accept and reject as true and as false. The compartmentalization of knowledge stipulates the boundaries of discourse—what is spoken and what remains unsaid—and provides the borders of interpretation.

For example, students may easily travel through their school subjects without a thought as to how these subjects interrelate or how the social convention of fracturing knowledge into academic territories evolved. In this fragmented world, each subject is an island, supposedly unaffected by all that surrounds it. Thus curriculum organization is fragmented into instructional activities reduced to discrete blocks of time, thereby isolating subject areas and teachers, abstracting knowledge from its socio-cultural roots and political consequences, and decontextualizing knowledge and skills from their practical existence.

Compartmentalized knowledge is knowledge that is self-referential; it seems to hold no other context beyond its immediate presentation. History, for example, is reduced to a textbook account of noncontradictory events. Language, in the context of the English classroom, becomes equated solely with dominant conventions of grammar usage and the mimetic iteration of texts. When knowledge is severed from its socio-cultural context, all the qualities of contingency, authorship, and chronology that realize knowledge in the first place are lost. Indeed, knowledge severed from time and place takes on a fixed appearance, valued precisely because it does not change. The mystification here is that while knowledge is valued as timeless, its value is determined by "the test of time."

The movement to return to "the basics" in education is one example of how time and the value of self-referential knowledge is used to legitimate curricular selection. The return to the "basics" presumes a simpler time and a simpler view of knowledge as representing a singleness of purpose and an essential meaning. Such a desire, however, constructs a repressive myth. Yet this value on time hides the very human process of selection and valuation. As Raymond Williams explains: "To put on to Time, the abstraction, the responsibility for our own active choices is to suppress a central part of our experience."[23] When time supplants humanity, the ethical issue of human responsibility is abandoned. This discourse is not capable of addressing such questions as what and who determines the "basics," why such knowledge is desirable, and who benefits from the forms it can take.

When the problem of interpretation is never explicit, knowledge appears to speak for itself and supposedly possesses a fixed meaning. The conditions of both knowledge and knowing are thus set: knowledge is not expressed as, in Philip Wexler's phrase, a "transformative social activity."[24] Given the limitations of compartmentalization, Wexler goes on to argue that what compartmentalization may in fact teach is "fragmentation as a mode of thought [that] blocks the potential for synthetic integration and the capacity to imagine totality."[25] What becomes fragmented is not just our conceptions of knowledge but our relationships—both possible and given—to it. We lose our ability to theorize about the consequences of social activity and our own power to effect and understand its effects.

James Donald refers to this coupling of knowledge and power when he argues that agency "can only be understood (and changed) if it is conceived not just as the source of social change, but above all, as an effect of particular social and institutional practices."[26] That is, the compartmentalization of knowledge presents not just a vision of knowledge and a vision of persons, but a set of discursive practices that make unavailable other practices. Compartmentalization, as presently lived, thwarts the development of critical relationships to knowledge and stalls the awareness that things could be different and that action can be taken to make that difference.

For those who arrive at the university, the compartmentalization of school knowledge reaches new heights. This is no coincidence, since the knowledge taught in compulsory education has its roots in the academy.[27] For those who enter the world of secondary teacher education, much of their program depends upon accepting the rules and rites of specialization, claiming and guarding a piece of academic territory, identifying with an academic department, and taking up a particular discourse and its accompanying practices.[28] Admission into the world of secondary education requires such specificity because compartmentalization defines not only knowledge but the work and status of teachers as well. Such territoriality sets the boundaries of what is accepted as "expertise" as it insures the isolation of teachers.

Pedagogy and Content

Inasmuch as the work of secondary teachers is defined by subject specialization, those learning to teach must "master" particular subject areas, as well as immerse themselves in the direct process of teaching them. However, the historic separation of knowledge from practice in the university centered around liberal arts prevents the student from formally learning about pedagogy and academic content in tandem.[29] Indeed, knowledge and practice are presented as a dualism. This separation tends to mystify the actual and potential relations between the "how" and the "what," and limits pedagogy to a mechanical problem of transmission.

But pedagogy, as David Lusted rightly argues, is productive and should be understood as an intimate moment of knowledge:

Why is pedagogy important? It is important since, as a concept, it draws attention to the *process* through which knowledge is produced. Pedagogy addresses the "how" questions involved not only in the transmission or reproduction of knowledge but also in its production. Indeed, it enables us to question the validity of separating these activities so easily by asking under what conditions and through what means we "come to know." How one teaches is therefore of central interest but, through the prism of pedagogy, it becomes inseparable from what is being taught and, crucially, how one learns.[30]

Pedagogy demands and constructs complex social relationships. Through exchange, pedagogy becomes productive, constituting the forms of knowing, the conditions for knowing, and the subjectivities of knowers. Pedagogy points to the agency that joins teaching and learning. Any practical discussion of pedagogy should address the discursive process of producing knowledge and the strategies for interpreting the knowledges that can and cannot be produced. This dialogic view of pedagogy is one that invites consideration of the social negotiation necessary for the production and interpretation of knowledge.

While the concept of pedagogy remains potentially powerful, its status is low. Indeed, future teachers and those who work with them perceive course work in an academic specialization as providing the real credentials for expertise in secondary teaching. Course work in education may offer opportunities for acquiring teaching skills, but an academic specialization permits the assumption of particular forms of cultural authority. This is because the academic myth of becoming an expert assumes that knowledge is instructive in and of itself. Indeed, as experts, secondary teachers may be perceived or perceive themselves as custodians of culture and as transmitters of cultural knowledge.

Mina Shaughnessy's stages of teacher development suggest this tension—the ways that content shuts out the agency of teacher and students—and identifies pedagogical consequences of viewing the work of teaching as custodial. Two of her stages are relevant here. "GUARDING THE TOWER" positions the teacher as a watchdog when "the teacher is in one way or another concentrating on protecting the academy (including himself) from the outsiders, those who do not seem to belong in the community of learners."[31] "CONVERTING THE NATIVES," a preceding stage, begins with the assumption that students can learn but do not possess their own knowledge. Consequently, they are taught as if they were empty vessels. "Learning is thought not so much as a constant and often troubling reformulation of the world so as to encompass new knowledge but as a steady flow of truth into a void."[32] Shaughnessy rightly argues that if uncritically assumed, the supposed cultural authority of the teacher translates into a pedagogy of imposition. This situation is inevitable when content is valued over pedagogy and over the lives of students.

Affecting more than one's teaching methods and one's epistemological visions, the low status of pedagogy is inscribed in the relationship between schools of education and other university departments. Like secondary schools, hierarchical organization defines the world of the university. Schools of education—and in particular teacher education programs—have been ghettoized by the larger university. They are low-status places and, according to Barbara Schneider, continue to be the brunt of significant criticism from the larger university community:

> Reproved for low admission requirements, technical rather than liberal arts focus, and questionable commitment to scholarship, schools of education have been labeled by some to be the "slums" of the academic campus.[33]

Three key dynamics are at work here, all of which grow out of the dichotomy of theory and practice, when theoretical knowledge is viewed as the property of an academic department and schools of education are viewed as only capable of hands-on practice. First, the elevation of academic knowledge over practice banishes practice to the realm of the practical. From the perspective of the larger university, the work of the teacher is viewed as technical rather than intellectual. Second, schools of education are not thought of as capable of producing scientific knowledge unencumbered by values and beliefs. Indeed, the knowledge of school practice is devalued because it is contingent, situated, and resistant to unitary truths, immutable laws, or universal generalizations. School knowledge is thus seen as disruptive to the push for unitary knowledge. The problem is not that unitary knowledge is disrupted. Rather, it is with how dominant conventions valorize knowledge as if it was unencumbered by interests and investments. Finally, the deeply held myth that one learns to teach solely by experience works against teacher education, because if teachers learn by experience, why should they attend classes in schools of education? Indeed, pedagogical knowledge is typically dismissed by those who have never considered or contributed to it.

Most teaching academics believe they have learned to teach on their own. In addition, a majority of university professors view knowledge, not pedagogy, as instructive. Trained as "experts" in particular content areas but not in the production of their accompanying pedagogies, many accept the view, instanced by the university reward system, that teaching is secondary to the "real" work of scholarly research. This third dynamic—the dualism between pedagogy and academic knowledge—works to dismiss the efforts of those learning to teach. In a very poignant sense, this dismissal forms the subtext of learning to teach: student teachers must struggle to validate their own efforts amid a population of disbelievers.

A different dynamic of the disdain for teacher education is produced within the historic struggle between whether the function of university education is for elite or mass participation. Historically, elite participation has meant the participation of upper-and middle-class white males who were educated to manage the society they studied. Juxtaposed to this is the fact that teachers work in mass institutions, and that for women education constitutes a "universal job ghetto." Since 1975, for example, women have comprised eighty-four percent of all elementary teachers and forty-seven percent of all secondary teachers.[34] In other words, women students constitute the majority of students in teacher education programs. The entrenched sexism and classism of university culture may well account for part of the devaluation of teacher education and the generally low status of the profession.

Knowledge and Interests

The struggle between elite and mass participation is also played out in the liberal arts curriculum where conceptions of knowledge are fragmented from its represented interests and deep investments. To separate knowledge from interests is to present the former as value-free or objective, and to mask the power implicit in the latter. This is the third way that knowledge is divorced from lived experience. Curriculum, however, means more than the texts under study; to neutralize its definition as a mere course of study prevents a critical understanding of the functions of curriculum during the teaching and learning encounter. As Henry Giroux and Roger Simon rightly argue:

> [Curriculum] represents an expression of struggle over what forms of political activity, orders of representation, forms of moral regulation, and visions of the past and future should be legitimized, passed on, and debated in specific pedagogical sites.[35]

Emphasized above is the very notion of curriculum as a signifying practice of placement and displacement. Yet the underlying politics of selection are typically obscured through the ways knowledge is presented and organized. That is, curricula, as a consequence of selection, organization, and interpretation, symbolize not only what is privileged as real knowledge, but shape the discursive practices that infuse this knowledge with power.

For example, in university settings, the lecture format is typically employed to dispense knowledge, and examinations are the chief means for exchanging knowledge for credits leading to credentials. Here, knowledge inevitably appears as self-referential, something transmitted to students who have no voice in determining its relevancies and who have gained no insight into the struggles of selection or their own power to interpret. This form of presentation bestows both knowledge and the teacher representing it with an immutable quality of certainty, efficacy, and authority. Knowledge is positioned as monological.

While selection is an inherent feature of any curriculum, the process of canonization is one type of selective impulse that structures traditions of university knowledge. The liberal arts canon, or the body of knowledge deemed "sacred and great," valorizes the worldviews of white male writers to the extent of significantly excluding all other views. The presentation of European and North American white male authors as the faithful transmitters of universal experience obscures their cultural specificity, socio-historical context, and the political interests served and perpetuated by the canon's selective biases. It is taken for granted that the Western classics speak for everyone, and that meaning can be stabilized and fixed in time. The canon excludes the historic and contemporary voices of women, ethnic racial writers, or writers who significantly challenge what Bob Connell calls "the hegemonic academic curriculum," knowledge that "dominates people's ideas of what real learning is about."[36]

The canon represents "the selective tradition," a particular intellectual heritage that is supposedly drawn from the best of a culture.[37] The politics that legitimate such selection, however, are not a part of the conversation. Nor are the assumptions and structures of power that authorize its discourses and practices made evident. Rather, canonization is a process whereby selection implicitly devalues the cultural expressions that do contest its hegemony.[38]

Barbara Herrnstein Smith, for example, in analyzing literary studies in the United States, traces the politics of selection (and omission) to two mutually enforcing conservative traditions dominating the university: positivistic philological scholarship and humanistic pedagogy. The former posits a neutrality in its supposed separation of fact from value, while the latter attempts cultural maintenance in its preservation of selected traditions. Each tradition may appear diametrically opposed, fostering two worldviews, but they are really different aspects of the same academic argument:

> While professors of literature have sought to claim for their activities the rigor, objectivity, cognitive substantiality, and progress associated with science and the empirical disciplines, they have also attempted to remain faithful to the essentially conservative and didactic mission of humanistic studies: to honor and preserve the culture's traditionally esteemed objects—in this case, its canonized texts—and to illuminate and transmit the traditional cultural values presumably embodied in them.[39]

What is recommended as value becomes the determinant of value.[40] That is, when a work that is valued takes on a defining force and authorizes the criteria for other works, knowledge is not just bestowed with value, it also bestows value. For example, literary genres originating from England determine how other genres are judged. This teleological process partially accounts for the persistency and power of certain modes of interpretation disguised as authoritative. Built into this process of valuation is the exclusion of contrary interests. In such a cycle, the politics of value are mystified as one mode of knowing shuts out a multitude of lived experience. The canon, then, is not so much an object as it is objectifying. It asserts rarified meanings and interpretations, but is presented in such a way as to cover its own narrative tracks.

The selectivity of the curriculum represents what Manuel Alvarado and Bob Ferguson term "preferred discourses" on knowledge rather than knowledge itself.[41] Preferred discourses offer representations of the world, not the world itself. These signifying practices are typically mistaken for—because they are presented as—the practice itself. For example, a history text can never be a chronology of "brute facts." Instead, historical narratives are always written through the prism of the author's perspectives that are effects of the discourses available. Regardless of the teacher's intent, representations of school knowledge are neither ideologically innocent nor bound by an essentialist interpretation:

> There are a whole host of factors which can serve to mask the nature of a specific discourse. . . . An example would be the classic approach to the causes of the First World War which manages to avoid any reference to the concept of *imperialism,* but discusses the quite "natural" competition between powerful nations. The teacher's task should be to denaturalize various discourses rather than to endlessly validate them by a complicity with the unspoken norms of a powerful ideological state apparatus.[42]

For teachers to deconstruct various discourses, however, they must cultivate a critical awareness of perspectival boundaries. Yet this epistemological sensitivity is rarely a part of the teacher's education. To counter the dominant view of knowledge as neutral and capable of "speaking for itself," knowledge must be approached as problematic in its social construction, and the problem of representation, interpretation, and meaning—that is, the question, how do we know what we know—must become a central theme in disciplinary studies and in school classrooms. To admit such a theme, the social construction of canonical knowledge and how such material becomes the measure of convention must be questioned.

Educational researchers are theorizing curriculum as another form of ideological practice and recognize that the cultural authority of university and school knowledge is hardly universally accepted or neutrally received. Those researchers who critically study school life in classrooms, as well as those who live their lives there, understand the tensions—engendered by curriculum and its practice—between received knowledge and lived experience. These tensions are ideological; they include notions of power, status, and competence, and represent a cacophony of values, beliefs, ideas, investments, and discursive practices that shape knowledge and its interpretive possibilities. The movement to reconceptualize curriculum as ideological practice makes accessible an examination into how knowledge is produced and the contradictory ways students and teachers mediate it. The assumption is that students do not simply absorb cultural authority. They mediate it, refuse it, or refashion it with their own significance. This approach to school knowledge recognizes the contexts in which knowledge is produced and interpreted and attends to the subjective investments of those who produce it.

The study of school knowledge as problematic began in the early 1970s. Geoff Whitty traces the beginning of the "New Interpretive Sociology" to the publication of Michael Young's edited volume, *Knowledge and Control: New Directions for the Sociology of Education*. It is distinguished from other sociological writing by its attempt to situate school knowledge within its wider social context, uncover the social interests residing there, and return to the study of lived experience in classrooms. The authors in Young's collection also attempted to understand the contradictory relations among social class, the organization, transmission, and interpretation of knowledge, and school achievement in ways that moved beyond both individual culpability and theories of social inevitability. Whitty summarizes the new sociology's central concern:

> To explore the possibility that there was some contingent relationship between prevailing definitions of school knowledge and the broader social structure. The intention was to establish, and indeed expose, the "interests and values" implicated in prevailing curricular arrangements, usually with a view to changing them.[43]

Those who position curriculum as ideological practice—such North American critical theorists as for instance Jean Anyon, Michael Apple, Henry Giroux, Philip Wexler—have attempted in different ways to ground the study of curriculum in the lived experiences of those who daily encountered it.[44] These researchers share a commitment to a textual analysis of curriculum and to the theorization of how the dynamics of power and knowledge can render natural a social structure characterized by an unequal distribution of material and social wealth, social inequalities, and institutionalized forms of oppression. Such an analysis is meant to render problematic the taken for granted views of knowledge and power operating within the curriculum. In addressing these inequalities, these authors have sought to restore a sense of agency to the ways in which teachers and students respond to the push for cultural reproduction.[45]

Wexler, for example, advocates an approach to curriculum as ideological practice that attends to the *object* of practice as well as the social relationships it inscribes. Here, the object of practice refers to the production of knowledge during the teaching and learning encounter. The ways in which teachers and students interact with knowledge and the meanings produced by such interactions can reveal something about what actually happens to school knowledge when it is acted upon. Here, knowledge production is defined as:

> A chain or series of transformative activities which range from the social organization of text industries, to the activities of text producers, through the symbolic transformation of the text itself, and to the transformative interaction between text and reader, or school knowledge and student.[46]

By focusing on the production of knowledge, curriculum theorists can move beyond a study of constraints to the study of activity as productive and transformative.

Just what exactly is produced during the teaching and learning encounter, however, is not without contradictions and is not always transformative in a democratic sense. Persons can voluntarily act in ways that diminish their own possibilities despite personal intentions to do otherwise. Here I am referencing those discursive practices that authorize institutional imperatives for social control.

Linda McNeil provides an example of this contradictory reality in a study of school knowledge and school structure. Her study documents the teachers' and students' acceptance of bureaucratic constraints. Her ethnographic investigation of high school life shows how teachers maintained discipline and the consent of students by the ways in which they presented course material. Labeling this dynamic "defensive teaching," McNeil analyzes how teachers came to mask their own relationship to the subject matter and chose to simplify knowledge and thereby reduce teaching demands, all in exchange for classroom order and the students' minimal compliance to assignments. However, in the minds of these students, school knowledge lost all semblance of credibility. Everyone was aware of the meaninglessness of school routine:

> Defensive, controlling teaching does more than make content boring; it transforms the subject content from "real world" knowledge into "school knowledge," an artificial set of facts and generalizations whose credibility lies no longer in its authenticity as a cultural selection but in its instrumental value in meeting the obligations teachers and students have within the institution of schooling.[47]

Defensive teaching and learning masks the vulnerability of both knowledge and knower. Behind the dreary routine of turning textbook pages is a
psychic disengagement from knowledge and the learning process. During defensive teaching and learning, the activity of covering the material is literally
realized; meaning is veiled for the sake of an appearance of progress. In such
a scenario, where learners agree to be less than they could be, each participant
must hold in abeyance the potential relationships between knowledge and lived
experience, a relationship central to the production of meaning and voice. When
this occurs, students and teachers give up their ability to author learning. The
cost of consenting to this tacit agreement—if you go easy on me, I'll go easy
on you—is an actual de-skilling on the part of those involved.

To approach curriculum as an instance of ideological practice means to
study its contradictions as it is lived by teachers and students, but to understand these contradictions as necessitated by school structure and sustained by
larger cultural dynamics. Such a direction can help us untangle the social
construction of knowledge and the performative rituals that naturalize it.

When student teachers encounter a curriculum, they are always encountering more than a body of traditions. They have the difficult work of helping
their students make sense within a context that stifles interpretive risks and
creative thought, and of constructing relevancies and common ground necessary for the creation of effective pedagogies. Simultaneously, student teachers
must also confront their own subjective experience with school knowledge,
how their own deep convictions, investments, and desires have been structured by it.

The tension is that the normative discourse of teacher education and the
discursive practices it makes available does not admit such complexity. The
last form of fragmentation, that in effect, renders theory and practice a dualism, expresses this contradiction more fully.

Theory and Practice

That knowledge has the capacity to appear both meaningless and meaningful
is a dilemma that underscores the structure of teacher education and the lived
experiences of those who work there. The trivialization of knowledge becomes most evident when prospective teachers leave their university course
work and attempt, through classroom teaching, to render this knowledge
pedagogical and relevant. It is here that student teachers must not only make
sense of theory but attempt to experience practice theoretically. The last form
of fragmentation—between theory and practice—is most apparent when
prospective teachers live the dramatic shift from learning about teaching in

university settings to teaching in actual classrooms. Throughout student teaching, it becomes the work of prospective teachers to put into practice the knowledge obtained from college courses. At the same time, they are expected to transform this received classroom knowledge, shifting from a student's perspective to that of a teacher. However, this transformation—of both knowledge and identity, and hence involving the transposition of knowledge and experience—is highly problematic. For it is not just the university that fashions the student teacher's pedagogy; the student teacher's life history, both in and out of classrooms, offers definitions of what it means to learn and to teach.

As was briefly outlined in the first chapter, prospective teachers enter teacher education with practical theories about the work and stance of teachers. Their view of the teachers' work—grounded in their student perspectives, constructed from their prolonged experience of classroom life—is incomplete insofar as it is simplified to mere classroom performance. Yet this partial view is a significant tension in shaping prospective teachers' desires for a practical training experience.[48] The problem, however, is not so much their desire for practical methods as it is their understanding, authorized by vocational models of teacher education, of teaching methods as an end. The "methods as ends" model of teaching reduces the complexity of pedagogical activity to a technical solution and "forgets" that methods are a means for larger educational purposes.

Methods courses that focus on mechanistic applications and view knowledge as a form of technical rationality implicitly encourage conservatism among student teachers in two ways. First, knowledge is presented as an accomplished fact, separate from discursive practices and the relations of power it supposes. Second, the curriculum and its presentation are not considered in dialogic relationship to the lives of students and teachers. These tensions delay an understanding of how students and teachers create new knowledge during their curricular encounters. Both knowledge and students are repressed when methods courses do little more than aid the student teacher in getting large groups of students through the same lesson in a prescribed period of time.[49]

If school reality appears as given, so too does the knowledge it conveys. The research of Mark Ginsburg, on secondary prospective teachers' conceptions of and experience with curriculum in teacher education, begins with the question of whether teacher educators "encourage students to treat curriculum knowledge as given or as problematical."[50] If knowledge is taken up as given, it is presented as unencumbered by the problem of construction, interpretation, or subjectivity. In counterdistinction, knowledge as problematical posits a tentative view of knowledge as socially constructed, subject to political, economic, social, and cultural forces, and contingent upon communities of discourse, relations of power, and social change.

In Ginsburg's study, most university-based education course work focused on writing instructional objectives and preparing lesson plans in order to permit a smooth transition between university and classroom life. The assumption here was that the role of teacher education is to insure the maintenance of school structure. And while the students in this program were told that teachers make decisions, typically they had no decisions of their own to make. Their participation was reduced to spectators who received the presentations of others. How to teach obscured the more messy questions of what to teach and why particular methods are suitable. Consequently, the discursive practices made available prevented these students from theorizing about the potential relationships among pedagogy, content, and social interactions. "Preservice teachers were, for the most part, educated in how to follow orders—i.e., to take a prescribed curriculum and deliver it with a variety of techniques."[51]

The dominant organization of teacher education that presupposes an acceptance of the way things are tends also to reinforce the ideas and images of education that prospective teachers bring to the university. It is a cycle that powerfully affects prospective teachers' understanding of the relationship between pedagogical practice and theory. Prospective teachers want and expect to receive practical things, automatic and generic methods for immediate classroom application. They bring to their teacher education a search for recipes and, often, a dominant concern with methods of classroom discipline, because they are quite familiar with the teacher's role as social controller. These implicit needs preclude the desire for theory.

Martyn Descombe describes these socialized "desires" as part of the dynamic of the hidden pedagogy:

> An implicit theory of teaching . . . based on the assumption that without first establishing classroom control and being able to establish it without help from colleagues, there is no chance of being able to put across the subject matter of the lesson, and consequently, little chance of being regarded as a competent member of the teaching profession.[52]

This implicit theory is housed in the teacher's school biography: students daily observed the consequences of the teacher's private battle to maintain classroom control. The popular image of teaching as an individual activity, privatized by the walls between classrooms, is an image students bring to their teaching practice. These "walls" serve a metaphorical function as well: teachers are expected to work alone, without any help. In such a privatized world, the teaching methods required to sustain it are specific and unchanging. Consequently, education course work that does not immediately address "know how" or how to "make do" with the way things are and sustain the walls we have come to expect, appears impractical, idealistic, and too theoretical. Real school life, then, is taken for granted as the measure of a teacher education program, and, as such, the student teaching semester is implicitly valued as the training ground, the authentic moment, that mystically fills the void left by so-called theoretical course work.

While alienation from theory is highly documented, much of the traditional research does not examine what, precisely, theory means to those learning to teach. What images of theory do prospective teachers hold that make it appear so untenable? Part of the problem may well be that theory is often dispensed in a language separate from the student teacher's reality, or is encountered as an accomplished fact, unencumbered by disputation, rival theories, or the subjectivities of theorists. Moreover, theories are typically presented as abstracted from the experiences they seek to bracket. At the same time, theories are universalized to such an extent that they homogenize— through the process of generalization—the very qualities of indeterminacy, contradiction, and struggle that give shape to the exigencies of the theoretical impulse. That student teachers rarely have the space and official encouragement to consistently theorize about their lived experience further distances theory from practice, and diminishes student teachers' capacity to theorize about the sources of their pedagogy.

THE RENOVATION OF THEORY AS SOCIAL PRACTICE

The academic separation of theory from practice is another manifestation of knowledge fragmented from lived experience. This dualism, however, can be transformed dialogically if we pose questions about theory that include the voices and experiences of practitioners. For example, the question, "What are the sources of theory?," allows us to consider a range of relationships: between the practice and the practitioner, between the theory and the theorizer, and between the circumstance and the lived experience.

We can consider the process of theorizing not as an isolated activity separate from the experience of teaching, or as a grand truth one attempts to impose, but rather as a lived relationship, grounded in the practical existence of persons and dependent upon the process of interpretation and change. Seen in this way, theorizing is a tentative and potentially transformative instance of practice. To theorize about one's experience means to engage one's reflective capacities in order to be an author of that experience. The relationships between theory and internally persuasive discourse can also be examined. The sources of theory, then, are in practice; in the lived lives of teachers, in the values, beliefs, and deep convictions enacted in practice, in the social context that encloses such practice, and in the social relationships that enliven the teaching and learning encounter.

The research of D. Jean Clandinin, Michael Connelly, and Freema Elbaz, for example, provides such a view of theory, one that is more informal and situated in the "heads" of real teachers.[53] Their research depicts teachers as theorizing agents and argues that whether teachers see it as such, they implicitly hold and routinely enact theories of teaching and learning. By listening to the voices of teachers, these researchers have been able to ferret out what Connelly and Clandinin term the "personal practical knowledge" of teachers, or a combination of theory and practical knowledge born of lived experience.[54] Such knowledge is contextual, affective, situated, flexible and fluid, esthetic, intersubjective, and grounded in the body.

Clandinin describes personal practical knowledge as a means to regain a "person-centered language and perspective for accounting for school practices":[55]

> By "knowledge" in the phrase "personal practical knowledge" is meant that body of convictions, conscious or unconscious, which have arisen from experience, intimate, social and traditional, and which are expressed in a person's actions. The actions in question are all those acts that make up the practice of teaching including its planning and evaluation. "Personal practical knowledge" is knowledge which is imbued with all the experiences that make up a person's being. Its meaning is derived from, and understood in terms of, a person's experimental history, both professional and personal.[56]

The investigation of personal practical knowledge results in narrative accounts of how particular teachers come to know and understand classroom life. These accounts are useful because they authorize meanings, forms of theorizing that suggest a sense of ownership and voice in the theorizing process. In this case, ownership does not refer to the acquisition of private property, but rather to a sense of participation and connectedness to one's social practices. This style of research expresses the prevalent dilemmas of the teacher's work and the insights garnered from social practice. Through study of the perspectives, practices, and contexts of teaching, teachers are represented as complex beings, struggling to make sense of their work.

When the moral and existential dilemmas that are so much a part of the work of teachers, and the rich complexities born of social interaction, subjective experience, dependency, and struggle that characterize life in and outside the classroom are examined, reality does not take on an immutable and unitary presence. When teachers are viewed as sources of knowledge, a more constructivist notion of knowledge evolves. Peter Woods characterizes this type of knowledge as:

> Not simply an extant body of facts and theories, but a living, experimental, processual, flexible, creative, compilation of insights, memories, information, associations, articulations that go into resourcing on-the-spot teacher decision-making and action.[57]

To construct such knowledge, researchers have moved beyond the authority of positivistic methodology and the search for what C. Wright Mills calls "grand theory"[58] to qualitative ways of understanding experience. Studying the personal practical knowledge of teachers, for example, requires a research relationship based upon mutuality, respect, and the recognition of vulnerability of both researcher and teacher. No psychometric measures distance the researcher from the teacher. Indeed, it is for researchers to narrate and interpret the words of others and render explicit their own process of understanding. This type of knowledge production requires the researcher to be sensitive to representing the voices of those experiencing educational life as sources of knowledge, and to be committed to preserving their dignity and struggle.

Here, the concept of voice spans literal, metaphorical, and political terrains. In its literal sense, voice represents the speech and perspectives of the speaker; metaphorically, voice spans inflection, tone, accent, style, and the qualities and feelings conveyed by the speaker's words; and politically, a commitment to voice "attests to the *right* of speaking and being represented."[59] Finally, attending to the voice of teachers attempts to remedy the traditionally imposed silences of research subjects as primarily spoken about but rarely speaking for themselves.

The work of Madeleine Grumet and William Pinar in autobiography, and Peter Woods in life history, for example, are methods of reflexivity that make available the discursive practices necessary to the critical theorization of teachers' "experiential continuum," their construction of meanings, and their subjective development. Two significant intentions characterize this style of research: to open research to its transformatory potential and to establish the teacher's ownership of and centrality in the research process. While these approaches are somewhat different from the ones I employ in this study, it is useful to consider briefly how such methods work.

Madeleine Grumet, for example, employs the methods of autobiography stressing how future and present teachers come to know.[60] For teachers to be authors of their experience, "the teacher [must] learn to hear, formulate and articulate her own questions about her experience of teaching."[61] The autobiographical method, as a means to self-analysis through social interaction, opens up such questions because it is there—in the life of the teacher—that these questions are fixed. But more than raising questions and the recounting of experience, Grumet seeks, though interaction with teachers, "the transition from concrete experiences to the theory that addresses them."[62]

Whereas Grumet's work provides a social opportunity for guided reflection, William Pinar's method of "currere," from the latin root *curriculum*, attends to individual autobiography. Pinar's four-stage strategy encourages teachers to trace their intellectual antecedents.[63] Currere is a conceptual and temporal approach to autobiography that requires one to engage with and become critically distant from one's lived life in order to trace the dialogic relations among one's past, present, and future. "There are many related questions," Pinar writes, "but the dominant one is: what has been and what is now the nature of my educational experience?"[64] The purpose of doing currere is transformative; it is an approach to gain insight into "the process by which one becomes less parochial, more understanding, more interesting, more humane."[65]

A different style that depends on the theories of symbolic interaction is offered in the work of Peter Woods. Life history is based upon conversations with teachers. These conversations are informal, an attempt, on the researcher's part, to understand the teacher in relationship to that teacher's life. Life histories, as described by Woods:

> Tune into the process and flux of life with all its uncertainties, vicissitudes, inconsistencies, and ambiguities. . . . They reach the subjective realities, pull in the historic and contextualize the present within the total framework of individual lives.[66]

As similar and disparate themes across participants are identified and analyzed, collections of life histories are likely to allow the development of a grounded theory of teaching experience. A fundamental assumption, then, of research that attempts to renovate theory is that examined life is educative. The act of simultaneously recounting and re-creating one's cumulative experiences should provide critical insight into lived lives. Likewise, in reading about others, we may learn something about ourselves and come to value our own struggle for voice.

These research directions attempt to restore the centrality of teachers to the theorizing process. However, they should be approached as a place of departure in that the process of studying practices cannot conclude once practices are narrated. When practices become a text, they must be read not as guarantees of essential truths, or recipes for action, but as *representations* of particular discourses that implicate the voices of teachers and researchers in larger interests and investments. Unless the narrations of practices are read through theories of discourse—that is, as representing particular ideological interests, orientations, and meanings, and of deploying relations of power—there remains the danger of viewing personal knowledge as unencumbered by authoritative discourse and as unmediated by the relations of power and authority that work through every teaching and research practice.

Cameron McCarthy and Michael Apple are quite clear on this point: "the production of educational theory and research is itself a site of ideological and political struggle."[67] The particular forms of knowledge privileged in the above research designs are not immune from this struggle. Indeed, such research is in part a response to the dominant research models that seek to normalize pedagogical interventions.

At the same time, it must be acknowledged that the research directions previously described are significant in at least four ways. First, images of theory as reflective practice can dissipate a view of theory as imposed from above and situate it as constructed rather than received. Both theory and practice can thus be viewed as a problem of interpretation. Second, in positioning theory as dialogic to lived experience, the traditional dualism of theory and practice can be reconceptualized as a problem of praxis. When this occurs, practice can be understood theoretically. Third, an emphasis on personal practical knowledge values the activity of theorizing as a tenuous yet transformative activity. Teachers can experience themselves as authors and interpreters of their lived experience. To see teachers as interpretors of theory dismantles the view of theory as monological. Finally, these research directions re-establish a qualitative understanding of the complexity of the teacher's work. Through the use of qualitative research methods, research grounded in the voices and in the contradictory realities of teachers implicitly opposes technocratic research directions that seek to "improve" education without the teachers' knowledge.

The dichotomy between theory and practice, which represents, in actuality, the fragmentation of knowledge from lived experience, is challenged when the context of theory is practice, not other theories. At the same time, these research styles, if they can be examined as discourses that produce discursive practices, may provide a way into the problem of how practices produce relations of power. Indeed, unless the study of subjective knowledge moves beyond its celebratory appeal, there remains the danger of abstracting the teacher from the social context and from the borrowed discourses one claims as if they were one's own. As John Willingsky suggests, "researchers must find ways of stepping from behind the disembodied voice."[68]

The idea of personal practical knowledge has strong parallels to the writing of Antonio Gramsci, an Italian theorist and political activist concerned with the problems of agency and consciousness in social transformation. Educators have looked to the writings of Gramsci for insight into the relationship between education and social change.[69] Gramsci's theories are attractive to educators because he emphasized the capacity to intervene in the world.

For Gramsci, the purpose of theory is to politicize common sense and thereby move to the realm of "good sense." The starting point of theory must be common sense, for it is there where passion, intellect, philosophy, activity, and subjectivity commingle. Many of the research styles described above help teachers articulate what is common. Common sense, however, is not reducible to any one form. Gramsci likened it to folklore, which contains a contradictory mix of metaphor, myth, wisdom, and dominant social values that operate in everyday life. If uncritically accepted, however, common sense serves as a subjective force of normalization and naturalization: it can sustain an appearance of the world as given and received, and of reality as existing on its own because "all 'immediate' or unmediated responses [are] inevitably . . . conditioned by dominant structures and values."[70]

Through the process of socially excavating one's implicit philosophy of the world, Gramsci advocates "renovating" common sense with "the philosophy of praxis," a dialogue between theory and practice, thought and activity, knowledge and experience:

> A philosophy of praxis . . . must be a criticism of "common sense," basing itself, initially, however, on common sense in order to demonstrate that "everyone" is a philosopher and that it is not a question of introducing from scratch a scientific form of thought into everyone's individual life, but of renovating and making "critical" an already existing activity.[71]

The act of theorizing is not an imposition of abstract theories upon vacuous conditions. Theorizing is a form of engagement with and intervention in the world. Theory always lives in the practical experiences of us all and yet must be interpreted as a source of intervention. Problems occur when we refuse to acknowledge this. However, recent directions in the "renovation" of theory can challenge those in education to locate theory within practical experience and within the interests and investments it signifies, develop relationships between grand theory and local knowledge, and assist in moving beyond the sway of common sense that routinely structures prospective teachers' and practitioners' discourse of theory.

FROM SOCIALIZATION TO SUBJECTIVITY

Development of the teacher's identity always involves competing chronologies of becoming. I use the term "becoming" because it conveys the simultaneity of time, place, events, and the meanings we give them. For example, there are at least four chronologies that constitute the process of becoming a teacher. Each sense of place and time presents different sets of demands and assumptions, and makes available a different range of voices and discursive practices. Students who enter teacher education bring with them their first chronology negotiated throughout their cumulative classroom lives. This sense of chronology is composed from their prior educational biography and particular ideas about the nature of knowing and the roles and performative rituals of students and teachers. Their student experiences in the university and teacher education constitute the second chronology. Student teaching furnishes the third chronology; once in the schools, student teachers become privy to aspects of the teacher's world and departmental politics, and construct relationships with teachers, administrators, and students that were unavailable during their past student lives. A fourth chronology begins once the student teacher becomes a newly arrived teacher. At that time areas of influence and negotiation broaden; the teacher must mediate the influences of the school system, students, the teacher union, the community, public policy, professional organizations, and the cumulative experience of their classroom lives. Each of the above chronologies represents different and competing relations to power, knowledge, dependency, and negotiation, and authorizes frames of reference that effectuate discursive practices in teaching. The sense we make of each chronology depends upon the discourses we take up.

Unfortunately, the normative discourse in teacher education reduces the complexity of competing chronologies by authorizing a functionalist version of socialization that is incapable of attending to the site of socialization as a contested terrain, and the ways in which the individual becomes the site of struggle. The problem is that traditional theories of socialization cannot account for the ways individuals refashion, resist, or even take up dominant meanings as if they were their authors.

Unlike Dan Lortie's definition of socialization as "a subjective process—it is something that happens to people as they move through a series of structured experiences and internalize the subculture of the group,"[72] the view of becoming that I advocate is not limited to what happens to persons. Instead, my concern is in understanding what they make happen because of what happens to them and what it is that structures their practices. Lortie's definition of socialization cannot account for this dialogic process or the complexity of negotiation and dependency that characterize the activity of learning to teach by teaching. Nor does the functionalist idea that student teachers internalize the subculture of the group provide any insight into the fact that culture is not a static and received script for the enactment of behaviors, rules, values, commitments, and perspectives defined elsewhere. Rather, in the words of James Clifford:

If culture is not an object to be described, neither is it a unified corpus of symbols and meanings that can be definitively interpreted. Culture is contested, temporal, and emergent.[73]

Culture is where identities, desires, and investments are mobilized, constructed, and reworked. It is the site where antagonistic meanings push and pull at our sensibilities, deep investments, and relationships with others. And consequently there is not one monolithic culture that communicates unitary meanings. Circulating within and persuading any culture are an array of contesting and contradictory discourses that vie for our attention.

To speak and act as if there is one monolithic culture of teachers, students, or schools is to take up a discourse that is at once authoritative and impossible. Within any given culture, there exists a multiplicity of realities—both given and possible—that form competing ideologies, discourses, and the discursive practices that are made available because of them. It is within our subjectivities that we can make sense of these competing conditions even as these competing conditions "condition" our subjectivity in contradictory ways.

Subjectivity, or "the condition of being a subject,"[74] can be examined in terms of the contradictory criteria individuals hold. It is constitutive of direct and indirect experience and mediated by the discourses that lend conceptual order to our perceptions, points of view, investments, and desires.[75] Subjectivity is both our conceptual orderings of things and the deep investments summoned by such orderings. It organizes an individual's ideas about what it means to recognize oneself as a person, a student, a teacher, and so forth, and arranges strategies for the realization of these multiple identities. A concern with subjectivity, or how we come to be subjects, can move us beyond essentialist notions of human nature, the ideal of possessing a noncontradictory self, and the push to embody these kinds of stabilities in spite of the complicated realities we live. In this way, if we shift our thinking from a static notion of socialization that summons us to take up the unitary, noncontradictory discourse of the completed self, and move to a provisional, contradictory, and multiple understanding of subjectivity as both individual and social, we may be better able to theorize about the problem of how the student teacher's subjectivity persuades and is persuaded by the conditions of teaching and learning.

The meanings of school life, like the multiple meanings of teaching, are not limited to unitary or self-evident definitions. Just as culture is always in the process of being reinvented, renegotiated, and reinterpreted by its participants, so too are the signifying practices of school life. Student teachers construct their own narratives but always in relation to the narratives of others.

Paul Willis suggests that the kinds of narratives they confront correspond to three competing dimensions of institutional life: the official, the pragmatic, and the cultural. These dimensions may be thought of as "stories" because they are, in a sense, multiple narratives about institutional life that are in continual dialogue with one another. Typically, institutions represent themselves from their official perspectives: what should happen, goals for achieving this, and an idealized representation of its workings. Official perspectives generally govern the effort of public relations but also contain fragments of the aspirations and hopes of the community. Official perspectives are found in such public documents as curriculum guides, system-wide learning goals, and grant proposals. The pragmatic level concerns how these "official ideologies" are mediated and lived by those who hold institutional power. They subsume the stories of everyday life and are charged by contradictory realities. At the pragmatic level, those who represent the institution:

> are likely to appreciate something of the more theoretical rationale for the prevailing ... "official" ideology, but they are also mainly interested in their own face to face problems of control and direction and the day to day pressures of their own survival within the inherited institution.[76]

These practical stories concern the contradictory ways practices make sense of the distance between the ethic and the experience. Alongside these dimensions are the cultural forms belonging to those whom Willis terms "the clients." While he refers here to students, it may well be that student teachers operate, at least partly, on this level as well, since their authority, while more practical than official, also takes cultural forms of opposition.

The stories of student teachers are charged by their marginality and otherness, and by their individual capacity to empathize with the classroom students' perspectives that continue to be housed in their own subjectivities. Clearly, the student teacher's opposition to the official and practical dimensions of the institution will take subtle forms that are more individual and privatized than those of their students. Nonetheless, given that student teachers attempt to carve out their own territory, and bring to teaching their own visions of becoming a teacher, oppositional strategies are being shaped and enacted. This is because, as Sara Freedman, Jane Jackson, and Katherine Boles point out:

> The rhetoric surrounding the institution of public education often proves to be in direct conflict with the function a teacher finds herself required to perform.[77]

That is, the official story is often deconstructed by the practical story and it is this rupture that permits the construction of cultural stories. Cultural stories may concern how the student teacher "got over," how her or his pedagogy and classroom routines resisted official perspectives, and moved beyond practical constraints to create a "free zone" of democratic learning. Such stories need not be victorious. They can narrate as well the more painful and private moments when student teachers fall back on useless routines, become confused and anxious when things do not go as planned, or become undone by how their classroom students understand them. To study the cultural stories of student teaching, then, is to study the uncanny, the creepy detours, the uneasy alliances, and the obvious clashes between authoritative and internally persuasive discourses.

To be touched by the traditions of teacher education, one need only step into its world. Student teachers may not necessarily be aware of the historic tensions between conformity and social change, but these tensions are lived during the practice of teaching. In classroom performance, university course work is relegated to the world of rehearsal. But the distance between lived experience and received knowledge that is so endemic to their education must be countered by their own ability to find some semblance of coherency. Once confronted by the exigencies of classroom life, the compartmentalized knowledge that student teachers inherit does not seem so fixed and immutable. Their relationship to the canon is not so tightly woven that it cannot be undone by a student's question, grimace, laughter, or refusal to be engaged.

Finally, once student teachers actually begin teaching, the visions of practice with which they entered are continually being reworked and reinvented. Given this complex instability in a role that still requires authoritative certainty, what does student teaching do to those learning to teach? What do student teachers draw upon to make sense of their efforts? And how then do their efforts act upon their subjective selves?

3

Narratives of Student Teaching
The Jamie Owl Stories

Jamie Owl is a small white working-class woman of Swedish ancestry. She was twenty-three years old at the start of her student teaching. That semester was her last. She graduated with a bachelor's degree in English in February 1984, but she did not qualify for secondary English teacher certification, because she chose not to complete all education course work requirements. She did, however, complete her student teaching and this is one version of what happened there.

The narrative of Jamie Owl unfolds chronologically. Her stories may seem framed—concrete and stable. But they can only signify the life of one unrepeatable public moment among the many more private, elusive, chaotic, and unaccounted moments that constitute the rhythms of life. This narration, constructed from the articulation of the ordinary, presents and covers interesting tensions. The ethnographic narrative glorifies the immediacy of the reconstructed present and in doing so freezes aspects of Jamie's struggle in a static and unyielding frame. This story may also suggest something completed and in doing so assert a unitary story line that has a beginning, middle, and end. The problem is that Jamie was caught up in multiple and conflicting stories and because of this there are constant disruptions and competing truths that work through Jamie's retellings. As I have attempted to show, Jamie is not the unitary subject of discourse, although she lives its dilemmas. Moreover, her stories and mine must be read as partial retellings, complicated by the push and pull of how the stories are told.

My narrative efforts concern reconstructing Jamie's experience as it unfolded; to try to understand how this experience became critically educative and miseducative, to uncover the hidden meanings, the unsaid, the multiple and competing perspectives, the discursive ideological terrains, and the contradictory realities that work through Jamie's material practices and become inscribed in her thoughts, deep convictions, and theoretical impulses. To accomplish this, there is a need, as Cortney Cazden advocates, for a particular approach:

> [One that] pulls back the micro-analytic zoom lens in two dimensions: pulls back in space to see interactions in the classroom in the larger contexts of school and community and society; and pulls back in time to see the present as a point in historical change.[1]

The narratives of Jamie Owl, then, are about her contradictory processes of becoming. That she did not continue to pursue a career as a secondary teacher should in no way signify that her teaching efforts were somehow less than those who readily enter the profession. Indeed, the fact that Jamie struggled with such self-doubt may illumine the private doubts of others. And like countless others, Jamie did through student teaching obtain glimpses of the work of teachers. Just what she saw and felt, and the meanings she was able to construct, are a part of her story.

Jamie Owl volunteered to participate in this study on September 12, 1983. Week by week, until December 14, 1983, Jamie and I did in-depth interviewing. My questions were characterized by inquiry rather than judgment, meant to invite, as they unfolded, Jamie's descriptions, interpretations, and theories about her teaching experiences. I was interested in understanding how Jamie understood her own process of becoming a teacher. This kind of intervention was not designed to help Jamie in her pedagogical strategies, although during our time together I often became a sounding board for her ideas, fears, and deep investments.

This process of questioning, however, did affect Jamie's understanding as she rehearsed her week's events. Two tensions must be acknowledged in this discussion. First, my work as an ethnographer means speaking for Jamie even as I re-read her words through the prism of cultural critique. Second, I am theorizing Jamie's identities, and in so doing constructing a textual identity that springs from two different narrators: Jamie and me. What these represented story lines should suggest, then, is my reinterpretation of Jamie's lived experiences.[2]

Originally, I also proposed to observe Jamie's teaching on a weekly basis, but the principal of Hurston High School and Jamie's cooperating teacher did not grant permission. They felt my presence in Jamie's classroom would be disruptive and cause her to feel too self-conscious. Most of all, they desired

Jamie to have a "normal" student teaching experience. They did suggest I might later request classroom observations, after—in the words of Mr. Barrison, the principal—"Jamie had her feet wet." However, three other circumstances foreclosed my entrance into Jamie's class. First, Mrs. Michaels, Jamie's primary cooperating teacher, was unexpectedly hospitalized in early October, not to return to her teaching duties for seven weeks. Second, by mid-October, the Hurston teachers voted for and implemented a "work to rule" job action that lasted for three weeks and dramatically altered the normal pace of both the school day and the work of teachers. Finally, by mid-October, Jamie's experience as a student teacher was becoming extremely difficult and these professionals felt it would best be played out without my classroom presence.[3] Thus Jamie's student teaching experience, despite the wishes of all involved, was far from "normal": life intervened.

Actors, Places, and Classes

Jamie Owl, student teacher[4]

Mrs. Carley Michaels, primary cooperating teacher and English chairperson of Hurston High

Ms. Karla Murr, secondary cooperating teacher

Jean Snough, university supervisor

Mr. Fred Barrison, principal of Hurston High

Hap Cleveland, instructional director of Hurston High

Mrs. Gretta Grettle, parent of a ninth-grade student

Gertrud Grettle, ninth-grade student

Gardenville, Jamie's hometown

State University, the university Jamie attended

Hurston, the town housing State University and Hurston High

Hurston High School, the site of Jamie's student teaching

Introduction to Literature, a ninth-grade advanced tracked class of twenty-five students. This class was originally Mrs. Michaels's class.

Persuasion, a tenth-grade basic tracked class of twenty-five students taught by Ms. Murr.

The Context of the Town: Hurston

Hurston is a college town. Surrounded by rural farmlands situated between mountains, the town itself reflects college rather than country life. This is because Hurston houses three well-known places of higher learning. State University is the largest public university in the region. Its total undergraduate and graduate population exceeds twenty-five thousand students. There are also two exclusive private undergraduate colleges located on opposite sides of the town. Hurston College, originally a men's college, serves the offspring of the country's ruling class. Campville is a small, private, experimental college. Although exchanges occur between institutions, each one appears as if it were a world of its own. It is the colleges rather than the land that are the largest employers of the town's population.

Colleges, then, provide Hurston with its major source of income and have created their own industry. Student-oriented businesses—such as bookstores, photocopy establishments, stationery supply shops, clothing stores, bars and restaurants, coffee houses, and computer stores—take up much of its center. Yet Hurston's major population is largely transitory. Its population swells when the colleges are in session, and shrinks each summer. Housing shortages, coupled with run-away rental fees and a recent move toward gentrification, are among the town's biggest issues.

According to the 1982 census, Hurston's town population is approximately 33,229. Of this number, 30,517 persons are white. The largest cultural minority is African-American (1,467), followed by Latinos (837), and Asians (620). Although the white population perceives Hurston as racially liberal, the experience of persons of color contradicts this perception. Recently, an influx of Southeast Asian refugees and a growth of the Puerto Rican community are challenging the town to provide multilingual services as well as bilingual and English as a second language instruction in the schools.

Although Hurston's median income in 1979 was reported as $22,119, it's racial minorities earn less than half that sum. Of the total population, forty percent of all families are at or below the poverty level. Yet, despite these statistics, the town's reputation is solidly middle-class. It is the presence of the colleges that support this myth.

Hurston's colleges have powerfully affected its public schools; many have the reputation for being innovative. The town has four elementary schools, one junior high school, and one high school. Many of its schools have been influenced by the philosophy of humanistic open education. At the time of this study, total management systems such as mastery learning and Madeleine Hunter were not yet in effect. Beyond the philosophic influence the colleges seem to exert over Hurston's schools, State University's school of education provides most of the town's student teachers; it also works with the Hurston

School Department in matters of evaluation, curriculum development, and in-service teacher education. Many State University student teachers believe Hurston schools will provide them with a unique although unrealistic teaching experience. Some have referred to Hurston schools as a "wonderland" in that the teachers seem open, the schools are not plagued with the issues of urban education, and compared with other school systems its schools appear to offer pedagogical freedom. The fact that Hurston schools are conveniently located also influences the student teacher's choice of school placements. When the colleges and university are in session, public buses are free.

Hurston High School is a modern structure; its architecture reflects the educational innovations of the early 1970s such as modular scheduling, and an emphasis on large group lectures and small group discussions. Approximately twelve hundred students are enrolled. Currently, the school is organized by a departmental structure, and uses a three-tier tracking system of advanced, standard, and basic to classify students and their courses. The school's racial makeup reflects that of the town. However, minority parent pressure and minority teacher support have encouraged moments of multicultural education. There is also a large foreign student exchange program, which affects the entire school. A majority of Hurston High graduating seniors move on to higher education. Of this group about three-fourths attend State University.

Although historically the town's taxpayers and teachers have worked in tandem for quality education, Hurston teachers have more recently pressed for economic and contractual demands. As in most school systems across this country, teacher layoffs have severely qualified teacher employability as well as increased class size. Each year, rumors hinting of layoffs, budget cuts, and the curtailment of extracurricular activities fill school corridors.

In 1983 Hurston teachers began their school year without a teaching contract. Negotiations had stalled since the previous spring. By mid-September the Hurston Teacher Association and the Hurston School Committee had reached an impasse. Teacher demands included an across-the-board pay raise, which had not been requested in previous years due to budgetary constraints. When negotiations broke down, the teacher association voted to implement a work to rule job action, which dramatically demonstrated the centrality of the teachers' labor in maintaining life inside and outside the classrooms.

Work to rule lasted three weeks. During that time, the teachers presented a united front and performed only those duties contractually specified. Each morning, teachers collectively walked into their respective schools at the specified contract time and left in unison, empty-handed, at the conclusion of the working day. Because no work was brought home, teachers used class time to grade and plan lessons. Further, all extra-curricular activities halted.

By the end of the second day of its implementation, the entire town felt work to rule.

Town loyalties were divided. Public school students, initially sympathetic, became angry with the loss of services they had taken for granted. Parents felt that work to rule diminished the education of their children. Many taxpayers were outraged at the teachers for adopting labor strategies in a profession perceived as selfless. Outside negotiators were called to help settle the dispute.

Three weeks after it had began, work to rule ended when the School Committee and the Teacher Association agreed on a new contract. Both parties had compromised. Community criticism against the teachers, however, was slow to fade. Further, many teachers were frustrated with their new contract. Although the schools soon returned to their normal pace, the bitter sentiment between both parties lingered. Still, the knowledge that other school systems had endured work to rule for as long as two years, and that the Hurston teachers' settlement seemed comparatively quick, helped to bring some relief. What was most significant about work to rule, however, was that the teachers were able to remind their students and the larger community that they, too, were workers.

BECOMING A STUDENT: STORIES FROM SCHOOL

Jamie Owl lived her childhood in a small factory town, Gardenville, approximately thirty miles from the State University she would attend eighteen years later. The town's noted chair factory employed both her parents. Jamie's father had an eighth-grade education and worked in factory production. Her mother, a high school graduate, worked in the factory's sales department. Jamie was brought up Catholic.

Gardenville's public schools provided for Jamie's compulsory education. Although she characterized herself as a "good learner" and a "popular kid" in elementary school, Jamie's recollection of junior and high school experiences was painfully narrated:

> Where I went to grammar school, it was a working class school. It was a neighborhood school. When you got to junior high, you were with everybody, for all the [town's] schools. And you know they were better schools. My classmates were smart, if not smarter, and learned faster, learned more, made friends easier. I became very shy, very withdrawn. Maybe it was class shock. [10-7-83][5]

As a young working-class child, Jamie's first memory of her class background is critical. She was made to feel marginalized, a girl somehow less than her middle-class counterparts, and consequently, in both the academic and social experiences of school structures, Jamie felt like a failure. This sense of "class shock" would reverberate throughout Jamie's academic career, causing her to feel like an outsider, poorly equipped to challenge the systemic constraints she would encounter throughout her student career. It was not until her sophomore year that Jamie began to feel that school—and in particular, her English class—could validate what she brought to her education:

> When I was sixteen, I remember one of my teachers had us do a short story. And it was the first time I ever wrote anything that I got an "A" on. I wasn't a good English student in high school. I always got "B's." There was something that never connected with me on how to write a good paper or how to read a book. I don't know where I messed up along the way that I didn't get that information.
>
> I remember writing the story and really enjoying writing it and learning a lot from it. And I got an "A," and I got an excellent, and I said, "Oh wow! I can do something." I was at that point when you're sixteen and you're wondering what you are going to do with your life. And OK, college was at the back of my mind. But what am I going to do?
>
> And I decided to be a writer. I think a lot of it was also because I was so quiet. I always figured, if I can't speak my thoughts, I can at least write my thoughts. So I hung onto that.

Jamie's idea that she had somehow "messed up along the way" reveals something about her burgeoning images of knowing and something about the power of "class shock." If knowledge is viewed as already out there, complete and waiting to be acquired, the process of "getting it" becomes an individual dilemma.

Yet at the same time, while Jamie believed she was ultimately responsible for her educational situation, she resented her educational experience for making her feel less than her self. These contradictory beliefs—being responsible for her education and feeling like a "victim" of miseducation—fashioned Jamie's struggle for voice. Fiction writing, however, permitted engagement with her private voice—viewed as separate from her public one—a voice she tried to protect from institutional demands. Hers is a struggle reminiscent of Bakhtin's distinction between authoritative and internally persuasive discourses: the authority of school discourse clashed with Jamie's subjective voice. Jamie's overreliance on personal experience as her primary way of coming to know, however, gave her insight into the impersonal models of learning asserted in school.

But the positive experience of her sophomore English class did not allow for any deeper sense of validation or entitlement; grades became enmeshed in her struggle for voice. Throughout her compulsory education, Jamie's relationship to grades remained self-depreciating and disparaging; she wavered between blaming the grading system and self-blame. Her intellectualization that grades have nothing to do with intelligence was overshadowed by her subjective acceptance of the power of grades:

> I never felt school was personal; I never felt I was looked upon as an individual. I was very susceptible to those grades because of my own problems with dealing with my image of myself or my lack of it.
>
> So when I got a "B," knowing full well I had really done nothing to deserve the "B" half of the time, it would still affect me deeply. I am stupid. I had a very hard time accepting the fact that I was an intelligent person. And those grades never helped me.
>
> But I stayed in school, partially because I know that a degree is the passport to a lot of other things in my life. But in my mind, I wanted to get out of thinking grades were so important. I knew it, but when I saw it, I would fall under it. And I didn't like that, succumbing so easily to that foolish little mark on the paper.

From an outsider's perspective, one can ask, Where does a young working-class girl receive the encouragement to view herself as intelligent, capable, and strong? How does she learn the discursive practices that would help to realize creative interventions? Given the power of institutional life to summon one's desires and investments, and simultaneously emphasize individual responsibility for development, it is little wonder that one's sense of becoming expresses these contradictions.

By the middle of her high school years, Jamie began experimenting with marijuana. Over the next five years, she socially participated in the drug subculture first during her senior year and later at State University. It was her way of breaking out:

> I did it because I think I knew I wasn't supposed to and also because I didn't like what was around me and I was turning off. When I first tried it, I'm somewhere else. [It] offered that escape. I was able to create my own world.

By Jamie's senior high school year, her overwhelming desire to escape small town life and the seeming inevitability of factory work led her to apply to college:

> College was an escape for me. It was an out. I didn't particularly care about going to college at that point. But I knew to get out of

Gardenville, I had to go to school. I knew all along that State University is where I'd end up because of its low tuition.

Life at State University

In early fall 1977, Jamie moved from Gardenville to a dormitory at State University in Hurston, where she began her life as a full-time undergraduate. Because all incoming first-year students must declare an area of study, Jamie chose English. Her intent was to become a writer, and an English major seemed to provide that avenue. However, social relationships with peers continued to be more rewarding than classroom life. Political ideas seemed to flow freely outside the classroom and talk—as internally persuasive discourse— became important. Through dialogue with others, Jamie was beginning to intone her own voice:

> It was the first time I met people who were concerned about things other than their immediate life. There was a deeper respect; there were people talking about politics, which I had never really exposed myself to, or been exposed to.
>
> There was a lot of people just tossing around ideas and what they wanted and their feelings and who they were and what they were going to do. And that was different and that was what I loved doing, just being with those people. And part of that environment included drugs and I started smoking pot heavily and experimenting with other drugs. And I met a good friend there.

Jamie reentered State University, after leaving for a year to travel and work, in the fall of 1979. Her second year was more intellectually challenging and personally validating. She began to look to academic knowledge as something other than a conforming force:

> I took some courses that I wanted to take instead of those introductory things that they make you take for your major. I took things like, "American Rebellion." I loved that because it related so much to what I had been through; people who sort of have to break out of certain situations they are in. It was about the Sixties, which I love. I was very mesmerized by that whole era and the events and the music.

However, even with this affirming semester, life at State University remained difficult and she left again for another year to work full-time.

The fall of 1980, when she began her junior year, Jamie was twenty-one years old. By spring semester, she was participating actively in her course work. That semester she enrolled in a series of politically oriented courses: "Culture through Literature" and "Marxism, Feminism, and Black Nationalism." The political context of these courses gave Jamie a framework and language from which to name and analyze past experiences and present constraints. Feeling less like a victim permitted her to consider her future. She thought about acquiring skills that would help her to escape the dead-end jobs previously experienced. She struggled too with the idea of doing something that could make a difference in the lives of others:

> I was scared. I knew I didn't have a lot of marketable skills out there in the real world and I didn't want to get stuck in a dead-end job. . . . There was no way I would end up working in a garment factory ironing belts for eight hours a day.
>
> And I read Kierkegaard. Told me all about self-deception and how you had to have social responsibility and social consciousness which I knew, but didn't know if I wanted to act upon it, or in what fashion.
>
> I was an English major. I guess teacher training wouldn't require a lot more of me. I met a woman in my apartment complex who told me about an Alternative Learning Center high school program. It sounded interesting and I decided to get away from myself, spent too much time thinking about myself. Wanted to see what was going on with other people. And considering all these things, I decided to go into teaching.

Jamie hoped teaching might help her achieve the critical distance necessary to move beyond the sway of her personal world. She did not think about how becoming a teacher might change her and in fact she did not perceive herself as wanting to learn to teach. But she decided to go into teaching. This distinction is important: ultimately, it was to thwart Jamie's ability to theorize about her own process of coming to know and to limit what she might draw upon during times of pedagogical decisions and distress.

Jamie was twenty-three at the start of her teacher education and had previously completed her English major before entering a secondary education program. That first year, she took five required education courses, three of which had in-school observation components. Jamie felt best about the one that examined the work of teachers, a course that required students to reflect on their educational biography and their reasons for wanting to become a teacher.

Throughout that spring semester, Jamie observed rural, suburban, and urban high school classrooms. Disenchanted with much of what she saw, these observations confirmed her belief that the school system was not very good. More poignantly, this perception returned her to her own painful biography:

> Most things I didn't like much [and it strengthened] my desire to learn more. I did not like the tracking system. I saw kids at one high school who had internalized this label, especially in Basics. I sat through classes where kids go, "We're not that dumb," and would turn to me and explain, "I'm only in this class cause I couldn't fit this and I'm really in business." And watching their lack of confidence and watching them beat on themselves and feeling so many times the teachers beat on them also, I found that upsetting.
>
> In the urban classrooms they lock the doors and don't let the students out. Perhaps because there's a lot of racial issues, flare ups, I'm not sure. That didn't seem right.
>
> I saw that whole conditioning process in so many classrooms. I saw humiliation going on. Teachers putting kids down, awful remarks to make to another human being who is trying to learn. That just made me more angry. It was rare to find a teacher who really liked what they were doing and really communicated to the students.

During observations, Jamie felt like an outsider. She did not have access to the perspectives of teachers or insights into their struggles. Yet these observations were a critical moment, a confrontation with the contradictory realities of the idea of becoming a teacher and the reality of student oppression. The oppression of students was far more evident than the idea of becoming a teacher.

Life in education course work did not seem that different from life in compulsory education. The social relationships in her education courses did not make available the practices necessary to reconstruct and transcend the sense of "victimness" that pervades student life. Without any acceptable strategies, Jamie continued to struggle with what it means to learn to teach in contexts that offer poor examples:

> I had Instructional Planning, which I despised. And not so much because I didn't like the professor. I didn't like the way he taught. I used to think, these are teachers teaching people to be teachers. And they're awful teachers themselves.
>
> [The professor] didn't listen. And not that I didn't think what he was giving us wasn't valuable. He's teaching you to do a lesson plan, objectives, activities. It was tedious work and you didn't want to do it at the time. The professor was very much willing to talk and tell you what to do, and keep you on task, but he never heard you

and that bothered me. And that's when I'd walk out at certain points. That's not teaching to me. That's not a classroom that I want to be in. Instructional Planning, I felt, could have merged with the methods class, or leave it to job training, something like that, on the job.

It seems ironic that a course named "Instructional Planning" prohibited the planner's voice. The course afforded Jamie no insight into the process of planning or her own participation in it, and she concluded that her real insight into teaching would come with the teaching territory. Evidently aware that there existed a body of pedagogical knowledge, Jamie believed she could acquire it best on her own. Just how this acquisition would progress, and how one makes the relationships between knowledge and experience internally persuasive, was not yet her concern.

The remainder of Jamie's educational course work seemed to reinforce the negative lessons of what not to do and what not to become. And this worked to disorganize her ideas about what a teacher is and does. One course did suggest a critical perspective from which to understand and construct the work of the teacher but, again, Jamie's criticism of the professor often overshadowed any potentially validating information:

> I would rather have just been given the information and go do it. Some of it was a waste of time. But other times, I can ask myself, "what is it I don't like about this?" and then start learning, well, I don't want to teach like this because of that. And teacher training doesn't compare to actually being in school and learning. And I don't know how much help that did give me, all those education classes.

The image of pedagogical knowledge as received, as a body of information out there, is a continuation of her previous experience of school knowledge as primarily calcified and instrumental. The process of acquiring this knowledge—depicted by Jamie as lonely work—is contradictory; while Jamie must learn it herself, she did not see herself as a potential source of knowledge. At the same time, she did not value received knowledge. For Jamie, really useful knowledge both permitted connections to others through dialogue and valued voice. While this was not her experience in university course work—because of the disjunction between personal knowledge and the impersonal voice required by the academy—Jamie's personal knowledge, drawn from the stuff of "negative" experience, became a major criterion for measuring the efficaciousness of teachers and her own process of becoming one. In this sense, Jamie's personal knowledge was not practical; it served as a warning signal but was not powerful enough to provide direction.

Like everyone in her teaching program, Jamie had a choice in her classroom placement. Upon advice from a professor, Jamie went to Hurston High. There she happened upon a teacher with whom she could relate.

> [That teacher] is the first person who really talked to me. I walked into her classroom and she was playing music to her class. So I approached her and asked her if she'd ever considered taking an intern.

Unfortunately, Jamie's first choice for cooperating teacher, Ms. Karla Murr, had not acquired tenure status and this disqualified her. So Jamie negotiated a compromise; she would work with two of Ms. Murr's classes and with the chairperson of Hurston's English department, Mrs. Carly Michaels, for one class. Mrs. Michaels, however, would have all responsibility in signing Jamie's certification papers at the conclusion of her student teaching. Both teachers agreed to provide Jamie with guidance and counsel.

That summer Jamie previewed her course material but had no idea what to expect in the fall when she would formally begin student teaching:

> I had never taught formally before my student teaching. I had only observed classrooms. I had no idea what to expect. It's not until you actually get in there and realize you're supposed to be transmitting, you're supposed to be teaching people, other human beings. And it didn't hit me what a responsibility that was until I got into the classroom situation and I actually met a few students on orientation day.
>
> And I was overwhelmed and I was very scared; partially because I had never been up there, and partially because I knew what an impact someone has in your life standing in front of a room. I knew I wanted to be there. That was a decision of mine, a very conscious decision.

Jamie conceived of teaching as a tremendous responsibility that had generational consequences. For this she felt ill prepared. Her image of her classroom stance as "being up there" expressed to herself both the awesome nature of the role she was about to assume and her view of the knowledge she was supposed to possess and distribute. The thought of the teacher as conduit, however, further mystified just exactly what this performance entailed. Like countless others, the condition of being a student teacher did not resolve the deeper conflicts about the meaning of teaching and learning. In Jamie's case, now she must do battle with an identity that could not be uncoupled from the structure she disavowed.

Jamie clearly recognized the boundaries of her struggle and early on identified the major question she was to confront:

> I haven't fully reconciled being a teacher [while] hating school. Partially I think I dislike my own school so much and because I dislike my education and what I see going on, that perhaps there's some way. . . . One is to understand how much of it was me and how much of it was the educational process I underwent that made me think as I thought about myself and the lack of skills I took with me to college. And partially because I feel that things can be different. And they should be different and perhaps I can do it different.

Jamie was involved in that messy process of rejecting normative visions of what it means to be a teacher and negotiating visions yet to come. She became the site of struggle between her past and present, between rejection of dominant cultural norms and the potential to reconstruct acceptable and validating ways of being in the educational world. This is the struggle between authoritative and internally persuasive discourses, trying to make relationships between knowledge and experience in order to extend the power of both. The poignant question—Can one become a teacher *and* hate school?— is one that is hardly asked. But it is from this question that Jamie began to negotiate the contours of her identifications in teaching.

DOING STUDENT TEACHING

Grand Questions

Jamie Owl entered Hurston High as a student teacher the second week of September 1983.[6] Although she began by observing classroom teachers and the classes she would eventually teach, her sudden immersion into school life was overwhelming. She characterized these early weeks as a time of being "scared to death." On September 26 Jamie "took over" her first class, "Introduction to Literature," a ninth-grade advanced track English class originally taught by Mrs. Michaels. Jamie selected the first novel the class was to read. After considering three novels, she decided to begin with *The Ox Bow Incident*, chosen because of the social issues it raised. Despite her relative ease with selecting curriculum content, deciding on her pedagogical approach was not so neatly resolved.

During these early weeks, Mrs. Michaels provided support, suggestions, and some initial structure for Jamie:

They give you a folder, complete with all sorts . . . quizzes, essay tests, multiple choice [tests]. There's Monarch Notes and someone's own notes as to how they approached it.

Mrs. Michaels asked me to have a week's plans, a week of planned lessons, before I went into the classroom. As I started to do them, I found it difficult. I don't know what was going to happen day one. So to go to day two, three, and four without knowing how day one is going, was difficult.

These guidelines served to tame content but they did not illumine the peda-gogical process or, more significantly, the "intrusion" of a different reality: that of students. Jamie characterized her early pedagogical experiences as "trial and error," attempts to regulate that which cannot be predicted, controlled, or manipulated. In so doing, Jamie confronted the vicissitudes of chance. Teacher education faded into the realm of vague recollections precisely because it did not equip her to deal with the mismatch between institutional requirements of writing lesson plans and her developing theory of what constitutes good teaching.

So too did her idealistic goal of attempting to change the educational system. Faced with her own inexperience and the exigencies of the present, Jamie redefined her social responsibility to that of raising questions and hoped that this strategy would open the possibilities she desired:

Maybe I used my teacher training. The only reason I say that is I felt my first weeks I went through a very instinctive level as far as how to approach teaching. Whether any of this has sunk in from those teaching courses, maybe, maybe not. I don't feel a lot has. The most you can do is stimulate thought, and you have to ask questions first.

Stimulating the thoughts of students immediately became problematic. Fearing she would be misunderstood, a fear that inscribed her own educa-tional biography, Jamie expected misunderstanding. Moreover, neither cur-riculum guides nor teacher education provided any insight into the teaching relation, the dialogue among the teacher, the students, and the curriculum. Nor was the humanity of students—their fears, passions, and deep convic-tions—a part of her previous education. The ordinary problem of how stu-dents accept or reject the curriculum, and the teacher's labors to deliver it, became the extraordinary subtext of Jamie's teaching. She was genuinely concerned with understanding the experiences and thoughts students brought to her class and desired her class to be an interpretive community.

Accomplishing such goals seemed impossible, particularly when Jamie confronted the myth of homogenized learning, that all students must learn the same thing at the same time:

> There's twenty-five in the ninth-grade class; that was my challenge, getting up there and speaking to twenty-five people. And one of the things I find incredibly difficult is, I may have one idea about what I want to get across, but knowing that these twenty-five people are coming from so many different places and so many thoughts in their heads. They're at different places even when they come into my classroom. And all of a sudden, how am I supposed to get them to focus on one thing? This is a tremendous challenge. Whether it can be done or not, I don't know.

Jamie began to cope with her self-doubt by integrating it into her ninth-grade curriculum. At first glance, themes from *The Ox Bow Incident* should have lent themselves first to an investigation into justice, socialized bigotry, and its consequential mob violence, and then on to a student's own life and investment in social justice. During these classroom discussions, Jamie's primary objective was to communicate with students. This was missing in her own education. So raising grand questions and soliciting student responses to them was her primary pedagogical approach.

The problem was that Jamie took up a discursive practice in which her students could not participate. The philosophic nature of her questions must have seemed puzzling to the students; Jamie's questions were often met with their silence. The silence of the students was puzzling to Jamie. She identified and empathized with them, and presumed herself to know as they knew. And yet Jamie did not understand the way in which classroom discourse is done, that classroom discourse makes certain things sayable and others not. Her discursive practices went against the grain of established routine and she did not know how to help students participate in this different style.

Although she had other sources to turn to for ideas, the strongest source was the students themselves. Much of their power to influence Jamie's ways of being in the classroom occurred because of their daily and immediate contact, and Jamie continued to identify more with the students than with the teachers. Official and unofficial student communication, however, was fraught with contradictory advice. Unofficial communication was expressed through the students' bodies. It was Jamie who had to make meaning from their symbolic interactions. She read student grimaces as indicating disagreement with assignments, classroom discussion, and classroom activities: blank stares reflected boredom, unanswered questions meant personal rejection.

To alter the emerging routine of classroom discussion, Jamie introduced role-playing into the class. She thought it would structure more student participation and encourage self reflection. The role-playing activity did not work; students became silly with giggles and laughter. Rather than investigate the contradictory meanings of laughter, Jamie dropped the activity. In her frustration, she blamed the school structure for producing passive students and blamed the students for their inability to try new ways to learn. Subjectively and pedagogically, Jamie was ill-prepared to struggle with student resistance.

Students' official communication voiced other contradictions. During class, Jamie asked students directly how they felt about the class. First they said she covered the material too quickly. When she slowed down, the students felt the class moved too slowly. The students told her the material was too hard and they did not understand the novel. Others had already finished the novel, while some had not yet begun. Many voiced their own exhaustion with talking about its meanings. This "Goldilocks" approach to negotiation proved frustrating to all involved.

In an attempt to establish a less contradictory communication, Jamie decided to take class time and talk about the relationships between the explicit curriculum, the hidden curriculum, school structure, and her own teaching intentions. She meant to have students explore how their experience in school shaped learning expectations, their own sense of power, and their relationships with teachers and other students. During this classroom discussion, Jamie violated a cultural rule by stepping out of her teaching role: she attempted to critique the very system that, in the eyes of her students, she also represented:

> I decided we were just going to get into a circle and talk. I told [the students] how I felt when I was up there and that I was having a hard time reconciling a lot of how I felt about education, and what I was doing as a student teacher. I told them how I felt when I was in school . . . how Hurston High was different, how I felt teachers had a lot more freedom in approaching their classes, in contrast to when I grew up, as far as, desks were in a line, eyes forward, don't talk to your neighbors, speak when spoken to.
>
> I told them I didn't like the grading system and what it was and that I don't want it to be going on in this class if at all possible. And we talked about their anxieties over grades, which is very similar to any high school. And I just see it ruinous to people's learning. I was hoping they wouldn't let that occur with themselves.
>
> They don't want to read *The Ox Bow Incident*. I told them why I was teaching that. Three books were given to me and that was my choice. And I also felt it was a good book and there was some good ideas and that's why we had to work more at it.

I told them, well, I listened to them. They told me about their other classes and they had a lot more homework. English wasn't their only subject, and that's how they felt I treated it.

They felt I wasn't clarifying assignments. They didn't know what they were supposed to do. They didn't understand why they had to do those character sketches. They thought it was just busy work. And we had a long talk about that and then that's when some people thought it was a good idea. They talked about how they felt about grades and we talked about that's how the educational system is set up.

I told them I wanted them to work. And that being a student teacher, I wasn't going to be easy or lenient. That's not how it was in the real world, that's not how it's going to be in this class.

But I also told them it's hard work to be a teacher. It was also scary for me to get up there and face twenty-five people and supposed to have this wealth of information, knowing that I don't.

Jamie's recollection of this discussion opens the tension created by her desire to personalize learning in an environment maintained by objectified social relationships. More specifically, Jamie endeavored to come to terms with the deeper dilemma confronting not only English teachers, but every teacher:

> Whether it is more [in the students'] interest to accept the existence of the present social structure and to give them help to advance within it, or . . . to reject it, on the student's [and teacher's] behalf as stifling, competitive and exploitative.[7]

Jamie's understanding of this cultural tension was reminiscent both of her working-class background and of her present status as a student teacher: preparing for the harsh reality turned into simulating one. This reality, constructed as if it were "other," appeared as if it could not be changed. To take up this reality meant instituting authoritarian pedagogy. On the other hand, Jamie desired to create a learning environment that valued ambiguity, subjectivity, contradictions, and the struggle for voice. But because these features of humanity contest institutional values of stability, certainty, and control, and because Jamie was not familiar with the discursive practices that might provision a pedagogy from such existential dimensions of life, all she could express to her students was what she hoped they might do. Each direction of this dilemma signified a political reality. The former tends to be legitimated by the fusion of cultural and institutional authority, while the latter direction, as Jamie was beginning to discover, requires not only the rejection of authoritarian practices, but also the creation of counterstrategies where exploration of cultural tensions and contradictory experience lead to creative and dialogic thought.

Implicit in Jamie's stance was one counterstrategy, "the autobiographical impulse," the ways in which we use our personal experience to connect and engage with others.[8] She invoked the terror of her own educational biography and invited students to do likewise. But more than merely "swapping" stories, Jamie had faith that stories were instructive in and of themselves. The problem, as revealed in the student discourse, is that relevancy does not have a mono-lithic and self-evident meaning. Jamie expected her students to assume the value of their personal voices, but in a context that militated against such ownership. However, the students' stories rested in the pragmatic: they were overwhelmed and frustrated by the ways in which their work was divorced from experience. Jamie attempted to bestow meaning on their work by assuming that her experiences were synonymous with theirs, and by explaining her own ef-forts, intentions, and desires. She expected that if students were provided with what was lacking in her past education—real talk—their reactions would be like hers. She thought that if given the opportunity, students would naturally take charge of their education and be clear about their learning needs.

Jamie's organic theory of educational development, however, did not take into account the power relations of any classroom or the ways in which power is negotiated. Nor could she think about the problem of agency, that agency encompasses not just our capacity for social change, but the ways in which our interventions become populated with institutional imperatives and con-straints, and thus produce practices that betray our deep investments. Jamie expected that if she identified with the students' experiences, they would reciprocate. While none of these expectations materialized, they both orga-nized her perceptions of classroom life and contributed to contradictory in-terpretations of its meanings.

There still remains the pesky issue of the text. Jamie states: "They don't want to read it." What are the meanings of such a rejection? This novel, as Jamie believed, may have well been an interesting starting point for raising social issues. But again, the problem is pedagogical and the discursive prac-tices Jamie employed did not accomplish the kind of student participation she desired. Jamie must work to construct relevancies by doing more than re-hearsing literary devices such as plot, theme, character, and setting. Such activities, if disengaged from the production of meaning, reproduce a view of reading as a treasure hunt.

As Freema Elbaz and Robert Elbaz argue, Jamie must move beyond a notion of the novel as a work, or finished product, and instead explore the novel as determined by intertextuality. "The text (the sign, the curriculum) is permutational, ever-mobile space, and within this text a multiplicity of utter-ances or discursive events criss-cross and interpenetrate one another."[9] Had students worked to produce their own meanings rather than receive the meanings of a work, the dialogue so valued by Jamie might have had a chance.

In contrast to these early discussions, Mrs. Michaels offered another view: the perspective of a teacher. Attempting to get Jamie back on track, Mrs. Michaels suggested traditional techniques of classroom management to reassert the curriculum and, supposedly, Jamie's pedagogical control. These tips included: give students quizzes to "keep them on their toes"; walk around the room to ensure student attention; pace the curriculum more quickly; and, above all, "stick" to the material. Such techniques are reminiscent of Linda McNeil's construct, "defensive teaching," the ways pedagogy is employed to mask the vulnerabilities of both knowledge and the knower.[10]

Mrs. Michaels also encouraged Jamie to expect a lot from the students. After all, she reasoned, these students were members of an advanced English class, and thus, presumably, highly capable. Jamie did try some of this advice but its implementation felt more like policing than teaching. She was still uncomfortable with being the recipient and evaluator of student learning, because she was caught among the official expectations of her cooperating teacher, the students' unofficial hopes for negotiating classroom power, and her own philosophical explorations of the activity of teaching.

Despite being pulled from all sides, and despite the real institutional pressure to move more rapidly and cover the material, Jamie's first goal remained for students to appreciate the concept of justice in the novel, and in this way she resisted the "pedagogical speed up" engendered by covering the material. So she continued to move at her own pace. However, student resistance to the novel persisted and Jamie took this resistance personally; she felt the students were also rejecting her.

Part of Jamie's self-doubt was also engendered by her image of the teacher as omnipotent knower. This image is discursively produced in her description of "being up there" and works to diminish her belief in what she might have to offer. But rather than reconstruct this objectified role, without confidence and without practice, all that was available was for Jamie to react against it. This reaction encouraged Jamie's persistent return to her previous student self. Her self-doubt remained in a role that left little room for such ruminations:

> I don't know what I'm doing in so many respects. I have to say that. And I don't know if it's fair to be up there. I was telling friends the other night, trying to find out something about the judicial system in this country and realizing how ignorant I am on that subject. And here I am, supposed to be going in there and having some knowledge to give these students. I don't. I can help them with certain things, particularly with writing . . . I know that.

Constantly I'm always drifting back to high school, which is really strange. It's like, I'll see the teachers in my high school, particularly in English. You just sit. They ask questions, you paraphrase *The Iliad* and *The Odyssey*. There wasn't anything creative, there wasn't anything stimulating. You sit around and read your book and discuss it in class. In a lot of respects, that's what I'm doing at this point because I don't have a lot of resources to draw on.

Jamie felt condemned to replicate her educational past, for this was the only model she had mastered, however reluctantly. And as she relived her student past, Jamie continually reminded herself of all that she should have known, but did not. The "class shock" of her youth had come full circle. Whatever fledgling confidence in her subjective voice Jamie had mustered, it did not enable her to extend the knowledge residing there. In this way, she became the site of conflict where authoritative and internally persuasive discourses work as agony.

Should I Stay or Should I Go?

By the first week of October, after teaching for three weeks, Jamie began to consider seriously whether to remain a student teacher. While the first weeks were painful, filled with feelings of inadequacy and self-doubt, two unexpected circumstances beyond Jamie's control fueled new feelings of inadequacy. The Hurston Teacher Association voted to implement a work to rule job action, and Mrs. Michaels developed gall stones that required her hospitalization for the next seven weeks. These situations dramatically limited Jamie's access to her cooperating teachers and their talk about her own problems. Unexpectedly, Jamie's pace of assuming responsibility for learning to be a teacher was accelerated. So was the growth of her doubt as to whether she could make the grade.

The human drama surrounding Jamie forced her to confront the daily work of teachers. Her marginal student teaching role, however, prevented participation with work to rule. She was expected by both the university and the school administrators to carry on as if everything seemed normal, but these unfolding events meant otherwise. Work to rule did affect Jamie's quality of life at Hurston High. Now responsible for two English classes, she felt her life energies were being consumed by paper work and planning. At the same time, she began to look at the work of teachers from the perspective of a teacher:

Teaching seems so much like . . . it's rushed. It's crowded. I have a lot of respect for those teachers being in there. If one thing has

changed, it has been my outlook on teachers, as human beings, and
what they do have to undergo and what is expected of them. Cause
they're asked to do a lot. I know what it is just for one class. I know
I have to take over two, and then three. I should have my third class
this week, and I've barely taken over my second one, and I'm already
not sure about my first. [10-17-83]

There is that moment when all student teachers realize the complexity
of the work of teachers. While the meanings of such a moment shift throughout
the internship, the shock of recognition becomes enmeshed with feelings of
humility and anxiety. Jamie was now in dialogue with the actual work of
teachers. And much of this dialogue was characterized by surprise over and
fear of having to hurry up and become the teacher while her insight into this
work was so entangled with doubt.

At this point, Jamie began to consider leaving. The image she used was
"removing myself from the educational system." Jamie sought escape because
her attempts to redefine the teacher's role and hence remake the identity of
a teacher in a context overburdened with authoritative practices were thwarted
by students and teachers. She was continually surprised that students had
their own views about life and that these views challenged her own.

An especially perplexing classroom discussion with her ninth-graders
seemed to embody the clash of expectations and values as to what learning
to teach and learning are really about:

We were having a discussion and I asked them if they had any
questions about the book they were reading. No one said a word. I
tossed out a few more [questions] . . . and they looked at me and I
looked at them and they're waiting to have those answers and I don't
have those answers.

    And that's when I started realizing how ignorant I am about
certain things, knowledge about the world. I say I don't like the
system, but I also question how much of it do I even understand,
how much of it am I aware of. Whether it be the political system,
the judicial system, which was brought into question and I couldn't
answer, but I realized I could go out and find information. But at
this point, it's so complicated and cannot be answered by running to
the library for a week.

    I find myself not knowing what I believe in, not knowing what
I believe is right and wrong, yet we're up there talking about right
and wrong and laws and conscience of society and I don't always
know what I think about the world today. I've gone from a place in

my life where I've shattered my value system or the value system that was given to me and have reached a point where all my beliefs have been questioned to now. Where do I go? And being there in a classroom with kids who already seem to have such strong convictions about things which I question very much. I don't know if I should, if I can, if I will bring my own doubts and questions into the classroom, or even if it's fair that I'm standing up there struggling with my own knowledge.

And that class was when it really struck me what had been occurring and what I was doing as I stood up there. They had no questions for me. . . . And I looked at them, and they looked at me, and I looked at them, and it started becoming very uncomfortable. People started giggling and laughing, not knowing what was going on. I didn't know what was going on. I knew I had it in my power, I was going to bring this class back and put it into focus, or at least return it to normalcy, if that is the case. And I just looked and said, "I have nothing more to say to you, I really don't. What you can do is read and talk quietly."

And I remember someone sort of walking around the classroom during this very uncomfortable discussion. . . . And I'm watching him. And after I had given them the freedom to do what they wanted for the rest of the period, I saw him walk out into the hallway. The bell was going to ring in about a minute. And it was just an instinct reaction. I don't know where it came from, I don't know. I said, "Matt, please come back here." I stopped him. It was like, what? Why should he come back here? We're not doing anything in this room. . . . And there it was, my sort of immediate, you have to come back in here, and that whole sense of control, controlling people . . . and having that in certain respects, is power. . . . I don't know if I want that.

I came home, I started thinking heavily about what was going on. I wasn't sure if it was just one of those day things, or if all of a sudden, all of the things I had been feeling all along from the first day I walked into the Education Department made me question and consider.

Jamie's narrative is striking because she recognizes the absurdity of placing young ignorant persons in charge of the educational process. She refused to take up pretentious practices but also felt responsible for facilitating learning. But her insight is limited, because she situates the problem as her own failure to know rather than as an effect of the absurdity of the system that she locates. In this way the cycle of self-blame is discursively produced.

Jamie found herself in the painful position of grappling with issues of control as they unfolded. In her retelling of the above story, two dimensions of power interfaced: knowledge as a means to control and the teacher's authority to control. Within this tension, Jamie came to view not knowing as a threat to her credibility, as a private inadequacy rather than as a social dilemma. For example, what prevented Jamie from asking students to investigate the judicial system and teach each other what they had learned? Could such a strategy help uncomplicate the matter? Why did Jamie view it as her sole responsibility to know everything?

As long as Jamie took up an image of knowledge as the sole property of the teacher, she was compelled to hold an image of knowledge that required—as proof of its existence—stability and certainty. Here is the complication. Such an image cannot help Jamie think against the doubt and uncertainty threatening to overtake her. Part of what Jamie struggled with was her sense that the teacher's authority to control depended upon accepting this view of knowledge. Jamie wavered, however, between damning herself for not already possessing knowledge of the world and realizing how tenuous and fragile such knowledge really is.

This incident, then, forced Jamie to question her image of the teacher as knowledge bearer; she responded by constructing a teaching style grounded in her own deep uncertainty about the relationships between knowledge and experience. But this was uncomfortable. Jamie, for example, wished her inquiries might permit students to consider knowledge as socially constructed, but this meant readying herself for the vulnerabilities such understandings create. She hoped students would raise their own questions, but when they did, these questions became for Jamie instances of her ignorance. The problem was that Jamie could not interpret doubt and uncertainty as central to an intellectual process. In this sense, Jamie had not escaped the deeper effects of the normative discourse that serves up the myth of the teacher as sole bearer of knowledge. As long as Jamie took student questions as attacks on her credibility rather than as the inquiries they were, the possible relationships between knowledge and experience, between what is brought to the learning encounter and the knowledge constructed there, will remain beyond the reach of her pedagogical imagination. Taking up a discourse that was only capable of situating her struggle with knowledge as "lacking a foundation in the world," thwarted Jamie from valuing the students' and her own process of coming to know. The failure of her own preferred way of knowing—subjective knowing—meant that she fell back on an already institutionally preferred and legitimated way of knowing.

A few days after this incident, Jamie sought the advice of her two cooperating teachers and her university supervisor. In part she wanted these women to convince her to stay. Instead, each gave Jamie contradictory advice, and to a lesser extent, suggestions for survival, should she decide to stay. First, Jamie approached Mrs. Michaels, the day before the latter's hospitalization. Mrs. Michaels told Jamie that she had the stuff to be a good teacher, but the decision was Jamie's alone, declaring that there was nothing worse than being uncomfortable.

Ms. Murr took a different approach:

> [She told me] that many teachers go through the same kind of doubts, perhaps not question them as soon, cause [Ms. Murr] has been teaching for five years and has not started questioning a lot of these things until the last year. That they were concerns, but if you kept thinking about them . . . I got the sense she did enjoy what she was doing and there were a lot of good things in the teaching profession . . . that you just have to work around the things you don't like. And if you question, you go crazy.
>
> [She] didn't convince me to stay. I knew that what I was questioning a lot of teachers had questioned, and had somehow struggled their way though to allow themselves to remain in the profession. But again, I didn't have any answers. I don't know if there are any. It could be as simple as that.

The responses Jamie received reinforced the isolation and self-doubt she sought to assuage. Simply, Ms. Murr's response continued to assign doubts and anxieties to the individual. And with the advice of Mrs. Michaels, success seemed to be contingent upon will power, not pedagogy.

Upon hearing Jamie's chronology of despair, the university supervisor, Jean Snough, took an excessively pragmatic approach. She stressed the need to accommodate, at least for the time being, to the exigencies of school structure. For Jean, leaving was not an option:

> [Jean] was profoundly distressed and wanted me to stay. And I was so close and she asked me to reconsider a lot of things I had thought about but weren't my priorities, as far as being so close [to finishing] and two more months and you'll have your teaching certificate. And when things clear up in your mind, you'll have that permission slip to teach. That has to be considered. I know what she was trying to do, to encourage me to stay.
>
> I knew I was going to have problems when I walked in there with the educational system. I have problems walking around here and living in this society. I just didn't think they'd come up so quick and so prominent, so often. And then to find myself part of it,

thinking I could work within it, not knowing how easily I could get caught up in them, too. I don't think I was ready for that.

Here, student teaching was defined as an act of endurance, a consequence of the pervasive myths of "trial and error," "sink or swim," and "baptism by fire." Such visions of teacher education can only deal with doubt through an assertion of will power, and the mistaken assumption that sheer persistency makes a teacher. In this university supervisor's discourse, student teaching was positioned as if it was only an obstacle to the real work of teaching: once the hurdle is overcome, the student teacher magically moves from being authored to becoming an author. What is missing from this discourse and what Jamie desperately needs are the practices that can help her come to terms with the conflicts that are wearing her down.

I'm Not a Teacher

One of the positive effects of Jamie's process of deciding whether to remain a student teacher was that she began talking about her experiences and doubts with her friends and teaching peers. Talking with friends allowed self-examination and moved her beyond the tautology of her inner world. Talking with other student teachers, however, was not satisfying:

> I had gone out with two other interns hoping that at some point they would talk about their feelings. . . . And no one really brought up teaching. . . . I didn't feel like saying, "Don't you ever feel like this?" Or [sharing] all my doubts. Everyone knew I was leaving at that point.

The knowledge that Jamie might leave probably inhibited these student teachers from expressing their own doubts. They, too, may have felt the professional pressure toward omniscience, or at least acting omniscient, and were unwilling to engage in such "taboo" discourse. Her decision may have also animated their own fears of failure.

In mid-October, Jamie walked into her ninth-grade class and decided to announce that she was leaving:

> I didn't have anything prepared for that day. My ninth-graders asked to get around in a circle. And I was very pleased cause I was going to ask them to do that anyway. So we sat around and I said, "Well, I'd really like to talk to you for a minute. I have decided not to teach." And I went into a few reasons why.

Actually, I really didn't know how to express, I found I was at such a loss of words. I was very vague. "It's something to do with me and it's something to do with the structure and the way the system was set up." And they were wonderful. "Oh why? Why do you want to leave?" "Is it us?" They thought, maybe if we worked harder, you would stay. That was nice. They threw out ideas of what I should do, maybe I should be a psychologist, a counselor, or philosopher.

And I started to cry during the class after they had expressed these sentiments. I left the room and went out in the hall for a few minutes and thought about what am I doing? Do I really want to do this? If it's right for me to leave, why do I feel so bad? [I] walked back into the classroom. Someone said, "Where did you go?" They'd been looking for me. I said, "I went to cry." We talked about it for maybe a minute more and then we went to work. [10-24-83]

After this discussion, Jamie saw her ninth-grade class differently. Her students did care about her, expressing—in their career suggestions of psychologist, counselor, and philosopher—their understanding of what mattered to Jamie. That day, it seemed to Jamie, the students showed a rare enthusiasm for discussion. Later that evening, Jamie decided to remain a student teacher.

In order to continue as a student teacher, however, Jamie constructed an alter identity—that allowed for inexperience, vulnerability, and doubt. Rather than be trapped in a normalizing role, Jamie attempted to assert her subjective self:

> I have finally decided when I enter that school building in the morning, I am not a teacher. I'm a human being who's assuming a role that has been designated teacher. And I carry out some of the functions of that teacher. But when things go against my grain, I don't want to do it, I don't believe in it, or I just don't know, then I can admit that. And that way I save my own peace of mind and I can deal with the situations that arise. And OK, I don't know everything, but I'm not a teacher anymore, I'm a human being, which in a lot of respects was my own expectations of what a teacher should be when I walked in there.

Because she was now a "mere" human, Jamie felt entitled to her doubts. In this version of self, doubts are a natural part of the human condition but not yet an effect of social structure, history, discourse, and relations of power. This is the transcendental self of humanist discourse. However, in positioning herself beyond social roles by saying, "I am not someone who fulfills the role,"

Jamie attempted an impossible transcendence. For her, a human being and not a "teacher" could rise above the messiness of classroom life.

On the one hand, her definition of humanity may be seen as an attempt at harnessing that which cannot be stabilized. Such a discourse is problematic because it ignores the contradictions we all live in. On the other hand, her definition of the teacher remained ensconced in the normative image of the teacher as controller. Consequently, while Jamie might have attempted to transcend repressive notions of the teacher's identity, this process of rejection—itself dependent upon escape—did not lend insight into just exactly what Jamie could become. Rather, she was trapped in the persistent uncertainty between presence and absence, being there but not being who you are. The normative discourse could not help her out of this mess. Indeed, it could only keep her there.

Jamie attempted to dismiss the image of the teacher as expert. But what images of identity did she assert? What does it mean to be a human being? What kinds of relationship to knowledge does this identity effect? What kinds of discursive practice are possible once vulnerability, ambiguity, and doubt are admitted? What kinds of power and authority are taken up and not admitted? Rejecting the status quo is a precondition for social change, but so too are the discursive practices that make available different visions and actions. That Jamie retreated into her self must be seen as an effect of a discourse that compels her to take up an essentialist view of who she is, rather than help her act as if things could be otherwise. The problem is that the available discourse provides Jamie with a language to describe herself to herself in times of relative stability. It does not provide her with a language that can deal with contradictory realities. This can explain why, for Jamie, being a teacher means not being who you are.

A World without People

Jamie's "decision" to view herself as "a human being who happens to be teaching" may have permitted more patience with her own painful process of coming to know, but this tolerance could not be extended to her students. Rather, she still expected students to value whatever she herself valued: talk, vulnerability, and the vicissitudes of uncertainty. The tension is not in these values themselves so much as in their enactment and the power they effectuate in the context of school. School discourse does not work in these ways and students are well aware of this.

Jamie's expectations, however, did not take into account how the school context summons the subjective meanings of students. The following incident allows us to explore the hidden tensions particular to the English curriculum as it structures the production of voice and, in so doing, disorganizes the voices and practices of students and teachers.

In late October, Jamie was observing Ms. Murr's Advanced Persuasion class. There, the students were reading and responding to each other's persuasive essays that answered the teacher-assigned question: Is war necessary for human survival?

> One student wrote an incredibly excellent, well, a well organized, well written essay, "Yes, war is necessary to human survival." It seemed to me he had gathered all the information you would get out of a history class, as to why war was good. . . . And in the last sentence, he said, "Yes! War is necessary to life."
>
> I was shocked. Until then, I had not said a word in the class. After he read it, the interesting thing about it was everyone responded to it as, "Yes, that's an excellent paper, very well written. But it's so far above us all. Only political scientists could do something like that!"
>
> And I was like, My G-d! You didn't even hear what he said! And during that entire discussion of war, not one person in that classroom ever, ever, discussed the loss of lives in war. It never came down to human beings.
>
> I, for one, was appalled. I told them, "I will tell you, these are my opinions and I'm not attacking. I'm just disagreeing." And I went point by point through his paper and the fact that he was just considering [war] in materialistic terms. When I started to disagree with him, he said, "Yea. I wrote this, but I don't know if I actually believe this."
>
> I'm appalled that he'd write something for the "A" and not look at what he's saying. I guess if I were a teacher, I'd have to give him an "A" for the organization of that paper. And his content, it was perfect, he had all the facts. With the exception of one little contradiction which personally is appalling. I'd give him an "A" but I'd make sure I commented on the paper. If what means more to them is the "A" rather than what they're thinking about, what can I do? What can I say except I disagree? [10-31-83]

This student's essay, and indeed, the audience's response can be read as an effect of knowing how to cover the material and of knowing how discourse is done in the classroom. His arguments, assuming the "matter of factness" tone of a history text, expressed a narrative style that requires concretizing abstracted "facts" but in doing so, abstracting these "facts" from their human implications. Such an argument depended upon the ability to decontextualize, a process whereby meaning is severed from its historical and human context in order to appear objective. This orientation is valued in the normative educational discourse that students and teachers are expected to take up. This student understood that he would be graded on *how* something was said, rather than be held accountable for *what* was said. Here, technique was taken for granted as an objective category while meaning, a mere vehicle for organizational structure, became devalued as subjective and idiosyncratic.

A significant cultural tension in English education is reflected here: the separation of form from meaning is a dichotomy that implicitly organizes teachers' and students' views of objectivity and subjectivity. What is deemed objective is thought to be unencumbered by human values and beliefs, and to assert the objective, one must deny the subjective. Subjectivity, on the other hand, becomes a human limitation and hence is stigmatized. This opposition masks the ideological interests served by such a stance. As Paulo Freire explains:

> The separation of objectivity from subjectivity, the denial of the latter when analyzing reality or acting upon it, is objectivism. . . . To deny the importance of subjectivity in the process of transforming the world and history is naive and simplistic. It is to admit the impossible: A world without men [*sic*].[11]

In this student's paper and its reception, the impossible indeed was admitted: people play no role in their survival. But while this student's logic was, in part, a consequence of how he read the context, it also reflected his own powerlessness. Rather than viewing his composition as a way to "act upon reality," he took up an academic voice that required the suppression of his own. With this exchange, the student revealed a further consequence of divorcing subjectivity from objectivity: the separation of the subjective self from one's institutional role in order to assume the views, values, and voices of others. Yet it does not work smoothly. This student, for instance, did not believe in his production.

The structure of this assignment and the pedagogy of the teacher could have moved beyond this cul de sac. For example, the students could have created a dialogue where competing voices argued with the question. Through constructing a many-voiced discourse, students might have examined the power of language to construct, implode, and rearrange views about and activities in social reality. Drawing on the students' dialogic imaginations, such an assignment might have helped them understand their own power to convince, negotiate, and act upon possibilities unforeseen. They could have been challenged to uncover not only their own theories of the world—the subjective in themselves—but also the ways "logical language" can objectify humanity, conceal vulnerabilities, manipulate thoughts, and impose meanings upon the unsuspected, uninitiated, and unprepared. Such a production would have transformed this audience into agents making their own meanings.

Jamie, too, was caught up in the tension between subjectivity and objectivity, and thus could not interpret the pedagogical issues this dualism positions. Taking up this dualism was not helpful, because the choices it makes available—either the valuing of individual belief and then the rendering of the subjective as a simple matter of choice, or the relegating of power and authority to the teacher and the text, and then feeling powerless to effect change— are not complicated enough. Jamie was pushed toward the first choice and thus could view this episode only as a personal affront to her own humanity.

Taking Note

Although beginning a new unit on Shakespeare might have signaled a fresh start, Jamie as well as her ninth-grade students had difficulty breaking out of the previously established patterns. While still concerned with her identity as a teacher, beginning a new unit forced Jamie to think about the more immediate questions of pedagogy. Constructing relevant methods proved to be difficult, because Jamie was mandated to cover the material and took this to mean asserting classroom stability, not experimenting with methods. Jamie resorted to lecturing, a method conducive to covering rapidly large amounts of material and to authorizing the teacher's role as the sole bearer of cultural authority. Even when Jamie resorted to this traditional method, it did not cover the students' resistance, and her own internal doubts:

> It's at a point where everything I'm doing they don't see the point. To get into Shakespeare's background, I put an outline on the board, elaborated points. I didn't really want to do it in that manner, but I had nothing else accessible to me. I thought maybe they had to know this background. But there were many students who turned off immediately. Just the look on their faces, "Oh this is ridiculous," "What are we doing this for?" Some refused to do any sort of notes on it.
>
> We started to do notes and I found out they don't know how to take notes. They feel everything is important and I had to slow down everything. One person started to say to the class, "Not everything's important." And they all told him to shut up, just because he knows how to take notes and they don't.
>
> I felt at a loss as to how to deal with that. How to say, well, this is important, and this isn't important. But important to whom? To

me? To them? To the quiz? An important fact? A lot of it was just
trivia. But when I started to speed up, it was like, "Wait! Wait! We
got to get this all down." I didn't like that. They're supposed to have
a quiz on this. I thought about why I told them they were going to
have a quiz. In a sense, it was because I wanted them to listen and
take it seriously. And I knew if I didn't threaten them with something, it would just go by the board. [11-7-83]

As Jamie attempted to transfer her authority onto the curriculum, and
give the canon the floor, she still found herself in the uncomfortable position
of justifying the curriculum's power and relevance. Her story's language speaks
of disengagement: Jamie depicted herself as being trapped in a predetermined
curriculum whose implementation, as she read the situation, obligated her to
"police" student learning. As the press for social control became coupled with
pedagogy, the curriculum became an oppressive effect of institutional authority. Even this force, however, could not silence collective doubt, anxiety, and
frustration.

What became most important to students was their method of note-
taking and "getting down" every technicality. Jamie gave life to this dynamic
with her announcement of a quiz. Implied here were the rules that define
quiz-taking: anything said by the teacher can be transformed into a quiz
question, for the function of a quiz is to monitor attention and keep students
alert to the smallest of details. So while the students had no control over
which piece might return to haunt them in the form of a quiz question, their
attempt to take meticulous notes and slow down the number of circumstances
for which they were to be responsible was a means for gaining more control
over the arbitrary nature of the quiz. Consequently, the study of Shakespeare
was reduced to disjointed trivia, meaningful only insofar as it could be exchanged, vis-á-vis the quiz, for a grade.

In a very literal sense, Jamie covered the material, veiling its meaning in
order that it might be rapidly acquired. In its figurative sense, covering the
material signaled to all involved the institutional imperative to stay on track.
The note-taking activity, while initially implemented as a means to focus the
students' attention onto the material, displaced the material: the act of taking
notes became more significant than what was to be noted. Covering the
material, then, became a perfunctory production of glossing over meaning.
Neither the students nor Jamie owned this production. Each merely carried
out an imposed job while style defined function as it disorganized meanings.

The idea that Shakespeare could be meaningful was buried under the
rubric of compulsion. Mandating Shakespeare does not mandate meaning. Jamie
had not yet found her own meaning in the study of Shakespeare, let alone the
ability to provide others with a meaningful experience. Two unanswered ques-

tions collapsed this lesson: Why is Shakespeare meaningful? How can students and teacher render it meaningful? Had Jamie created a situation that valued students as interpreters of the text—through study groups—and investigated the history of Shakespeare to form their own questions, for example, she might have provided all involved with a means of producing relevant meanings. But again, these suggestions make sense only when they are made available to the newly arrived teacher. And the repertoire of strategies that were available— study guides, quizzes, and lectures—were not sufficient to help Jamie with the transformative pedagogies she desired. As the lesson stood, reproducing the details of others was merely an exercise in forced submission.

Being Noted

Episodes such as the above only reminded Jamie of all that she lacked. While her students did take some initiative, requesting they read *Romeo and Juliet* in lieu of *Merchant of Venice* —a request Jamie gladly accepted (despite the fact that the former was for the tenth-grade curriculum)—Jamie began counting her remaining days as a student teacher:

> There's only twenty-two teaching days left till December. I'm already thinking there's no way we can get through Shakespeare by the end of November.
> I also feel I have these ideas but I don't have the background to initiate classroom activities that would promote the type of learning environment that would get [students] involved in their own education. I go from points of being so frustrated the two weeks previously, to the last week, that I can't wait to get out of there. And I go from this past week, that that's not enough time. [11-14-83]

Although they stood on the sidelines, Jamie's university supervisor and her present cooperating teacher, Ms. Murr, also attempted to ease Jamie's growing doubts. Jean Snough was perceived more as a sounding board than a supervisor, despite her bimonthly classroom observations. In fact, much of Jean's energy was spent listening to Jamie's frustrations and advising her to take the path of least resistance. During classroom observations, Jean attempted to build Jamie's confidence; she focused on her strengths and occasionally would make irrelevant suggestions like having Jamie walk around the class as she spoke. Ms. Murr was viewed by Jamie as more a friend then a cooperating teacher. Besides, because Ms. Murr often confided in Jamie about her illicit affair with a Hurston high school student, Jamie was reluctant to approach her, for she seemed to have so many problems of her own.

By the first week in November, Jean organized the second mandated certification conference with Jamie and Ms. Murr to review Jamie's progress and set final goals for her last six weeks as a student teacher:

> Both Ms. Murr and Jean said I was organized, as far as presenting my materials and having a format for the day. That came as a surprise because I never feel organized when I'm in there. I always feel when I go in there something different comes up and we're somewhere else. [They told me] I have good questioning tactics. I come down on their level, which was nice to hear. It didn't particularly change me. It's not until I see a significant change in the students, perhaps an interest and involvement in what they're doing that I will feel like I'm doing something good.
>
> I appreciate what they tell me, especially at some low points. It's nice to hear somebody thinks you're doing something good. But yet I know when I go in there I don't feel I am at this point and I don't think my students are seeing that either. At this point, I'm realizing that I'm a very mediocre teacher, very mediocre. But that's OK. This is my first experience. In the next two months, if I can't bring anything different to that classroom and in so doing, interest them and myself, then I will not continue with teaching.
>
> Jean has a list [of goals]. This is all very nice, but what does it do for me now? I mean it still leaves me with me and my students and it still leaves me with a lot of areas I need to explore.
>
> I think it was from someone else, who, when I was talking about those kinds of feelings, said, "You cannot go in there expecting your students to like you and if I'm looking for affirmation in a personal sense, then I shouldn't be in teaching." It was another student teacher. I have questioned that. It's hard to separate my person from my teaching. And I'm not there to be a nice person and not have them learn anything in the classroom. But I do want to be respected as much as I would like to respect them. . . . At this point I'm working at a very personal level, as far as teaching. I'm not thinking about the system anymore. Well, I'm not focusing on what the system does as what my own actions are, which, I suppose, are inseparable.

Jamie dissociated herself from her supervisors' positive comments; their views were alien to her subjective reality, and at this point in her internship, Jamie was overtaken by her feelings of inadequacy and mediocrity and by her deep sense that being a teacher means being someone that you are not. She believed as well that her success as a teacher was more dependent on the students' actions than her supervisors' sporadic observations. Their talk could not create the respect and motivation she desired from her students. Neither did it make available any new practices. But Jamie's supervisors had observed her painful beginnings and tried to warn that taking oneself too seriously only increases anguish. The problem, however, was that this kind of advice could only situate the individual as the source of anguish. Without concrete strategies to help her act in other ways, these words of advice did not dissipate her deeper epistemological questions.

Jamie was firmly rooted in doubt and caught in a cycle of self-blame. Not even the promise of transcendence helped her define her work:

> I'm a human being who's undertaking the activity known as teaching and is at a loss as to what to make of it and what to call herself.
>
> Student teaching doesn't make it in any real sense of the word for me. Student teacher? Someone who is learning to teach? If I listen to Carl Rogers, I would say no way. No one can teach another person, everyone must teach themselves. I have all these feelings and doubts about it and yet I'm still trying to figure out what it's all about.

Part of this blurring of boundaries occurred because Jamie had such difficulty theorizing about her sources of pedagogy. She valued herself as one source, but when viewed as the only source, felt inadequate. There were times when students were seen as a source of pedagogy, but only at times when their contributions did not contest Jamie's values or expectations. Students could make suggestions as to their choice of text, for example; but on a daily level, Jamie was unable to integrate pedagogically their concerns and interests. Because Jamie's experience was so isolating, she began to view herself as solely responsible for developing into a teacher. But the problem is more than that, for Jamie was not clear about the kind of teacher she desired to become.

Give Them What They Want?

In early November, after two months of being largely on her own, Jamie's professional supervisory network suddenly reappeared; her university supervisor observed more frequently, her cooperating teachers held a series of meetings, Mrs. Michaels returned, work to rule ended, and a Hurston administrator took an unexpected interest in Jamie's classes. However, this renewed access to her significant others did not soothe Jamie's deeper dilemmas, for these persons urged Jamie to assimilate into her role and ignore her struggles with constructing an identity as a teacher.

Inevitably, the grand questions plaguing Jamie found their way back into her ninth-grade curriculum. Jamie returned to the strategy of integrating her philosophical questions into the class. A quiz on Shakespeare, for example, contained the sole question, "Write everything you think is important about Shakespeare." Thus the students rather than Jamie would decide the material's import. Jean Snough happened to be present during that particular quiz:

> That [question] really threw them because it was such an open-ended question. For me that was an interesting question and for them it was confusing. They were unprepared for the type of quiz it was. . . . There was a lot of uproar about the fact that this isn't what we studied for and this is unfair. During the quiz I told them I was leaving for a couple of minutes and to hold their questions 'till I came back. I left them there, 'cause my supervisor was in and I had another hand-out that I wanted to go and run off. And that was a very conscious decision knowing that during the quiz my supervisor was going to be there and I was going to leave the room.
>
> It was interesting because when I did leave the room, there was a mass grouping of people cheating. They jumped on one another and said, "What is this answer?" Jean was amazed. I wasn't sure if they would be discreet about it. Jean said apparently they didn't care. It was interesting to know what's important to them, the grades rather than any of the material presented.

In approaching both the quiz and her impromptu exit as an experiment in student reaction, Jamie broke two implicit rules. First, she attempted to hand over, to the students, control of the quiz when the function of a quiz is to ensure the teacher's control. Second, by absenting herself from the context, and hence abandoning her policelike role, inadvertently, Jamie gave students the right to do as they pleased. This absolved Jamie of any responsibility and prevented her from examining the deeper issues of using traditional evaluative measures in untraditional ways. Neither Jean nor Jamie explored the deeper implications of Jamie's exit in terms of supervision or evaluation. Instead, Jean provided Jamie more useless advice:

> Jean said, give them what they want to do, anything to get me through the next seven weeks. I remember walking out of there feeling defeated. And thought everything I've felt and thought and believed in was to be so easily thrown away.
>
> I went into the teachers' lounge, where I hang out, and Ms. Murr happened to be there and asked me how the class went. And I just looked at her and put my thumbs down. It was lousy, miserable. She asked me what had happened and why did I feel this way. And in essence, I just all of a sudden realized I felt defeated. I felt

like I had to compromise myself and become a teacher. I said, "I got to be a teacher."

The tension in Jean's advice was that even when Jamie acted in traditional ways, the contradictory realities of school life were not covered. And while Jean may have meant to help Jamie by encouraging her to stay, the former never suggested practices for helping Jamie be her best. It is no wonder that Jamie felt defeated. That each of these professionals seemed to position success in student teaching as an effect of the proper sentiment or the sheer persistency of an individual could only exacerbate self-blame. Consequently, no one helped Jamie move beyond the view of the teacher as either tyrant or comrade.

Maybe I Should Go out in a Blaze of Glory?

The week before the three-day Thanksgiving school break, Jamie had an unexpected meeting with Hap Cleveland, an administrator in charge of Hurston's curriculum. Although Jamie had briefly been introduced to Mr. Cleveland and the principal in early September, until this meeting she had not had contact with any school administrators. A question concerning the semester's grading procedures brought Jamie to Hap Cleveland's office:

> It was right around lunch. He was on his way out. And when he saw me, I said, "Oh, I just have one quick question." And he asked me to come into his office. He said, "I want to talk to you." He had only been in my classroom once, and that was for a brief minute.
>
> Hap Cleveland goes, "I realize there are certain people you can trust and certain people that you can't in this system. And I just want you to know that you can come and talk to me." And immediately, I was on guard. What does that mean? I should have asked him. That's my lack of confidence.
>
> He said it wasn't a complaint but a concern from a parent in my classroom and he sort of wanted feedback on that situation. And this meeting happened after the time I had mentioned in the ninth-grade class [about] abolishing the school system. I felt sure I was going to have parents in my class the day after, after I had thought about it.
>
> One day [in the ninth-grade class] we were talking about education and learning. It came out in the course of the conversation. They asked me what should be done about the educational system, and I said, "I think it should be abolished." And immediately one girl asks me, "Well, what would you do if you didn't have schools?"

At that point I sort of panicked and thought, should I have talked about that?

And when Hap Cleveland called me in, it was with that expectation. He said that Mrs. Grettle had called and Gertrude [her daughter] was in my classroom. She expressed three complaints.

One, there was some concern as far as I was leaving and then I was staying. And they didn't understand that. So I had to explain to Hap Cleveland how I had been very frustrated and at one point I decided I wanted out but eventually changed my mind. Mrs. Grettle had expressed concern that one day I walked out on the classroom. I mean these are ridiculous things to complain about. But it was also a realization that a lot hadn't been communicated to the classroom, the fact that I had left the classroom during the conversation with my students that I was leaving. I had gotten very emotional and started to cry and decided to go out into the hallway. I explained that situation to Hap Cleveland.

Then Mrs. Grettle had expressed concern over the fact that Mrs. Michaels had left on her operation and when was she coming back? I didn't know. How was I to express that to my students?

Then he expressed that Mrs. Grettle was upset over an assignment I had given them, as far as paraphrasing Shakespeare. And I said to put Shakespeare into real English. And she was aghast because Shakespeare is real English. I just laughed. But that's what Gertrude went home and told her mother.

Nothing about abolishing the school system, which is what I felt anyone would call about. I was astounded! And he knew I was helping him out by the fact that I was taking over Mrs. Michaels's class and they weren't paying a substitute. So I saved them lots of money. And he was real appreciative of that.

Since Mrs. Michaels left, which was a good six to eight weeks, no one had ever come into that classroom to find out what I had been doing. . . . I could have been telling those kids anything. I am an intern. That made me wonder about their concern for education, as far as no one had come in to observe me. [12-9-83]

What began as a circumstantial meeting became a critical incident. Jamie expected consequences for her controversial remark advocating the abolition of school, but the concerns Hap Cleveland raised on behalf of a parent seemed trivial. Most surprising was that Jamie felt these concerns had already been settled. Her decision to continue student teaching and the drama surrounding that was already a distant memory. Jamie had not imagined that her students would take those events outside the classroom, reinterpret them to their parents, and then have this new version boomerang back. She had considered her classroom as a hermatically sealed world. Now Jamie was confronted with yet another contradictory reality; what happens in the classroom can take on a life of its own.

The second concern, Mrs. Michaels's prolonged absence, was not in Jamie's control. The real issue, avoided by Hap Cleveland's paternalism, was Jamie's unsupervised student teaching. The third complaint was irreverence to authoritative discourse. In asking students to paraphrase Shakespeare in "real English," Jamie had somehow discounted canonical English. Gertrude's interpretation of that assignment may have also reflected her relationship to the text; the language of Shakespeare may have seemed so distant as to appear unreal. Perhaps Mrs. Grettle did not see the point in this exercise. But as with all these "complaints," there was really nothing Jamie could do.

Jamie left this meeting more perplexed and angry, but expected her explanations had settled the matter. Further, she was attempting to relieve student frustrations by assuming the teacher's role and getting back to traditional approaches of English education. But two days later, Mrs. Michaels phoned Jamie and reported that Hap Cleveland had called to tell her about the "barrage" of parent phone calls complaining about Jamie's classroom. Jamie was very much surprised, for Hap Cleveland had only mentioned one parent's concerns. Mrs. Michaels told Jamie to attend a meeting the next morning with Hap Cleveland, her university supervisor, Ms. Murr, and herself at 8:00 A.M. sharp. The meeting, however, although unattended by Hap Cleveland, was quite supportive and Jamie felt renewed by all the attention. With only two weeks of student teaching left, Jamie was suddenly surrounded by supervisors.

Jamie first began feeling more like a student teacher upon Mrs. Michaels's return. Part of what encouraged this recognition was that Mrs. Michaels provided a field of contrast. With her cooperating teacher back into the picture, Jamie noticed a difference in herself as well as her students. When Mrs. Michaels walked into Jamie's classroom, the students became more alert, more eager to contribute. Jamie described the difference when Mrs. Michaels observed and when she did not as the difference between "night and day." But most dramatically, Mrs. Michaels's return signified Jamie's temporary student teaching status; the class was not hers and Jamie was not the real teacher. For example, student behavior became transformed when Mrs. Michaels walked into the classroom. The past power struggles between Jamie and her students dissolved, and during observations Mrs. Michaels found no evidence of Jamie's classroom struggles. It was left to Jamie to reconstruct what really happened. In some ways, the students' dramatic behavior transformation personalized Jamie's social struggles. It almost seemed as though Jamie had imagined all that preceded Mrs. Michaels's reappearance.

Mrs. Michaels's return also allowed Jamie to reach new conclusions about the meanings of teaching. She began to view teaching as bound to teacher/ student relationships. However, like other ideas about teaching, Jamie was unclear as to how to form these relations. She attributed Mrs. Michaels's success to personality and to the condition of being a real teacher. Here teaching was reduced to a natural talent rather than a process of development tempered by lived experience. When Jamie viewed teaching as a function of personality, she easily concluded she did not have what it takes. In some ways, this perspective eased Jamie's feelings of guilt and self-blame. She could absolve herself of the responsibility for the quality of student teaching when she saw teaching as rooted in one's individual nature. In rendering as essential the teacher's identity, the real problem—the structure of the school and the way teacher education is organized to effect self-blame—was unrecognized.

In early December, Jamie again met with Mrs. Michaels and Ms. Murr and Jean Snough to renegotiate her last days as a student teacher. Mrs. Michaels's concern was that Jamie had not spent enough time in her newly acquired third class to meet state certification requirements. But Jean Snough assured her that indeed Jamie had met the classroom hour requirements. During this meeting, Mrs. Michaels told Jamie she would not write her a recommendation, although she would sign the final certification form that would qualify Jamie for teacher certification:

> The reason she would not give me a recommendation was not be-
> cause of the state requirements. She felt I had fulfilled those as far
> as capability on the job. It was she did not feel I had a happy
> experience and she did not feel it was something I wanted to do. In
> other words, my heart wasn't really into it. And that to her is the
> major part of teaching. And I agree. Teaching apparently was not my
> career.
> Mrs. Michaels said she would feel real good if I could start
> doing brilliant things in Persuasion [class]. Maybe I should go out
> in a blaze of glory. I still had a chance to redeem myself. The pres-
> sure was there and I felt it as I walked out and started thinking
> about brilliant things. But then when I came home, I felt really
> scared because now the pressure is on all sides, myself, my supervi-
> sors. I don't want to leave there feeling like I had done nothing.

Mrs. Michaels's decision not to recommend Jamie for a future teaching position confirmed Jamie's perceptions of her experience. Jamie tended to agree that her heart was not into teaching; this acceptance, however, individualized her struggles to matters of mere sentiment. Still, putting one's heart into teaching meant different things to Jamie and to Mrs. Michaels. Jamie came to believe she had not tried hard enough, as if sheer effort might have enabled a deeper insight into matters of pedagogy. As part of the dominant discourse of student teaching, experience was supposed to solve questions, not raise new ones. And perhaps Jamie's final attempt to achieve great moments seemed a possible remedy to a bad experience. For Mrs. Michaels, however, putting one's heart into teaching meant acceptance of the school structure, the teacher's role, and the relevancy of the curriculum—all of which Jamie deeply questioned and effort alone would not erase.

Jamie's desire to go out in a blaze of glory ultimately became an additional pressure, another impossible goal. That Jamie discounted the positive views of her cooperating teachers and instead believed she lacked a foundation upon which to build prevented Jamie from extending her strengths. Moreover, her wish to go out in a blaze of glory superseded any formation of concrete strategies or even scrutiny of what this wish represented.

School, School, School!

The pressure to be "brilliant" only served to magnify Jamie's shortcomings and mistakes. During her last two weeks at Hurston High, classes that did not go according to plan were disparaged as lost opportunities. Objectively, Jamie knew her expectations were too high; subjectively, however, she needed them to revitalize her hope.

Three days before her student teaching ended, Jamie experienced deep disappointment in her ninth-grade class. This incident became, for Jamie, yet another symbol for all that she lacked:

> I had a bad day and that's my own fault. I did my first unprofessional thing I've ever done in my whole life. I wasn't prepared for class while Mrs. Michaels was there. She wanted to watch one more time before I finished up.
>
> My intention was to finish up student projects and go back over certain Shakespeare characters for the test. However, not taking into consideration that the students really wouldn't be enthusiastic and not having any other back up, [I] just watched nobody having anything else to say, and then me not having anything else to say. There was, what seemed like a half hour, but was only three minutes where nothing went on. For me it was uncomfortable because I knew it was my fault. Mrs. Michaels picked up on it, and so I'm sure the kids did too.
>
> And at the end of the day, I saw Mrs. Michaels and I said, "What did you think of it?" And she said, "Well, I had the sense that you weren't prepared." And I said that was the way it was. She tried

to make me feel better. She knows me enough to know that I would whip myself, knowing how badly I even take my better classes.

With three more days of student teaching, why did I let even one class go? Being unprepared and seeing the consequences bothers me. It doesn't reflect for me quick thinking, or how can I get myself out of this bind that I'm in, which in teaching seems like a requirement. To be able to know, what next, what next. If something isn't working, or to make those transitions really fast to avoid unpleasant silences. [12-14-83]

What might have been an informal review before the next day's test became a formal teaching lesson for which Jamie had not prepared. For Jamie it symbolized her inability to think on her feet and transform a momentary silence into dynamic learning. Because every minute counted, three minutes of silence seemed like an eternity. Time became her worst enemy; it seemed to rob her of both experience and opportunity. She felt she had let down Mrs. Michaels, her students, and herself.

Jamie equated her inability to act with being unprofessional. If she had only prepared more fully and had only anticipated student responses, the class would have been successful. Preparation, Jamie had come to believe, was an essential component of professionalism.

But even if Jamie had prepared more fully, there was another contradictory reality: planning did not ensure success. Along with preparation, Jamie believed, teachers should possess the ability to anticipate and harness the unexpected. The teacher's knowledge must be immediate and unwaveringly certain. Like Houdini, they can get themselves out of binds. Yet this image of the teacher denies the uncertainty that infuses pedagogical encounters.

The last three-way meeting of Jamie, her cooperating teachers, and her university supervisor occurred a few days before Jamie left Hurston High. They reviewed her total experience and decided she had met the state requirements for teacher certification. Jamie viewed this meeting as largely perfunctory:

It was a matter of we had to go around and sign [the form]. We talked about our strengths and weakness, where I needed to improve. Mrs. Michaels [signed] all of the things on my certification [but did not] write my recommendation because of my unhappiness and my seemingly lack of desire to teach.

I remember Jean asked me, what did I feel would have to happen for me to go into teaching? As I put it, a surge of belief in myself. But as soon as I said it, I was echoing what everybody else said. I was uncomfortable saying that. I'm not sure what I'm catering to, whether I'm saying things because this is what they expect me to say, or because I really believe these things.

Mrs. Michaels asked me what would I do if I walked into a system that handed me a curriculum and told me that's exactly what I had to teach. I didn't know. I don't know if I can work around the system, if I could work within it. I don't know what I would do. They seemed comfortable with that answer.

I got my certification form signed. But it didn't seem, gee, congratulations, or gee, you did a good job. It didn't feel that way and I hadn't expected that at all. It didn't seem like a big moment in here, like graduating or getting your degree. It seemed a ritual for them but not for me. It was the least relevant to my student teaching.

It all seems so meaningless. It's a piece of paper. Like we signed this form and everybody says I can teach now. What does that mean? How many people were in there all semester long? How many people really saw me teach? Truthfully, I don't think anybody did. And in the end, I'm the one who should sign and say, Yea, I'm capable of doing all these things. [12-21-83]

The certification signing seemed like an arbitrary end to a bad dream. The questions her supervisors raised during the meeting addressed much of Jamie's struggle but they came too late to make any difference. Jamie was still not sure what she needed to be effective or if she would carry out a system's curricular mandates. In narrating this meeting, Jamie's disappointment and anger surfaced; she was angry at her lack of supervision and resented being evaluated by those whom she believed had no idea of her reality.

The Hurston High English department had a party for the student teachers on their last day. Reluctantly Jamie attended. She did not feel like celebrating and felt uncomfortable with her teaching peers. When the last bell excusing the last period of the day rang, Jamie left Hurston High. Her brief description of her exit was of one who feels defeat but is grateful for the opportunity to leave. This was how Jamie initially felt during that last day. It was not until later that Jamie began to feel differently and began to think about all that she had suppressed during her time as a student teacher:

There's one thing I remember on Friday. Went into the center of town after everything was done to pick up some things. All of a sudden, I just started realizing there's another world outside Hurston High School. There's a whole different world! It's so easy to just get caught up in where you're at the moment.

There's so much going on and you can isolate yourself and get
so wrapped up in that one place, and you think that's all there is and
that's all that goes on. And I started feeling a sense of relief almost.
Wow! Wow! I'm out!

School, School, School! That's all I've had in my mind for the
past two years. I don't even know where to begin to start sorting it
out. And one direction I want to bring myself to is to slowly go over
the things that have occurred and I can start thinking it out and
finding perspectives which I have not done all semester.

As much as I've tried to do, I've had to cut myself off at certain
points, and get the work that's at hand done. You're not allowed to
think in there. As much as I've tried to take the time, the pressure
not to do that is so incredible. Now I'm going to take the time.

A few days after her internship ended, Jamie was required to attend a two-
day debriefing workshop for student teachers at the State University School of
Education. There, she filled out the remaining certification forms, attended a
series of workshops ranging from how to prepare for job interviews to sexual
harassment at the workplace, and was confronted with a workshop that required reflection on the student teaching experience. But Jamie deeply resented
the workshop's underlying assumption that student teaching had been a good
time for all and now that it was over, everyone would naturally enter the
teaching profession. She felt the workshop's tone invalidated her entire experience. As a last form of protest, Jamie walked out of this last workshop session.

The Idea of Teacher

Jamie left with the questions she had brought to student teaching and continued to formulate her understanding of teaching and the teacher's identity.
But by the end of her experience, she began to theorize about the complex
forces that pulled her in so many directions. She situated her own process of
becoming in relationship to others and expressed how her present conditions
were always contingent upon past discourses:

I had a lot of freedom. I didn't have someone who told me I had to
teach this. I had suggestions . . . well, you could quiz them, keep
them on their toes. And I rebelled initially against that. I didn't like
that idea, but eventually I was doing that, giving them tests, because
at this point, being the student teacher and being here for one semester, I didn't know how to break through the expectations for
students, from other teachers.

You're learning more of the things you don't want to do than the things you want to do because you are feeling your way out and don't know quite where your beliefs, philosophy, your whole personality in the classroom, that you end up falling back on what's been done previously, the things you remember. And a lot of that just doesn't seem to work.

I don't have a view of the master teacher. I have an idea of what a teacher should be like . . . and then I rebel against it 'cause that's not right either. I don't know for myself what a teacher is. That was one question I started out with and one question I haven't answered yet. And yet, in between, I've always, whether from inside or outside, gotten those cross currents of, gee, that is a good teacher, and gee, this isn't a good teacher, and I'm not doing this right, and I'm not doing that right. I don't know if it's internal pressure or outside pressure.

Both good and bad teachers were a part of Jamie's subjectivity, part of the deep convictions, desires, beliefs, and investments that she carried into her teaching internship, and that in some ways became rearranged while she was there. Jamie could now begin to unweave her understanding of teaching in order to embrace displacement as a place of identity. Acknowledging these forces, Jamie was becoming more engaged with her own process of becoming, a process that requires dialogue with the past and the present, with other persons, and with the contexts and histories that coalesce in the process of coming to know.

While Jamie was beginning to analyze herself, she was not able to theorize about what one does to become a teacher. The structures that should have assisted her—educational course work, academic preparation, supervision, and accessibility to and support from a professional network—had miserably failed Jamie. Her perceptions of Mrs. Michaels only mystified how one becomes the teacher:

Mrs. Michaels really appeared to love teaching. And I loved going to her classes and watching her teach. And that was worse, in some respects, because she made it look so easy. She made it look fun. Why can't I do that? I'm not saying she hasn't had her moments. But overall, when she's in the classroom, it's wonderful to be there. And I realize there's a lot of what she does that I would not do. But as far as her overall personality and the atmosphere she brings into the classroom, it's really hard to compare or beat.

Mrs. Michaels's apparent ease as a teacher seemed to confirm Jamie's ideal of the natural teacher. Mrs. Michaels made it seem as though teachers were born, not made. Jamie did not consider lived experience as contributing significantly to Mrs. Michaels's classroom manner. To Jamie, Mrs. Michaels's knowing presence supported another popular myth that everything depends on the teacher, that the teacher even "brings" the atmosphere to the classroom. But Jamie's idealization of Mrs. Michaels only served to constrain her understanding of the heteroglossic in teaching, the ways in which antagonistic discourses push and pull to create new meanings.

Jamie also struggled with her images of school curriculum. It was not until Jamie began teaching Shakespeare to her ninth-grade students that she understood the problem of curriculum relevancy as a problem of pedagogy. These concerns were often obscured by the larger issues of Jamie's struggle to construct her identity as a teacher. But at times, especially when she questioned how teachers determined what was important, or important to whom, questions concerning the canon's relevancy dominated. By Jamie's last month, occasionally, Mrs. Michaels questioned her as to whether she believed the material was worthwhile. Jamie always answered in the positive, but still wrestled with the problem of making the material relevant:

> I've been thinking, is it worthwhile to teach *Romeo and Juliet?* Why is it worthwhile? Why do they have to know that? Big deal. So it brings in certain questions about parents. It's two rich kids. In some respects, I almost think there has to be some other material. But in other respects, you take away. I mean, you don't expose them to things like Shakespeare, the so-called classic books, there can be a loss, too.

Jamie's ambivalent acceptance of the need for students to be exposed to the classics did not illumine the reasons why Shakespeare may be relevant to students. Instead, the argument for exposure was partly entangled in her own university training as an English major. There Shakespeare classes were required for English teacher certification. Despite the fact that Jamie was personally alienated from Shakespeare's work, she also believed teachers must transform the seemingly irrelevant curriculum into dynamic learning. Again, the discursive practices that would have assisted Jamie were unavailable, and thus she was left on her own, unable to connect her own deep convictions with the inherited curriculum.

Jamie did understand the significance of teaching without convictions. She was painfully aware of the cost: her own sense of possibility.

> I think at certain points, I did become assimilated into school life but I don't feel a part of it. I don't think I ever did. I felt bad because I didn't like the school environment. I never felt it was healthy or natural, I never felt comfortable there.

And I did fulfill some of the expectations. But it wasn't me. And now I have to decide whether, well, is it because I'm not comfortable with myself that this discomfort came, or is it really that environment that is making it so uncomfortable for me? I don't know. That's something I may be confronting all my life. Is my discomfort because I'm not just comfortable with me, or is it everything out there that's making me this way?

Alienation from school, an effect of how school is structured, contributed to Jamie's strong feelings of displacement. She had difficulty embracing displacement as a place of departure, because she positioned the problem of becoming a teacher as being someone other than who she is. Such positioning, however, is not a personal problem. It is an effect of how power is lived within the school context and of the normative discourse of teacher education that reduces the complexity of learning to teach to that of merely accepting the teacher's role. While Jamie struggled to uncouple power and knowledge, much of her discomfort with the teaching role stemmed from the persistent image of the teacher as knowledge-bearer, yet another effect of the normative discourse. Throughout student teaching, Jamie felt the pressure to have answers for any questions raised:

> The pressure is there to know, whether it's from yourself or the students or other teachers. I mean there's a category on the teacher certification evaluation form. Is this person knowledgeable in her fields? Whatever that means. That's another thing. I've had these classes, but how much does anybody really know? As far as, one thing everyone always expressed to me, cooperating teachers, other teachers, you don't know something, just say you don't. Which is OK, but when you're in the classroom, initially you're trying to prove yourself and you want to know. And when someone asks you a question, there is that tug. Gee, why don't I know. I should know that. Oh, shit.

At the close of her student teaching semester, Jamie continued to raise the messy questions of the relationship between knowledge and uncertainty, and between power and powerlessness. When she perceived the classroom as a proving ground, any question appeared more like a threat than like an invitation to exploration. This persistent pressure to know was part of a cycle of tensions rooted in Jamie's educational formation and legitimized by the institution of teacher certification and the organization of school. During our last interview, I asked Jamie, "Is there a place for you in the public school system?" Her answer reflected her persistence and strength:

Right now? No. That was one of the things in the meeting Mrs.
Michaels asked me. Seeing I had such an unhappy time, seeing that
I was questioning the value of everything I was doing. And I got the
feeling from her if I did feel those things, then I shouldn't be there.
At one point, I was knocking myself down. Why can I not, what is
so bad about feeling those things, of having those questions, of not
having a good time?

I remember sitting in the final workshop and everyone was
saying it was wonderful. Student teaching was wonderful. And it
was like, what is wrong with me and what are they looking at?
What's happening here? And is it so wrong to see these things and
question these things and not have a happy time?

I think, maybe, sometimes, I don't have answers but at least I
was looking and maybe that's something that should be brought into
the school, that you don't see a lot of. There's a lot going on, let's
look at this.

Jamie was beginning to value her difficult teaching semester. But she was
on her own, for the dominant assumption that student teaching should be a
relatively painless experience, despite the fact that it is typically known and
lived as "sink or swim," denied the contradictory realities of learning to teach.

Part of Jamie's struggle concerned her attempt to mediate the disparate
experiences of curriculum practice: those between the set texts of the received
curriculum and the subtext of relationships with students; between the chronology of both the canon and institutional time, and the personal time required for sorting things through; between the ways in which we are, in the
words of Harold Rosen, "taught in educational systems how to cover our
narrative tracks and even be ashamed of them,"[12] and the exigencies of the
autobiographical impulse; and between past and present images of teachers
and her own deep convictions about what a teacher can be.

These contradictions affected Jamie's decisions about just what aspects of
classroom life might be drawn upon as sources of her pedagogy and as places
for her own validation. Her struggle demonstrates how difficult it is to work
against the dominant practices when one is provided only the practices that
produce authoritative discourse. The departmental press for covering the material against all odds subverted Jamie's attempts to establish meaningful relationships among the curriculum, the students, and herself. Her teacher education
course work focused on acontextual techniques without providing the discursive
practices and social encouragement necessary to counter the isolation of learning to teach. Her English background never concerned itself with the problem
of rendering content as pedagogical or of examining how the canon engenders
exclusions, silences, and resistances. Those who surrounded her felt it was up

to the individual student teacher to single-handedly learn to teach. Moreover, the disappearance of her professional network and lack of adequate supervision, at the time Jamie replaced her cooperating teacher without pay or guidance, proved to be so isolating that Jamie's privatization of learning to teach was an inevitable effect of a system gone awry.

Given this mess, it is no wonder that Jamie, herself, was unable to untangle the knotty problem of constructing her teaching self from the stuff of student experiences and to move beyond the constraining dualism that becoming a teacher means not becoming who you are. Caught between the mandates of institutional life and her own convictions and dreams, Jamie was compelled to privatize these socially generated dilemmas because this was the only available discourse.

Jamie Owl's story is particularly painful because, throughout her teaching, her work was to construct an identity based upon not fitting into the traditional roles expected of teachers. Her context was qualified by isolation and lack of discursive practices and critical dialogue in which to work things through. Jamie was absorbed by the terrifying process of rejecting normative visions of what it means to be a teacher while negotiating visions yet to come. Relevant here are two types of conflicting views on what it means to take up the identity of a teacher: the centripetal or normative voice, which defines what a teacher is and does in relation to the kind of authority and power teachers are expected to deploy; and the centrifugal or resisting voice, which speaks to one's deep convictions, investments, and desires. For Jamie, these two moments were in constant antagonism, positioning multiple identities and delaying the kind of pedagogical work necessary to realize her possibilities as a teacher. And while self-blame and thus privatization was a dominant dynamic, these tensions must be understood not as effects of personality but as a dilemma made from the ways that learning to teach is orchestrated and lived.

4

Narratives of Student Teaching
The Jack August Stories

In early September 1983, Jack August was one of six secondary social studies and English student teachers who attended a series of preparatory education workshops prior to their entrance into high school classrooms. There I presented my research plans in order to solicit student teacher volunteers. Immediately after my presentation, Jack August, a white working-class man, aged twenty-four, approached me to volunteer. I expressed my surprise at his immediate and receptive response. "Why not participate?" he grinned. "I have a soft spot for helping out researchers."

Jack August gave the immediate impression of being a mild-mannered, soft-spoken man. Of medium height and weight, he is distinguished by a ruddy complexion, slightly balding red hair, and a close-cropped red beard. Known by his peers and professors as a shy and private individual because he was rarely vocal in his education classes, his university supervisor and professors were puzzled by his decision to participate in this study. Later Jack expressed one of his intentions; coming from a background in psychology, he respected the process of research and throughout his undergraduate years, often volunteered as a research participant in experimental studies.

At the time of this study, Jack August was enrolled in a master of education program at State University, taking courses that would lead toward secondary teacher certification in social studies, and the advanced degree. Prior to this degree program, Jack's relationship to the field of education was marginal; his undergraduate background was in the field of behavioral psychology. How Jack decided to enter the teaching profession with a focus in social studies education, and what happened during his time there, is part of his story.

Another part of Jack's story concerns the evolution of his teaching and learning intentions, how these intentions became an interpretive lens through which his actions and the actions of others were invested with meaning. Indeed, the subtext of his story suggests the surprising struggle to render experience meaningful. Jack was deeply invested in the discourse that experience makes the teacher; he began his teaching with the hope that experience was transparent and guaranteed access to truth. He believed that experience was the most stable ground of knowledge. So while Jack assumed that he would come to know through experience the world of teaching, what happened during his time as a student teacher was hardly as self-evident as he had hoped and planned. As his experience appeared more and more arbitrary, and less stable than he could ever imagine, Jack retreated into his private world of intentions, rehearsing what he would have liked to have happened despite what in fact occurred. And what occurred was complicated by the reality that, as a student teacher, Jack had few opportunities to make the changes he desired. Indeed, Jack was caught between his own ambiguous desires and the seemingly fixed world of the student teacher. Such uneasy boundaries fashioned how he understood his lived experiences. Chris Weedon describes the vacillations of understanding experience:

> The meaning of experience is perhaps the most crucial site of political struggle over meaning since it involves personal, psychic and emotional investment on the part of the individual. It plays an important role in determining the individual's role as social agent. It affects both where and how the individual acts and whether her action is based on a consensual acceptance of the meaning and effects of an action, on conscious resistance to them or on the demands of other external necessities.[1]

Throughout his teaching, Jack would struggle with conventional notions of experience, pedagogy, and power in the classroom. External constraints certainly shaped Jack's sense of possibilities. But along with conventions and constraints, Jack also drew upon his own subjectivity—the deep convictions and beliefs, life experiences, sense of self, and his own theory of the world— to endow with purpose the inherited territory of student teaching and the meanings of the pedagogy constructed there. Jack unwittingly lived the argument that "teachers, by the nature of their work with often resistant learners, with always 'pre-formed' learners, are forced to address the issue of pedagogy with every working breath they take, even when unaware of it."[2] As Jack's situation suggests, the sources of pedagogy are not an automatic feature of experience because experience is never the stable, transparent, or knowable phenomenon we hope it will be because the pedagogy is not the property of the teacher.

Jack August's story is composed from one hundred ninety-seven hand-written interview transcripts and classroom observation field notes. I met with Jack twelve times throughout, of which nine involved classroom observation and interview sessions in Greenville High. Three in-depth interviews took place in Jack's apartment.[3] Weekly classroom observations extended from October 6 to December 14, 1983, during his most active student teaching weeks. From the back of the classroom, I observed Jack and took detailed "running records," descriptive field notes that focused on Jack's presentation of curriculum, his formal and informal interactions with students during this class time, and the activities that ordered his class. My field notes recorded verbatim classroom dialogue in order to capture the texture of discourse as it unfolded.[4] Time notations ordered my field notes, for I was interested in understanding the flow of discourse, the diversity of activities, and the necessary transitions Jack employed in his efforts to maintain curricular cohesiveness. Moreover, time notations served as a reminder that it was literally impossible for me to capture everything that was said and done in Jack's classroom and that even at my most conscientious, these running records were partial and incomplete.

Each observation was formally scheduled, allowing interview time before and after a specific class. In-school interviews focused on Jack's general experience as a student teacher, his instructional intentions, and his impressions of a particular class. I usually met Jack in the social studies office, where he was given a small work space. Occasionally, we met for lunch in the teacher's cafeteria or in an afternoon study hall he often supervised for his cooperating teacher, Roy Hobbs. Each week I spent approximately two hours in Greenville High, although by late October my time there increased as Jack assumed additional history classes. I observed a total of fifteen of Jack's history classes which provided the opportunity to view each of his history sections a number of times.

Jack's story unfolds chronologically; it follows and comments upon how he saw his development as a student teacher. Like the preceding story of Jamie Owl, Jack August's narration magnifies the immediacy of ordinary classroom life. Again the reader is warned to approach Jack August's stories cautiously and remember that at best they represent particular moments frozen in time. Whereas the context of Jamie Owl's narration was largely shaped by the literature she taught, the history in which Jack and his students lived, because he taught social studies, became part of Jack's pedagogical struggles.

A second, and perhaps more important, distinction between these two stories concerns my methodology.[5] Because I was permitted to observe Jack's classes, I was able to compare how Jack saw his classes with what I saw happening there, how Jack struggled to enact his intentions and values, and the meanings Jack's students made because of his efforts. Observation allowed me to grasp the dimensions of conflicting meanings constructed by Jack and his students.[6]

Actors, Places, and Classes[7]

Jack August, student teacher

Burt Rerun, chairperson of Social Studies

Roy Hobbs, primary cooperating teacher

Edith Daring, secondary cooperating teacher

Alberta Peach, university supervisor

Thorn Parker, professor at State University

Joe Probe, professor of education

Greenville, town that houses Greenville High

Greenville High, secondary public school, site of Jack's student teaching semester

United States History (1492–1865), section one, level two. (U.S.H. I, II) Originally taught by Roy Hobbs, this course serves standard tracked ninth- and tenth-graders.

United States History (1856–1983), section two, level two (U.S.H. II, II). Jack took over Edith Daring's class in late October. The course serves ninth- and tenth-grade standard tracked students who passed the first course.

The Context of the Town: Greenville

For much of its history, Greenville has been a relatively quiet town. Its typicality is a source of official pride. During the late 1950s, the town seemed to be on the "up and coming." It boasted of jobs and decent housing. An apparent economic boom promised a good life to its citizens. Indeed, at that time Greenville adopted its official slogan, "Greenville, a typical town to live in."

Approximately twenty thousand persons live in Greenville. Of these, sixty-three percent are over eighteen years of age. Whites comprise well over ninety-nine percent of the population. African-Americans are the largest minority but less than two-tenths of a percent of the total population, followed by Asians (one-tenth of a percent), and Native Americans (one-fiftieth of a percent). Initially, Greenville did not suffer from the extreme urban problems of larger cities. Because the town is ninety-nine percent white, race has been an invisible issue; class divisions outweigh those of race. These divisions can be observed in its housing patterns; neighborhoods are economically segregated. After World War II, federally funded low-income housing projects were built on the town's outskirts.

By the mid-1970s, Greenville was in economic decline. Its major factories closed, to relocate either in Southern non-unionized towns or in other countries that guaranteed cheaper labor costs. After the factories closed, wholesale and retail manufacturing outlets absorbed some of the unemployment. Currently, clerical work employs the greatest number of persons. Beyond its few movie theaters, the main street downtown shopping area offers little beyond daily needs. Although Greenville has public transportation, it is costly and limited.

Those born in Greenville tend to live out their lives there. In fact, most town residents were born in the state. Greenville Community College absorbs most of the town's high school graduates, offering an affordable two-year post-high school education. Although universities throughout the country send recruiting personnel to Greenville High, only one percent of its graduates leaves the town for higher education. Army recruitment personnel have been more successful in their recruiting efforts; each year, approximately forty percent of the male graduating seniors and eight percent of the female seniors enlist.

Over the last fifteen years, social service agencies have been established in Greenville. They seem to come and go depending on the current political administration and the availability of federal funds. Unemployment tends to run high in Greenville despite job retraining, adult literacy, and head start programs. But its day-care centers are not sufficient in meeting the needs of the working class. Over half the school-age families of Greenville are headed by a single female parent. Persons working in such programs perceive Greenville as a troubled city with social problems reflective of the larger country, such as unemployment, child abuse, wife abuse, alcoholism, teenage pregnancies, illiteracy, and rape.

Greenville High, the town's only high school, enrolls approximately eleven hundred students. Like the town, its student population is predominantly white; it also reflects the town's social class divisions. Ethnic and racial minorities are rendered invisible. The few Puerto Rican students, for example, are placed in the academic Spanish class; no bilingual or English-as-a-second-language services are available despite the recent arrival of a small group of

Southeast Asian refugees sponsored by a local church group. Yet it is the high school more than any other institution that brings the town's four corners together.

The school's structure reflects its modest student population growth in the late 1960s. A new school wing, primarily servicing vocational students, stands in stark contrast to the original structure built in the late 1940s. The school organizes and processes students into a three-tier tracking system of advanced, standard, and basic. Its classroom architecture is traditional; each classroom is square, lined with individual student desks. Each academic department has its own corridor and office. It is in these offices that teachers congregate each morning with their departmental colleagues.

From Greenville High to an area of fast-food restaurants and shopping centers is a short walk. Although Greenville is a closed campus, it is not uncommon to see students there during the school day. They are permitted to congregate outside the main school entrance to smoke cigarettes. Another popular hangout after the school day is the large indoor ice skating rink housed in the school parking lot. Ice skating is a year round sport but becomes especially popular during the hockey season. Indeed, most of the administratively sanctioned social activities revolve around sports, which are used to cultivate school spirit and community.

At the time of this study, both the school's student enrollment and its economic support were in decline. The town's shrinking tax base, coupled with a property tax revolt, greatly affected school offerings. Beyond athletics, few extracurricular activities survived budget cuts. Each academic department drastically cut special interest courses and teachers. The social studies department was especially hard hit with budget cuts; in the early 1970s, for example, its course offerings reflected the New Social Studies Movement. At that time, courses in oral history, contemporary society, anthropology, and psychology revitalized both teachers and students. As funding diminished, so too did course offerings. Traditional United States history courses dominated the department's offerings. There was one special topics class, but it was limited to advanced-track students. Every social studies teacher carried two to four sections of United States history.

The basics, then, defined Greenville's curriculum, which in turn qualified its teaching staff. Few new teachers were hired. Approximately ninety-five percent of its teaching staff was tenured. Because of teacher layoffs, few teachers have been at Greenville High for less than fifteen years. Most teachers were known by the town and had been educated in the state. They have often taught generations of the same families and have reputations that precede them. Students usually predict which teachers they will have before officially enrolling in their class.

BECOMING A STUDENT: STORIES FROM SCHOOL

Jack August was born and raised in the small rural village of Plainfield, forty miles north of State University. Known as a farming community, Plainfield's population is predominantly white. He attended public schools throughout his formal education. Jack's social class background is working class; his ethnicity, Irish.

Jack barely remembered his early childhood. Characterizing himself as a loner, having few friends, his childhood and adolescent activities remained solitary. He played in the woods, rode a trail bike, and was interested in mechanics. He has no memory of close friends before senior high.

What seemed to matter to Jack most during our first interview was his early relationship to the teaching profession. He began the interview by fashioning his life story around how he decided to be a teacher:

> I can remember wanting to be a teacher even in elementary school. I thought at different times that maybe the only reason that I wanted to be a teacher was it was the only professional job that I was exposed to. And when you're in school, you see a lot of teachers. You see teachers all the time unless you've been to the hospital, or something, doctors, or some other kind of professional person. [9-21-83][8]

Jack's early desire to be a teacher seemed to depend more on his perceptions of teachers as role models and their accessibility than on his success as a student or his enjoyment of school. He described himself as an average student, doing just enough work to pass his courses, although he did remember scoring well on an achievement test and being placed in his junior high school's upper-track classes. But apart from looking up to these familiar figures, Jack could not explain what it was that drew him to the profession or remember particular incidents that illustrated a teacher's influence.

The summer after Jack graduated from high school, he began his first two years in higher education at a local community college. While Jack focused on fulfilling the general liberal arts requirements for the associate degree, he began to explore the discipline of psychology. An instructor drew him to this field:

> He was somewhat outspoken and a little less than conventional. And he really didn't last that long. I got the impression that they sort of wanted him out. He didn't have tenure or anything. But I liked the way he taught. In fact, he taught one of the psych courses. But he had sort of an unstructured approach to the classroom, not to the

course, but the classroom. If it were a nice day, we could go sit outside. A little more freedom and common sense. Why sit inside as long as you can keep people's attention? I can remember thinking at that point that a career like a community college teacher would be great. I hoped to hold a job a little longer than he did.

During his community college years, Jack began to identify the types of educational structures most stimulating to him as a student. He appreciated the responsibility and freedom that college afforded:

One of the things I've liked is when the teacher sort of treats you as, gives you some vestige of being adult and having some responsibility. I still think that would be something to strive for, to treat students as semi-adults, at least. I realize there will be some times when that approach really won't work. I'm sure there will be times when a little bit of freedom and a little bit of responsibility will be abused. But I'd still like to give it to the students who will appreciate it.

Jack depended on his student educational experience to inform him of the kind of teacher he would like to become. Early on, he realized his goals as a teacher might be too idealistic, at best affecting only a small minority of students. But educational philosophy was important: for Jack intentions were more significant than necessary adaptations or even the process whereby intentions become enacted.

After receiving his associate degree in liberal studies, Jack entered State University for his junior year. He had completed all general university requirements with his work at the community college, and declared himself a psychology major in the college of arts and sciences. During the next two years, Jack became involved in both psychology courses and internship work. He was strongly influenced by his psychology professors' emphasis on behaviorism, and there he focused his studies:

Behaviorism just seemed like a succinct, scientific, simple kind of way to deal with maladaptive behaviors. The principles are supposedly universal, you could use one to help just about anybody. One of the things I used to think was good about it was that you really didn't have to know why there was a problem. All you had to do was deal with the problem.

The interest in behaviorism was kind of like jumping on the band wagon. . . . It was sort of a way to identify myself with something. I can remember wanting to be a radical behaviorist. Once I found that initial interest, I continued it without really diversifying it or without really exposing myself to anything else.

Jack's attraction to behaviorism began with the theory's promise of effectiveness. If practiced correctly, behaviorist theory seemed to guarantee concrete and predictable results. Beyond the theoretical attraction, Jack had the need to belong; the psychology department offered a community. During the two years Jack spent at State University, his energies went into his studies, leaving little time for extracurricular activities.

Jack did not become disillusioned with behaviorism until a few months after graduating from State University with a bachelor's degree in psychology. He had secured a full-time job as a case worker in a private residential school for autistic children and it was there that he witnessed the children's treatment:

> My attitudes were changing. You come out of school with textbook ideas of how things should work. And about how principles and procedures should be implemented. And when you see how they are actually done, it's not the same. I didn't like the way the principles were implemented at the school. And the school is considered to be the best of its kind in the country.
>
> I guess the reason I got turned off to it was the behavioral procedures. I get the impression anyway, that the school tends to attract people who are just kind of mean. Or enjoy feeling power over these kids and would use excessive force in physically promoting kids to go through the procedures. And I got a little disheartened, a little disillusioned with the behavioral procedures implemented there and sort of got turned off to the field of psychology.

Once contextualized by social practice, behaviorism lost its ideal qualities. Significantly, Jack began to consider the dilemmas of working with people. As he contrasted the type of educational relationships most personally significant to his own development with the practices of the school, he could not reconcile the use of this method. At this point, he returned to the idea of becoming a teacher and played with the possibility of special education because of his work with autistic children.

The M.Ed. Program: Life in Teacher Education

When Jack went to the School of Education, he knew he wanted to be a teacher, but was not quite sure just exactly who or what he wanted to teach:

> Actually, I sort of wandered into the certification office. I was lean-
> ing more toward elementary and I had that idea. But I was intro-
> duced to Joe Probe and Thorn Parker and they were secondary people.
> I hadn't made a firm decision, anyway.
>
> I was thinking elementary because I thought it would be a little
> less, it wouldn't be . . . well, you hear all the horror stories about
> controlling the classrooms and I thought maybe elementary school
> because I'd be a heck of a lot bigger than them.

Even before becoming committed to secondary education, Jack's concern
was with issues of classroom control. Initially, the extent to which a teacher
could exert physical intimidation made elementary education more attractive.
However, the certification office assumed males to be best suited for secondary
education. Jack did not reflect much on this tension and instead appreciated the
attention he received from the men of the secondary education program.

Jack decided to enter the master's program for secondary education with
the goal of completing course work leading to secondary teacher certification
in the behavioral sciences and social studies. The dual certificate was pragmatic: Jack could apply his undergraduate psychology credits to the behavioral science certification and take four history courses for the social studies
certification. Of the thirty-three credits required for this degree, twenty-one
credits would be taken in the School of Education.

That fall of 1982 Jack enrolled in four undergraduate history courses
from State University's history department. A stranger to the discipline of
history, he was, by the end of that semester, deeply affected by his studies. For
the first time, Jack learned of African slavery resistance, women's history, the
United States government's genocidal policy toward Native Americans, and
the Reconstruction period from African American perspectives. He came to
understand how interpretation and perspective position not only historical
writing but the individual's understanding of and relationship to history, and
he lamented the poverty of his own education. His professors helped rescue
history from between the pages of textbooks; looking back, Jack traced his
newly emerging historical awareness to these courses. Challenged to recon-
sider and question his own educational biography and the relationship to
history cultivated there, and determined to spare his future students from the
myopia of historical conventions, Jack was determined to take this "new"
knowledge into his own student teaching classroom.

Rather than recall specific course titles for the five education courses Jack
took during spring 1983, he remembered instead their general themes:

> They're all theory courses, outside of the one where you develop
> something. None of the courses are like, this is how you fill out a

grade book, or this is how you teach. I guess they more or less assume that you're going to develop your own style or you're going to do it your own way, anyhow. All they can do is hope that you'll be creative and use creative teaching methods and strategies and ways to develop critical thinking. But as far as actually having a course that says, this is how you grade papers or something, you just don't get it there.

I think that approach is pretty good because it doesn't make much sense to waste much time. How you're actually going to teach or run a classroom, it's something you're going to develop on your own, anyway. I think it's something that I'm going to learn how to do myself. Nobody's going to be able to teach me, tell me how to do it. I don't think you become a teacher by going to the university or any place else. You have to rely on your own experience. I think you have to do it and develop your own style.

Educational theory appeared more like an intellectual exercise than an instance of practice. Indeed, Jack's burgeoning vision of theory was quite subjectivist: everyone will develop her or his own individual theory and style because truth and theory, like experience itself, can be known only subjectively. Consequently, Jack looked to experience as automatically providing insight into practice. Because of this valorization of experience, Jack hoped student teaching would offer on-the-job training and a teaching style. The idea seemed to be that style could metamorphose into knowledge about pedagogy.

Jack's belief that experience makes the teacher may have been supported by his educational classes. There teaching seemed more like a craft, learned from direct and personal experience. His impression of teaching was that it was a highly individualized activity, dependent upon the person rather than negotiated within social contexts. Such a supposition—that teachers make themselves—may have been based upon the program's refusal to reduce pedagogy to a series of decontextualized and controlling recipes for instruction. The problem is that this refusal to simplify pedagogy seemed to be coupled with the pervasive argument that it is impossible to teach anyone to teach. Jack focused on this impossibility; he looked forward to the real experience that teaching would provide. That experience could be treacherous in either activity or interpretation was not yet his concern. Rather, Jack assumed he could automatically be a teacher from the experience of teaching.

Of all the required education courses, curriculum development offered the practical advice Jack accepted gladly. The professor's formula for creating curriculum was routinely specified. It reduced curriculum design to its smallest parts and then provided strategies for long-term planning. In many ways, this approach to curriculum design is similar to the behaviorist strategies of control. Each method offers specific and simple steps toward accomplishing observable goals. Each depends more on the practitioner's directives than on social negotiation. Both fragment solutions from problems. At the root of each method is an assumed hierarchy that positions persons as clients. The temptations of the practical, however, influenced Jack's uncritical acceptance of it.

As with his history course work, many of Jack's education classes did attempt to provide a critical lens through which to view educational life. Critical thinking was valued as the key to personal and social awareness. Throughout his education courses, Jack read critiques of current educational practice and began to understand how social inequalities became structural features of high school life. His burgeoning critical awareness encouraged his desire to do something creative, something other than the traditional lecture model so endemic both to the high school classes observed recently and to his own educational biography. Yet how this desire would be translated into practice was subsumed by Jack's assumption that because he was a critical thinker, he could teach others this same process. He also assumed that students would be open to question what they took comfortably for granted. However, uninitiated in communicating these new thoughts—in dialoguing with others about what it means to be critical and in constituting critical conduct—Jack's desires for critical awareness remained only that.

Upon completing these courses, Jack decided to teach at Greenville High because it was close to home and because he believed the school would give him the most typical and generalizable teaching experience. He preferred to teach in the behavioral sciences, an area where he felt knowledgeable, but because a taxpayers' revolt had seriously affected school funding, most social science courses had been eliminated. Instead, Jack inherited three sections of United States history.

Of the six social studies teachers Jack observed during those two weeks in the early fall of 1983, he chose to work with two. His first cooperating teacher, Roy Hobbs, had been teaching in the social studies department for seventeen years. While Roy's fluent articulation of history impressed Jack, his primary approach, the lecture format, was a method Jack wanted to avoid. But because Roy was personable and friendly, Jack decided to begin his formal teaching by taking over the first of Roy's two United States history courses.

Jack's second choice was Edith Daring, a veteran of thirty years teaching, and the only woman faculty member of the social studies department. What drew Jack to Edith was her creativity. She involved students as much as possible and integrated popular culture, women, and persons of color into her history curriculum. Bright posters, maps, photographs, art work, and plants filled her classroom, in stark contrast to other social studies rooms, empty except for desks and standard maps. But Edith Daring struck Jack as less approachable and had the reputation, among the men of the social studies department, of being a loner. He would eventually take over one of Edith Daring's classes, United States history from 1865 through the present.

Jack's decision to have two cooperating teachers during his student teaching semester served conflicting desires. First, he desired to develop his burgeoning historical awareness into expertise, and he believed he should learn the content of history before doing any creative work. Roy Hobbs appeared to personify such traditional knowledge, routinely teaching history through its military exploits, and Jack turned to him. Edith Daring, his second choice, was to meet Jack's desire to be creative. But why Jack chose Roy Hobbs as his primary cooperating teacher and Edith Daring as his secondary teacher can only be surmised. Certainly Edith Daring's approach to history was more congruent with Jack's commitments and values. On the other hand, Jack needed social acceptance and social compatibility. Roy Hobbs was one of the "boys" of the social studies department; Edith Daring was not. She neither participated in the social studies department's daily gatherings, nor joked about with "the boys." Edith Daring separated herself from her teaching peers and in turn was ostracized by them. Indeed, Edith was preparing for a lengthy legal battle over sex discrimination in the hiring practices of the social studies department. Her case was about to go to litigation, and although she did not speak of it, it was common knowledge. Perhaps Jack August thought choosing Edith Daring as a primary cooperating teacher would be too great a price to pay. Despite his selection, Jack continued to maintain that the problem of establishing himself as a teacher would be his alone:

> I really don't have too much idea of what student teaching is like. I sort of thought it would be like substitute teaching in a sense. You have the difficulties of a substitute teacher. . . . You know you have to establish yourself with people. They are going to see how far you'll go and put you through some tests. So I assume I'll have to go through a period where I'll have to establish myself with students. I'm not going to have the same sort of control that my cooperating teacher who has seventeen years of experience in the system. It doesn't bother me. You have to go through it.

By the end of September, Jack had settled into an initial routine. Each morning he would go directly to the social studies department office and have coffee with the men. During coffee, before the first bell of the school day, the men would joke together, discuss sports, and talk about the school. Jack would then observe three or four classes, spend time in the library reviewing material, have lunch in the teacher's cafeteria, and occasionally walk with Roy Hobbs during the latter's hall duty.

Stressing critical thinking skills, which meant critically questioning any information by analyzing it as one mode of interpretation, was Jack August's main teaching goal. He knew one model of how to translate his own critical awareness into curricular objectives and procedures, the university model, that worked for his student self. This model presupposed the student had ascertained advanced literacy skills, maturity, self-motivation, and an interest in the material. At State University, Jack's professors lectured and handed out critical articles for classroom discussion; they focused on the course content rather than on the students or the pedagogy that brought them together. Jack entered student teaching with the idea of organizing his history classes like the university seminars he had so enjoyed. Perhaps Jack hoped to meet the student he was becoming.

DOING STUDENT TEACHING

Shouting out Ideas

Officially, Jack August began student teaching on October 5, 1983, when he "took over" Roy Hobbs's United States history class. The course was known by everyone as "U.S.H.I, II.," an awkward acronym that seemed to erase the content and context of the course.

Prior to Jack's official takeover, this class was under the tutelage of Roy Hobbs, who organized the material chronologically, focused on pivotal events emphasized in the textbook, and examined these events by highlighting a specific concept. Students received this information by lecture and returned it in recitation. A complex point system ordered his grading procedures. Students earned points by participating in class and taking frequent quizzes and tests based on the text and class lectures. Roy determined participation points by comparing his present students to his past students. Although Jack would have this class for fifteen weeks, or two graded quarters, he decided to continue Roy's structure with the reasoning that continuity would be in the students' best interest. Accordingly, Jack structured his presentations chronologically, dispensed the tests Roy designed, and covered the same concepts Roy covered in all his history classes. Yet these adjustments were neither painless nor automatic. Following Roy's plans meant holding his own in abeyance.

During that first day, Roy Hobbs introduced Jack to the class. Then, as Jack expected, he immediately left the room:

I asked [Roy] how he'll turn the reins over to me. He said, "I'll introduce you and leave for a week or two." Roy's philosophy is to have me start on my own and then come back. [10-6-83]

Jack's analogy of his new classroom stance as "taking the reins" signified his acceptance of Roy Hobbs's original classroom structure. On the other hand, Jack decided to hold these reins loosely, giving the students the slack that might encourage their participation. However, because Roy taught in the same room the period before Jack's class, Roy was often still sitting behind the teacher's desk as Jack's students filed into their history class, a symbolic reminder of who really held the reins.

Jack began his history class with the year 1763, focusing on the events that led to the American Revolution. In a few short weeks, Roy had already "covered" three hundred years. During these early weeks, Jack, through Roy's instruction, stressed the concept of the colonists as natural rebels. The term "natural rebel" also occurred frequently in the history text, the eighteenth edition of *History of a Free People* (1970).

I observed Jack's second class meeting, sitting in the back of the class-room, without being introduced and largely ignored by students. Twenty students were present, nine females and eleven males. Although seats were unassigned, the males sat in the front of the class, the females, toward the back. The students entered the room highly animated, boisterous about the events of the previous night. Roy Hobbs was in the front of the room col-lecting student papers. Two minutes after the bell rang, he left. On this particular day, the cooling system was malfunctioning; loud clanging noises reverberated throughout the classroom, overriding individual speech but blend-ing into the general din of loud student conversation. Jack began the class in a soft, barely audible voice.

10:38

Jack: I'm going to take attendance so I can learn everyone's name. Jack Damon?

Class: WRONG CLASS!

Jack [searching through a stack of papers on the teacher's desk]: I don't have the class list.

[The class continues talking among themselves. The cooling system commotion makes everyone talk louder.]

Jack: I want to talk about the concept of natural rebel [writes "natural rebel" on the board]. Does anyone have an idea of what a natural rebel is?

[The class, ignoring Jack, continues talking among themselves.]

Male student to Jack: Could you speak a little louder please?

[Jack says sure, but continues to speak softly.]

10:44

[Jack hands out a two-page, fourteen-paragraph photocopy article to each person in the class. The reading, taken from one of Jack's university courses, described the social and racial makeup of the early colonial society. It depicted the colonists as socially and culturally alienated from England.]

Jack: Who'd like to start reading? [Jack points to a male student in the front row.]

Male: Not me.

Jack: Go ahead.

[The male student begins reading in a soft voice which can barely be heard above the clanging cooling system. The student has great difficulty reading the names of countries.]

[No student volunteers to read. Jack picks each reader until fourteen students have read one paragraph each. Each student reads for approximately forty seconds, and most students, when called upon, slump in their seats and stumble through their paragraph in low quiet voices. A few students punctuate each sentence with, "I can't read." Some students joke about not hearing the readers, while Jack summarizes each paragraph.]

11:00

Jack: OK, what's this all about?

[A few students summarize the reading.]

11:04

Jack: All right. I'll give you the rest of the period to work on your time line.

[10-6-83 field notes]

For the remaining twenty minutes, students continued to talk and joke among themselves. Jack attempted to get the students back on task twice, warning them to work quietly. But student conversation continued, at times escalating into loud noise. Toward the end of period, Jack slipped out momentarily to return with the correct attendance list. He read the student names out loud while two students were throwing rulers at each other. A few minutes before the bell rang, students began gathering their books and crowding around the classroom door. As the bell rang, those few students not waiting by the door jumped over desks and ran out of the room.

After class, Jack wondered about the students' noise level but felt he was off to a pretty good start. If he could create a more relaxed atmosphere, Jack believed, students would feel free to participate.

> I want to encourage responding in class. They're not used to it. I wanted to be a little bit different. My cooperating teacher had more a lecture, a certain structure. More formal. I don't want to become preoccupied with discipline. I'd rather have free responding. I'm trying to incorporate some of the ideas in the education theory courses, that discipline isn't that all-consuming goal. I'd rather be more lax in exchange for participation. I want them to shout out their ideas if they want.

Jack wanted to conduct an exciting history class, where, similar to his past university seminars, ideas determined classroom structure. He was aware that the students were not used to this form of discourse, but did not foresee its implementation as problematic or concern himself with constructing the discursive practices that would allow students to participate in this kind of exchange. Rather, Jack settled on a tacit bargain: his foregoing a traditional classroom approach that stressed order through teacher control, for student freedom and their participation. Yet reconstructing power relations is never so simple as deciding not to use the prerogatives of the teacher's institutionalized power, or of hoping the material is powerful enough to transform students' alienation toward history. Moreover, while Jack selected what he believed would be a highly stimulating article, he had not considered the literacy skills of his students or even thought about ways to help students discuss it. Instead, he assumed the self-evidence of the material. This particular reading, however, presumed a complex acquisition of critical literacy as well as prior historical knowledge; his students possessed neither.

What seemed most important to Jack was that this article appeared to challenge directly the dominant ideas of the required text. Jack wanted to put history on trial with the students as the jury, but did not see that he needed to take up practices that would help students grasp the complexities demanded by such a stance:

> At some point, I'd like to introduce the idea that students should be more critical of historical accounts. Just because it's in their book doesn't mean they should believe it. I have to use it but I can use it just as well and point out it's not perfect but bring in other sources. I don't want to just stick with the textbook. I also don't want them to learn just what I say, but to consider it.

Jack longed for students to consider history for themselves by questioning the authority of the teacher as well as the text. This was missing from his own education. While being a laudable goal, until Jack could translate this goal into a practice that could permit students to see the relationship between history and themselves, Jack's goals remained private desires.

Keeping Them on their Toes

On the advice of Roy Hobbs, Jack gave his history class weekly quizzes. Usually students had prior notice but occasionally Jack surprised his class with a "pop" quiz. These quizzes asked students to list, define, or recall the received details of historical events. Students had twenty minutes to take each quiz and then Jack discussed the correct answers. Such quizzes filled the entire history period.

Jack intended a quiz to serve two purposes: first its warning function. He borrowed Roy Hobbs's phrase, "keeping the students on their toes," that implied both an expected student readiness based on preparatory study and the teacher's power to coerce. The quizzes were a way to check up on whether they did their homework, but they really served to authorize the teacher and the material. Second, the quizzes were a way to reward students for taking notes during class, because students could use their class notes during the quiz. If students took good notes, Jack reasoned, they would do well on the quiz. However, the students then understood the purpose of note-taking as a means for scoring well on quizzes. As a result, during every class, students would punctuate Jack's historical explanations with the questions, "Do we have to know this for the quiz?" or "Should we write this down?" In this way quizzes rather than history structured pedagogical relations.

Jack gave his first quiz in early October. He announced the quiz at the start of the class. Immediately students began negotiating. They asked to go to the library instead, told Jack they did not have enough time to read the chapter, and denied having previous knowledge of the quiz despite the fact that it had been announced and posted on the board days before:

12:50

Jack: The quiz is a little different than Mr. Hobbs. It's worth only one point, not two, and it will take about fifteen minutes. OK! Let's get quiet!

Male: Can we use our notes?

Jack: OK. You can use your notes but not your books. [As Jack hands out the quiz, students are talking loudly.]

Female [holding her head]: Oh my G-d! I have no idea!

Jack: This is a quiz. Let's get quiet or I'll have to take your paper away. . . . You want me to read over the questions? [Jack begins to read each question out loud.]

Female: Give us some hints.

Jack: That question is pretty straightforward. I took it right from the book.

Male: Do you want us to list or explain?

Jack: Just list it.

Male: Can we get extra credit if we put more down?

Female: OH SPARE ME!

Male: Can we use our notes?

Female: Who takes notes?

Female: That was easiest enough to flunk.

1:06

[The quiz is over and Jack collects the papers. A female student asks Jack when the time line homework is due.]

Jack: I'm not sure.

Female: YOU'RE NOT SURE!

Jack [to class]: Alright. You wanna go over the quiz?

A few students in unison: NO!

1:08

[Jack reads the questions in a soft, barely audible voice. Although a few students answer, Jack ends up answering his own questions. Few students are listening to Jack. A few minutes later, Jack takes off his sport coat and rolls up his longsleeve shirt to his elbows. He is now talking about the colonists' boycott of British goods.]

Jack: You don't have to have the word "boycott" in your answer. You just have to explain what it is.

1:16

Jack: Anyone has any questions on economic growth? [The class is silent.] No one has any questions on economic growth? Especially since we haven't ever gone over that? Karen Tarr, can you tell us about economic growth?

Karen Tarr: We didn't go over that.

Male: Oh yes we did.

[10-13-83 field notes]

After this class, Jack expressed deep concern over his procedures for communicating material to his students and spoke of the distance between knowing a concept and explaining that understanding. He knew his quiz had been ineffective. The student's sub rosa discourse told him as much. However, Jack did not perceive the quiz's purpose as contrary to his goals of creating an environment of free-flowing discussion where authority was questioned. Neither did he consider, as contrary to his goals, the detail-oriented quiz questions and the absence of student interpretation.

Jack attributed his classroom difficulties to inexperience with both the material and the methods of presentation. With little experience to fall back on, Jack was hard pressed to do anything but follow in Roy's footsteps. In actuality, this meant "sticking" to the text:

> I'm trying to stick to Roy's [plans]. I'm talking about the same things he is in his other classes. You have to start somewhere. He's eventually going to have this class back and I can't get too far away from his ideas. They seem like valid ideas.
>
> I don't want to just become a lecture teacher. I think I'm getting frustrated because I seem to be doing that. I don't want to model everything I see. I haven't been inventive enough. There's a bunch of things I'd like to do but I don't know how to organize it.
>
> There is a couple of things that Roy doesn't do. I'm going to try them. But then again, it's not like it's my own class. Not that I could probably organize my own class. It's a little bit difficult when you take over someone else's class. I look forward to the day when I have my own way of organizing. I don't know if I'll be able to do that, but I guess it will be easier to be consistent with things.

In some ways, Roy Hobbs's classroom structure served as Jack's safety net, allowing Jack to practice his new role, yet entrapping him in an identity he would rather avoid. Despite its contradictions, initially Jack rationalized Roy's structure as a means to organization. But the techniques became an end in themselves. For Jack, the only way out of this vicious cycle was to become a real teacher, something possible only after completing the internship. If Jack could not take ownership now, he could at least be the author of his future. In the meantime, Jack found himself in an identity that was the opposite of what he wanted to be. Although Jack expected to pick up teaching techniques on the job, he had not reckoned that the techniques offered would be so contrary to his philosophy and goals. But the problem was not Jack's inexperience. Rather, Jack could not view his present experience as contributing to his development. Experience seemed to thwart his attempts to understand teaching; it was a treachery he did not expect.

Even when Jack considered the practical circumstances confronting history teachers, he was at a loss as to how to make history relevant or balance the demands of the curriculum with the needs of students:

> The material should supplement what you're doing, not dictate what you're doing. . . . I'm wondering about what realistic goals are. Some of the social studies teachers are under the opinion that you're not going to turn any of the kids into historians.
> Another social studies teacher believes you can spark an interest. The ways others talk, they think it's all futile, that they're wasting their time. Maybe the goals and means need to be reassessed. I'm going to grapple with that when I get my own classes.

The question, "What is social studies for?" is a dangerous one. It requires critical interrogation into not just the student capabilities, but the processes and contents of pedagogy. Neither Jack nor the majority of his colleagues were prepared to explore such considerations. Such a discussion, however, might have helped Jack construct relevancies, moving beyond a rigid notion of skills to the relationships that concepts have to thought and to practice.

One social studies teacher did offer support and creative suggestions. Edith Daring rarely lectured. Instead, she used games, projects, and styles of discussion that engaged her students. She also gave Jack a book on games to help classroom discussion and to build community. For Edith, organizing her students to work as a community was a prerequisite to meaningful discourse. But while Jack appreciated the book, he also complained, "I don't want to spend the whole period moving desks around." Edith Daring may have reminded Jack of his own struggles, between covering the material and having some semblance of control while establishing an open, free-flowing classroom.

Jack's immediate present was out of his control. Even the curriculum seemed to take over. He was beginning to feel trapped by curricular demands, student resistance, and the social studies department's unreasonable goals. This powerlessness led Jack to continually imagine his future as a real teacher where he hoped for more control and the insight to achieve a balance between curricular demands and student needs. At this early stage, however, Roy seemed to keep Jack on his toes and the students seemed to be stepping on Jack's toes. More specifically, Jack felt no ownership in his process of learning to teach, and hence discounted the experience he was in fact living.

Part of Jack's early struggle concerned the distance between authoritative and internally persuasive discourse. He was struggling to construct his own historic voice while the history text and Roy's directives asserted an authoritative discourse that disorganized Jack's intentions and populated his activities to the extent that ownership was impossible. Juxtaposed to this was the sub rosa discourse of students, the discourse of negotiation, cynicism, parody, and embarrassment. The students' continual banter was as defensive as it was protective. Having to answer to these two extremes was Jack's own voice, one that valued disputation, critical response, and multiple perspectives, but remained private; influencing his subjective self, this voice was hardly heard by the students.

How Do You Sway People?

By the end of his third week, Jack was beginning to feel more comfortable with the curriculum. He had been teaching the same concepts about the American Revolution and the more Jack rehearsed this material, the less overwhelming were the details. Jack was also observed by his university supervisor, Alberta Peach, who managed to help Jack feel better about his efforts by encouraging him to think through his own classroom methods:

> The only thing Alberta didn't like was when I did the reading. I just passed it out and then just picked on somebody, mostly the kids who I knew their names, and looked at the name sheet and just grabbed people at random to read a paragraph at a time. And I hadn't given any thought to doing that. That was something being done in Roy's class. He suggested that but I didn't put any thought into how to disseminate the reading.
>
> Alberta thought it wasn't a very good idea to grab people and force them to read. I said I wouldn't force anyone to read. And she said it's powerful coercion, even if they hated it they'd still do it and be hating it. I thought about that for a little while and it makes sense to me. I asked for any volunteers first. Nobody volunteered so I began reading it myself. [10-20-83]

Jack's solution to the problem of "disseminating information" was to teach the students how to take notes and outline their reading; he provided instruction in traditional study techniques. Because Jack frequently employed outlining as a means of understanding and remembering material, and referred to these notes during his classroom presentation, he believed this same technique would benefit his students. So he designed a series of detailed study guides for students to complete as homework or as in class seat work. Like the outlines, Jack drew on and projected his own means of learning onto his students and then structured his teaching techniques accordingly. The problem, however, was that Jack's purposes in learning the material was quite different from his students and different purposes effect strategies of learning.

However, Jack experienced two new problems because of his stress on note-taking and outlining. First, he learned that both techniques were time-consuming and boring. For example, Jack attempted to read and outline a four-page article with the class. Four class days later, students still had not completed this work. The more Jack struggled to explain the article, the more the class tired of the routine of reading a paragraph, answering surface comprehension questions, and then outlining its main ideas. Although Jack tried to plow through, after spending four days on three pages, the article's meaning evaporated and his history section now fell behind the ones Roy taught. The second problem was related; note-taking tended to heighten disjointed details at the expense of meaning. Likewise, students understood the purpose of note-taking as a means for improving quiz and test grades. To all involved, history appeared as flat, predictable, and routine as the techniques themselves. Jack's approach seemed to tell students that history is a finished product, unencumbered by ambiguity, contradiction, or partiality.

The third strategy Jack employed was more compatible with his values: class discussion. During discussion, Jack attempted to have students consider the perspectives of the historical participants studied in order to understand their motives and actions. Jack's implicit goal was to deromanticize the early colonial rebels; he wanted students to crack their patriotic and sentimental casing and see their human frailties. To get the students' attention, Jack depicted the colonists as "terrorists."

The following description of Jack's class embodies these tensions. His goal was to introduce the idea of propaganda and Roy Hobbs's concept of "the politics of confrontation." The major point was that propaganda was employed to sway persons to support an independence movement they had previously ridiculed:

1:38

[Jack is silently taking attendance.]

Female [very loudly]: The majority of us are here physically anyway.

Jack [addressing the class]: Has anyone started the outline I gave?

Male: What outline?

Jack: The outline I gave.

Male: When is the time line due?

Jack: The time line is not even going to be collected. It's for your own good.

Female: You mean we've been doing this for nothing?

Female: Can we hand it in for extra credit?

Jack: No. It's not to be handed in.

[Students groan loudly.]

1:45

Jack: Does anyone know how many people wanted an American Revolution?

[Students call out numbers and percentages.]

Female: We've already went over this.

Jack: Let's have a vote.

Female: We don't want a vote. Just tell us.

Male: What's he talking about?

Male: It's one percent. That question was on the quiz.

Jack: In 1776, how many people wanted a revolution?

Male: Thirty-three percent.

Jack: Did we go over this before?

Male: Yes.

1:50

Jack: How might you sway people from their ideas to get them on your side?

Male: Propaganda.

Female: Prizes.

Jack: Does anyone know what propaganda is?

Female: Jerry does.

Jack: Does anyone know besides Jerry?

Female: Jerry knows everything.

1:55

Jack: Where did the Boston Massacre occur?

All students shout: BOSTON!

Jack: It obviously happened in Boston, but where? What kind of building?

Female: A big one.

2:00

Jack: What do you think the soldiers do if they see a mob?

Female: Shoot them.

Jack: And then what happened?

Female: A shot was heard around the world.

Male: No. Not that one.

Jack: So was it a massacre?

All students shout: NO!

Jack: What's a massacre?

Female: More than five.

Jack: Were they just innocent people?

Class: NO!

Jack: They were asking for it, right? Why do you think that word [massacre] was used?

Male: Propaganda.

Jack: It was blown, what?

Female: Out of proportion.

2:10

Jack [describing how the Sons of Liberty burned an effigy of a Tory supporter]: Sounds like nice people? What do you call them?

Female: Terrorists.

Jack: Can anyone think of terrorists we have today?

Students: Iran, PLO.

Jack: Do we like terrorists?

Class: NO!

Jack: The founders of America were terrorists. So, you think it was right?

Male: End justifies the means.

Jack [not responding to the male]: What happened to the woman in Goldfinger? You don't have to know that for the test.

As a result of Jack's "seminar" style, there seemed to be at least three simultaneous realities in this class. First was Jack's agenda of covering the material in a way that would engage the students. Yet the discursive practices he employed subverted his goal. Second, students who did participate felt free to take Jack seriously or respond with humorous answers that reflected their experience, such as the comment about changing people's ideas by offering them prizes. These students, in actuality, demonstrated their bantering skills. Finally, during most of this class, one to two-thirds of the students either waited the period out, did homework from other classes, talked among themselves, slept, wrote letters, drew, or just sat quietly. Jack's main strategy for reaching these students was to circulate around the room and individually ask them questions.

In this lesson, Jack's discourse mirrored his students: the shorter the student answer, the more specific were his questions. And the more specific his questions, the more literal students became. By the middle of his lesson, the majority of Jack's questions could be answered in phrases, one-word answers, or slogans such as "A shot was heard around the world" or "The ends justifies the means." Students were rarely encouraged to speak in sentences, theorize about motives, move beyond the obvious, or even explain their ridicule. Instead, they ended Jack's unfinished sentences fill-in-the-blank style. Indeed, most of Jack's questions permitted students to say less; they required no thought and reinforced the notion that history is already completed. Consequently, a mechanistic discourse pattern supplied a facade of meaning; it asserted the appearance of participation with no real investment in making sense.

Jack struggled with the problem of making history relevant to students' lives but was not availed the practices to help him achieve this goal. His main strategy was to detail situations by, for example, either having students vote on what already occurred—as if their votes could change history—or weaving sensational tales about tar and feathering, and then asking students what they thought about the tactic. It seems Jack thought that the "blood and gore" approach to history would engage students. His focus on the Sons of Liberty as terrorists, while originally meant to depatriotize these men, contradicted the earlier theme of natural rebel.

Jack's implicit argument—that it was natural for people to want to overthrow oppressive conditions, but unnatural or bad to use terrorist tactics—provided no interpretive clue as to the complexity of oppression and the contradictory responses to it. At no time did students gain insight into the multiple meanings of terrorism. For example, Jack asked students to take on the perspective of a British soldier at the scene of the so-called Boston Massacre. These students agreed that if they were soldiers at a demonstration and were hit by rocks from demonstrators, they too would shoot the demonstrators. No questions were raised as to the meanings of authority and power. Neither did a discussion ensue concerning alternative strategies—on the part of the colonists or the soldiers—to challenge the students' conclusions by comparing contemporary situations in this country, or elsewhere, to the past. But to realize such a discussion, students would have had to engage with a kind of knowledge that would move them beyond the taken-for-granted world of appearances. Jack did not provide this, and indeed, at this point in his formation, he too may have lacked the knowledge to advance such discussions. Rather than question authority, his lesson acted it out.

Jack's professional support network—that is, his cooperating teacher and university supervisor—focused on techniques of classroom control. The suggestions that he agreed with, or had no prior experience with—such as letting students volunteer to read, or his walking around the room—were easily integrated into his routines. The techniques he disagreed with philosophically, such as raising hands, were halfheartedly tried in an effort to comply. They did not help Jack with the deeper issues of working with the concept of ideology or making available practices that would help him do so. Although Jack seemed to be aware of the overt power struggles between teachers and students, he was unaware of how knowledge mediates such power struggles or even his own participation in and contributions to its ideological structure.

Grist for the Mill

With the first snow flurries of late October, Jack acquired his second United States history class, originated by Edith Daring. Until then, he had been sitting in the back of her room, observing Edith's style and classroom structure. Now that he was responsible for two classes, Jack was beginning to feel overwhelmed by the pressures of teaching. Prior to his recent takeover, Jack had used the majority of the school day to observe a few classes and prepare for one class. Because he tended bar at a local tavern at night, he rarely took home school work. Now he was even more pressed to use his school time wisely. Further, the rotating schedule of Greenville High guaranteed that these classes would be taught back-to-back. Jack would have to rapidly transform his frame of reference at the sound of a bell. When one class concluded, he immediately walked into the next one.

Even at this early stage of teaching a two-class schedule, Jack could not help making comparisons between classes. Foremost in his mind was the difference in student maturity. Unlike in the first class, Jack did not feel forced to assume the role of disciplinarian. In fact, now that he had classes to compare, he became more troubled over the direction his first class seemed to be taking. There Jack found himself becoming more authoritarian, setting limits on student behavior, creating consequences for infringement of class rules, and taking the advice of Roy Hobbs—that is, keeping students on their toes with a barrage of quizzes.

The second class was accustomed to discussion. For the last two months, Edith had encouraged a community where students interacted with each other and with history. These students were older than those of Jack's first class and, although they were also in the middle track, their basic skills seemed more developed.

Jack now had to learn post-civil war history. He began the start of a new unit on United States imperialism. Here Jack saw a sanctioned opportunity to investigate United States foreign policy from a social issues perspective.[9] Edith Daring seemed open to Jack's experiments; as far as she was concerned, Jack was now the teacher.

On his first official day, Edith Daring formally introduced Jack to his new class. It was a brief introduction and then she immediately left the room:

10:40

Edith [to class]: People. Mr. August will collect the abstracts from you. People, Mr. August is going to be your intern and I will be in and out. But it's going to be his face that you see everyday.

Female: Are you going to have another class?

Edith: No. I'm going to be in the library to do our files.

10:43

[Edith leaves the class and students begin loudly talking among themselves. One student loudly whispers, "SHHHH" to get the class quiet.]

Jack: Let's come to order. My name is August and I'm a student teacher from State University. You probably noticed me in the back. This is my second class.

Female: He's a permanent fixture.

Jack: I'd like to take a few minutes for you to tell me about you.

Male: Can we just say our names?

Jack: How about one thing about yourself?

Male: My name is John.

Class: HI JOHN!

Female: SHHHH! We have to be quiet.

[All students say their names but nothing about themselves; others make jokes about the name exercise. The noise level is rapidly rising.]

Jack [repeating this twice]: Can I have it a little quieter? I can't hear.

Female: SHHHHHH!

10:53

[Jack hands out to each student a large cardboard "flashcard," each bearing a phrase that partly defines the concept of imperialism. By the end of the game, students have to agree to a particular definition.]

[Jack writes the following definition on the board: "A government policy, deals with control of an empire, extends a nation's rule, deals with territory outside its boundaries, involves rule of other people and races and involves commerce and trade."]

11:10

Jack: So what happened in Grenada?

Female: There was a communist government.

Jack: Who was building the airstrip?

Class: CUBA!

Jack: Who's Cuba friends with?

Class: RUSSIA!

Jack: So maybe there's some connection. It's run by Castro and he's a communist. What was controversial about the airstrip? Does anyone know?

Male: It's two miles long.

Jack: How long does it have to be for a commercial jet? Maybe a mile long? So what's it used for?

Class: JETS!

Jack: So what happened then?

Male: The U.S. found out about it.

Female: They had a coup.

Jack: What's a coup?

Female: Coup d'etat.

11:16

Jack: So what did we do? We took it upon ourselves to do what?

Male: Troops.

Jack: What did people say when a big country like the U.S. brings in troops to a little country. What are they acting like?

Class: IMPERIALISTS!

Jack: Are we imperialists? I'm not saying we are.

Male: We're capitalistic pigs!

Jack: According to the definition, what are we going to do?

Male: Expand our territory.

Jack: Alright. Some people are saying we're imperialists. What's the big excuse we're there for?

Female: We're the peace keepers.

Jack: Do they sound like valid excuses?

Male: They're valid.

Jack: Are those justifiable reasons? I'm not going to make a decision either way. It's a controversy.

11:23

Female: Are you going to be our teacher everyday?

Male: You've got to keep this class quiet.

[10-26-83 field notes]

Later that day, Jack's first impressions of his new class were positive. He liked the students and felt they were mature enough to handle a seminar-style class. And whereas Jack's first class seemed more a testing ground for classroom techniques, he perceived this class as a proving ground. In fact, with this class, Jack felt he had improved some of his classroom methods. For instance, Jack had students introduce themselves, something he wished he had done in his first class. By his second month of student teaching, he realized the value of knowing students' names. He also began this new class with a loud voice and circulated easily around the room as he spoke. Finally, unlike his first class, Jack's goal was to establish rapport with students.

In Jack's mind, the recent United States invasion of Grenada seemed to occur "at the right time," in that it would "fit" right into his unit on imperialism:

I'll use the definition of imperialism throughout this semester. It's the dictionary's definition. The text talks about imperialism but it doesn't give a definition of it per se. But this definition seems like a reasonable one to me. It talks about expanding territories and taking over cultures that are unlike your own. It's unfortunate, but the recent events [i.e., the Grenada invasion and the U.S. presence in Lebanon] make for good—the way Thorn Parker put it—good grist for the mill, as far as the discussion 'cause the word [imperialism] has been brought up recently. They seemed to be aware of it.

Ironically, Jack's borrowed metaphor describing historical events as "good grist for the mill" reflected his classroom handling of the U.S. invasion of Grenada. It was almost as if the invasion afforded an opportunity to grind history down into consumable parts, chew them up, then spit them out.

Jack did not perceive his acquired definition of imperialism as problematic or as ideological. That the definition appeared unbiased seemed to obscure its neutralization of aggression and its separation of governmental policy from its effects on daily life. This definition erased oppression and exploitation with its technical emphasis on policy as neutrally managing people and places. Jack's intention, however, was to lead students to apply specifically his definition to an actual situation and then construct their own proof. Students were to consider whether the invasion of Grenada fit the formula for imperialism. But to construct such reasoning required that students understand more about Grenada than was established by Jack's questions.

However, Jack's implicit anticommunist stance subverted his intentions of critical inquiry. One student's comment, for instance, referring to United

States citizens as "capitalistic pigs," seemed to parody the anticommunist tenor. Again, student answers were reduced to slogans, phrases, and one-word replies, a pseudo participation similar to that of a quiz-show audience.

Jack seemed to mystify this invasion further by chalking it up as a controversy, refusing to take any stand, and thereby dissipating the potential purpose of the question-and-answer episode. The tension may well be that while Jack had his own opinions, he did not understand how to create the conditions for students to extend their own. The question here is, What happens after students name the U.S. invasion imperialistic? Should this lead to moral judgments or resistance to governmental policy? Such questions suggest that pedagogy embraces both a problem of producing knowledge and analyzing the knowledge that is produced. Without the discursive strategies to consider pedagogy in complicated ways, it is no wonder that Jack was unsure about the discussion's real effects. Indeed, he was consistently uncertain about his efforts:

> I don't have any way of knowing if I made any headway toward the points I was trying to get at, especially since my closing statements were made after the "leaving the period uproar" had begun. I've got to learn to get my major points in well before the period ends.
>
> I went all through history courses in high school without even questioning anything. It didn't dawn on me. Obviously, the questions were never raised. . . . I can remember a rude awakening. At some point, I realized that books don't have all the answers. It probably sounds ridiculous now. I think it could have been shown to me earlier. . . . That's sort of the roots of it. Just because teachers say that these are important points to look at in history, or even that the points are accurate, is always questionable. . . . I'd like to develop it through the course that they shouldn't just believe anything they read. . . . I'd like to get them to have a personal reaction on some things. Ask them what their opinions are rather than having them tell me the dates and facts.

The questions Jack did raise never really asked students to explain themselves, elaborate their views, or interpret the consequences of the views they held. To do this, Jack would have had to think through the purposes of each lesson and begin to theorize about how to understand the students' perspectives and invite them to take the interpretive risks he so valued. He would have had to think through, with the students, what it is that structures personal opinions and how opinions carry traces of authoritative and internally persuasive discourses. But while lamenting his own uncritical development and disillusioned with his own education, Jack was still a history neophyte, struggling with the details necessary to reconstruct his historical voice and attempting to remediate his own historical education at the same time he was forced to teach it. Torn between his own struggle for a critical voice while attempting to help students construct their own, all Jack could do was describe what he hoped students would do.

How Am I Supposed to Judge Class Participation?

Greenville High's first grading period ended in early November. Throughout the school, teachers calculated their students' final quarterly grades. Students expected to receive their first report cards before the end of November. For the majority of students, this was the school's first formal contact with their parents. Anticipation characterized the atmosphere and many students rushed to make up three months of academic work in a matter of days, cajoling their teachers for one last chance.

A few weeks before Jack began averaging grades, he reminded students about their participation. If students were reminded that their participation counted as part of their total grade, Jack reasoned, students might be motivated to become more active in class. So when Jack spoke with his first class, he had this goal in mind:

> I said, "How am I supposed to judge class participation?" And then I had them come up with a definition of it. Like taking notes in class, having read the material. We came up with four or five things. And then we talked about how I might judge them and give out the points. [11-14-83]

After that discussion, his first class seemed more responsive. Jack was pleased with this strategy for it was congruent with his philosophy of student involvement. When he worked on the quarterly grades, he had their recent participation efforts in mind; students were generously rewarded. Jack then gave the results to Roy:

> First I figured out their averages and I told the averages in class. I figured in class participation. Then Roy came in and he asked me for the grades. So I gave him what I figured out. He said, no, he wanted the test grades and everything. He wanted to figure them out himself. So he refigured the averages and gave students much less in class participation than I did.
>   So we all talked about that in class. The kids said, "Why did we spend all this time talking about the definition of class participa-

tion?" And Roy said he's never given out more than six points to anybody in the seventeen years of teaching. Nobody ever gets ten points. The kids said to Roy, "Well, you haven't been a teacher in this class. How do you know?" And he said, "Well, I know. I've seen enough."

It was just kind of a lousy situation. I have given something like eight points. But Roy turned around and gave, I think the most he gave was two points to anybody. Because that's the way he does it. It was kind of a case where I guess I overstepped what I should have done and he stepped on my toes. . . . It would have been nice if he spent a little more time and explained that to me. . . . Obviously, he's going to have the class back. He'll have it through the end. So it should be consistently done his way 'cause he's going to have them for the majority of the time.

What made this situation "lousy" was that Roy's request for the quarter grades occurred while Jack's class was in session. The students watched as Roy admonished Jack and relieved him of any vestige of authority. Although Roy rarely observed this class, he let both Jack and the class know that he had seen enough to determine participation points. In many ways, Roy's point determination seemed more punitive than valuative, especially compared with Jack's original estimation. Any power or credibility Jack had negotiated crumbled beneath his very feet; his previous negotiations with students now appeared a waste of time. Dramatically, Roy announced and demonstrated that he alone was the "real" teacher. For Jack, this incident signified another moment of discontent. It did not serve as the basis of resistance, because Jack knew the territory was not his alone and felt he had no choice other than to accept Roy's encroachments.

To understand Jack's complicity, however, one must also consider the literal and figurative power of the cooperating teacher. The experience of student teaching means entering a preestablished territory and negotiating for power within that territory. Sharing territory, however, goes against the grain of the institution's departmental structure, and indeed the entire organization and ethos of schooling. And in the case of student teachers, without permission and encouragement to carve out their own space, typically, each student teacher ends up reproducing the style of another while resenting such impositions.

The end of the first quarter supposedly signals both closure and new beginnings. It promises feedback on the first few months of school and provides students with a rudimentary understanding of how the rest of their year might progress. In the case of teachers, the first marking period signals something different; it may either guide reevaluation of their own performances or place the burden of grades on the students themselves. But for Jack, the first marking period barely affected him as student or as teacher; his participation was marginal and his efforts were erased.

That painful interaction made Jack turn to the history curriculum with renewed vigor. At the very least, his classes allowed him to bring different perspectives into the history curriculum as long as he covered the expected material. In this way, selecting supplementary reading gave Jack a semblance of autonomy and power. However, his cooperating teachers believed the readings were too detailed for the students and encouraged Jack to move on. Still, Jack was determined not to "stick" to the official text.

But Jack's overriding concern for relevant content continued to obscure the complexity of relations this content assumed. Jack believed his teaching methods would emerge from the content he presented; he approached the content as if it were pedagogical in and of itself. He had not considered whether, for example, orally reading each article and asking surface comprehension questions aided student understanding. Nor did Jack reflect on how this written text precluded the students as text. His valorization of content over pedagogy did not deviate from the traditional separation experienced throughout teacher education. There, content superseded pedagogy and positioned a dualism that must have effected his privileging of the material as more significant than the students. Jack believed the material was worth the time even if he was losing the students along the way. Consequently, the more Jack taught, the less he knew about his students and the less he knew about the discursive practices that might involve them. His goal of teaching critical thinking ignored the agency of the thinker.

The Day after *The Day After*

Occasionally, there appears a made-for-television movie that assumes the proportions of a media event. A program may be so highly promoted for its controversial content that it becomes news, and hence the "talk of the town." Such was the case with the American Broadcasting Company's made-for-television movie *The Day After*, a two-hour extravaganza chronicling the horrible days following a nuclear attack on an unsuspecting midwestern farming community.[10] It was almost impossible not to know about *The Day After*.

Media promotion began with the film's inception and continued throughout the year. Weeks before its television premiere, nightly announcements portended its appearance. Parental viewing guidelines were issued by both the network and the schools. Some schools made their first venture into the world of television censorship, advising parents to prevent their children's viewing. Other school systems sent home detailed viewing instructions and prepared for their own day after. The real issue, then, was not whether it would be viewed, for curiosity ran high, but rather who would view it with whom and how these viewers would be affected. Because the film promised graphic depiction of the consequences of nuclear war, viewers had strong expectations for witnessing the horrible.

The day after *The Day After*, Jack's usual morning routine of early morning coffee in the social studies department was disrupted. That morning, Burt Rerun, chairperson of the department, informed Jack that the history curriculum would be suspended and in its place Jack was to discuss the film. No guidelines were suggested as to how to proceed. Although the film had been broadcast at the bar where Jack had been working the previous evening, he had been busy mixing drinks and missed the showing. Luckily, Greenville High's media department had videotaped the program and Jack's first class did not begin until mid-morning, giving him time to view the film. So Jack hurried to the media center and for the next two hours viewed *The Day After*.

The day after *The Day After*, Jack found himself in front of his history class, attempting to discuss a film he had barely had time to view, let alone to reflect upon in tranquillity. But because he had been told to do so, for the next two periods Jack attempted to discuss the film in both his classes. For this period, his cooperating teacher, Roy Hobbs, sat in the back of the room. Prior to the bell, students were animated in their discussion of the film:

10:44

Jack: We can talk about the study guide or talk about the movie.

Class: TALK ABOUT THE MOVIE!

Jack: Did everyone get a chance to watch it?

[Class breaks out in loud talk.]

Jack [repeating this twice]: Let's hear it from one person at a time.

Kim: The reason nobody was scared was everyone thinks it will be worse.

Celeste: The movie wasn't as severe as what would happen. Only cockroaches will live.

Jack: OK. Celeste was saying that the movie wasn't as severe as what would happen. If you saw footage like that, could it really be like they said? No. The footage was only indicative of a small disaster. What do you think the purpose of. . . .

Bonnie [interrupting Jack]: To make them aware.

Jack: Is survival a reasonable strategy?

Female: It's not worth it. We're all brought up having things here. If everything is blown up, we wouldn't know how to build it.

Male: They won't bomb Greenville.

Jack: Let's have one person at a time.

Nobel: They'd be going after military posts.

Jack: Nobel's question was, Where would they strike first?

10:51

[From the back of the room, Roy Hobbs begins talking. The students do not turn to face him. After his first sentences, Roy perches himself on the desk top.]

Roy: The area they struck was dotted by minuteman missiles. It was theoretically an offensive nuclear attack. . . . The whole idea behind the nuclear arms race is their idea of launching a preemptive military attack, the reality being NATO does not have large-scale troops. . . .

10:54

[Roy is still talking. All students are quiet although few students appear to be listening. No student turns around to face Roy.]

Roy: There was no attempt to absorb that attack without retaliation. I don't know where that leads us.

Jack [picking up on Roy's cue]: Anyone else have some comments about the film?

10:55

[For the next twenty minutes, no student speaks. Roy Hobbs has the floor. He recounts the horrors of nuclear winter, describes the four ways nuclear war kills, compares historical devastations, and discusses the technical features of nuclear weapons. Finally, Jack regains the floor.]

11:15

Jack: Well, it doesn't really paint a bright picture, does it?. . . . Do we want to have the situation? How about the normal people in Russia? Who makes up most of the people in the world? Is it the leaders? People like who? People like you and I. So who should have a say?

Female: People.

Jack: How can we do that? Did somebody vote in the idea of nuclear war? Did we have a say?

Class: NO!

Jack: But where did they come from?

Male: World War II.

Jack: Right. It was kind of dumped into our laps.

[11-21-83 field notes]

The remainder of the class was characterized by Jack's asking a series of yes or no type questions and Roy Hobbs's addressing the class from the back of the room. After the first ten minutes, the actual film and students' responses to it were no longer the subject. Instead, the technical aspects of nuclear war, as described by Roy Hobbs, became the curriculum. The bell interrupted Roy's final speech and the students, who had been largely silenced by the expertise of Roy, quickly fled. Despite the students' hasty exit, Roy continued talking, primarily addressing himself to Jack. He concluded by telling Jack the students did not have the historical background to discuss the film. Jack saw similar problems when he briefly mentioned: "They seem to want to discuss it but don't know how."

Jack's perception that student interest did not necessarily ensure know-how in the discussion could not provide insight into the particular problems of discussing a difficult issue. Part of the problem was that the subject of nuclear war warranted a different pedagogy, one that would carefully elicit student investigation of student feelings and fears. Although Jack personally recognized students by name, and paraphrased aspects of their responses, his paraphrasing strategy was conclusive, and did not invite student dialogue. The way in which he raised questions created further difficulties; it permitted students to shout out responses without being personally accountable for what they said. Further, Jack's questions continued to be phrased in a fill-in-the-blank formula, thus structuring and limiting student discourse to slogans or superficial responses. The uncomfortable nature of the topic, combined with Jack's routinized pattern of classroom discourse, exacerbated avoidance behavior from everyone. Indeed, after the first few minutes of class, everyone stopped using first-person pronouns as if to distance themselves from their own responses.

The unexpected monologue of Roy Hobbs further dissipated student involvement. It is clear that Roy felt important points needed to be made. However, whether Roy felt Jack was faltering, or whether he became impatient with the discussion's progress, is difficult to know. Regardless, Roy's powerful body cues signified to all involved that he was the teacher and when he spoke, he had the floor. Although students did not acknowledge Roy visually, they remained respectful. Encouraged by such silence, Roy spoke rapidly and authoritatively, leaving little space for the voices of others. By the third time Roy took over the "discussion," he had moved to the front of the classroom, continuing to make highly technical points without explanation. He focused on the physical and environmental effects of nuclear war, and on the unstable personalities of those who possess nuclear materials. This approach sealed the discussion's fate; nuclear war was presented as a technical fact and the lesson became one of mechanics.

Each time Roy took the floor, his monologue ended as abruptly as it began, forcing Jack to create sudden transitions to his own delayed discussion. It became Jack's task to coalesce Roy's monologue. This was a struggle between authoritative and internally persuasive discourse; whereas Roy's voice signified an instrumentalist reality, Jack, realizing student despair, attempted to lead students to the idea of the power of a critical mass: students, as part of a larger humanity, could monitor their government's military and social policies. However, Jack's questions and statements subverted his goal of transforming despair; to dislodge student powerlessness demanded a pedagogy that would disturb the hopelessness engendered by the film.

Jack's second U.S. history class was not much different except that his cooperating teacher, Edith Daring, while also sitting in the back of the class, never said a word. Before the class began, however, Edith confidently told Jack: "You don't have to do a thing; they discuss it themselves." As the class began, one exasperated student exclaimed: "Do we have to talk about that movie again?" Jack took a vote and the majority ruled in favor of the film.

After establishing the movie's sequence, Jack launched into a technical monologue, mirrored after Roy Hobbs, on the ways nuclear war kills. He then tried to build an argument for the futility of nuclear buildup, for there were already enough weapons to destroy the world ten times over. From there, Jack began to discuss the political tensions between the Soviet Union and the United States, and how these tensions might contribute to nuclear war. Keeping in mind Roy's concern about student knowledge, Jack attempted to lead students through a bird's eye history of the Soviet Union:

11:51

Jack: Does anyone know the fundamental ideas of communists? [No one responds]. We're talking about fundamental differences. There's enough material to make a whole college major about it. So we'll talk about it today.

11:54

Jack [pointing to a world map]: Alright. Take a look where Russia is. Is Russia different from the Soviet Union?

Female: Russia is part of Europe and the Soviet Union is something else.

Jack: The Soviet Union has territories that were forced to join under duress. The land mass that we call Russia is surrounded by what? Is it surrounded by oceans?

Female: Land.

Jack: Russia is landlocked. What do we have to the east of the U.S.?

Female: Water.

11:58

Jack: Is Russia a new country? How old is Russia?

Female: Old.

Jack: It's a pretty ancient country. I don't know too much about Russia but what was Russia's government like?

Female: Dictatorships.

Jack: They were ruled by the Czar. Has it ever been democratic?

Female: No.

Jack: So they're fundamentally different that the U.S., right? They're landlocked, they have a hostile history. . . . What kind of people is Russia likely to have? The history of Russia tends to produce a suspicious people in the sources I have read. We, on the other hand, have produced a relatively stable system. . . . Is that true of Russia?

Class: NO!

Jack: So when Russia and the U.S. leaders meet, are they coming from the same place?

Class: NO!

Jack: So this discussion isn't really leading any place, because we keep coming against walls, right? This discussion isn't leading to any positive points. Let's go back to the movie. . . .

In depicting the differences between the United States and the Soviet Union as irreconcilable, Jack had reached a cul de sac in a number of unintended ways. First, he had argued a good-guy verses bad-guy scenario. This cold-war representation of comic-book communists, trapped by geography and history, could only support the then dominant view that negotiation with the Soviet Union was impossible. Second, cultural differences were defined as harmful. His handling of this discussion unintentionally reinforced both a cold-war mentality and a xenophobic perception of world history. In these ways Jack concurred with the underlying message of the film, that nuclear war is indeed beyond human control.

It may well be that the discursive practices of gender identity thwarted Roy and Jack's attempts to explore the human issues of nuclear war.[11] Rather than discuss the depression, fears, and vulnerability—the subtext of the film— Roy and Jack distanced their emotional response with an excessive focus on the instrumental features of nuclear war. With this mechanical focus, both students and teachers switched into the third-person voice. This behavior was congruent with Roy and Jack's experience as men; males are socialized to repress both fear and powerlessness, situations filled with stigma. Both men appeared to overcompensate for their felt powerlessness by stressing the destructive power of nuclear weapons.

Gender identity may have also contributed to another feature of Jack's discussion tone: his authoritativeness about a subject of which he had little knowledge. Jack admitted time and again that he was unprepared to discuss Soviet history, yet he continued to do so. On the other hand, Jack's position as a student teacher may have also pressured him to appear certain in a situation charged by uncertainty.

As with the first class, students formed a Greek chorus to Jack's monologue. After both classes, Jack was depressed and just as despair led students to regard survival after nuclear war as futile, so too did Jack conclude that discussions on this topic were pointless. In contrast to Edith Daring's initial prediction of the ease of the discussion, Jack found the opposite to be true: he felt as if he had been talking to himself:

> I really don't know what the point of these discussions were. We seem to be arguing. They just became very negative. We discussed what would happen and that it is impossible to change the situation. Not a very positive outlook. But as far as the alternatives, I have no more idea than I think they do.
>
> My knowledge of the situation isn't that great either. I had something else planned. I really wasn't prepared, it was a lesson in how to punt. Today was the day when I really didn't know what to expect. I certainly didn't have a lesson plan. It seems as a teacher you're going to be able to do that, have to react then and there.

This was Jack's first experience with "forced" spontaneity. Leaving behind his lesson plans meant encountering the unexpected, while being in a role that demands certainty. The second class seemed to instantiate Jack's rudimentary expectations of ideal teacher behavior. Real teachers are expected to deal authoritatively with the unexpected. This belief is commonly ascribed to "thinking on one's feet," a stance that implies concrete answers and purposes can be conjured automatically to order a seemingly chaotic situation. Because Jack was not the real teacher, especially in his first class, his perceived "pseudo status" permitted him to rationalize his hesitations and directionlessness. Rather than consider how the subject itself contributed to emotional paralysis or cathartic reaction, Jack turned to his ideal role expectations. A "real" teacher would know what to do. How it is that one achieves this instantaneous transformation, and whether such a hope is even desirable, was never theorized. Instead, Jack maintained a vague hope that somehow experience would tell him what to do, because the meaning of experience should be as self-evident as common sense. Had Jack viewed experience as a problem of meaning, an effect of discourse and the discursive practices we offer, he would have been better prepared to theorize about not just what occurred but what it was that structured the practices of those involved.

Jack's tendency to distance himself from his teaching strategies was clearly evident in this lesson. Most apparent by the last stages of his student teaching semester was that he had no analytical framework from which to theorize about his experience. His experience appeared trapped in immediacy, subject to the pull of uncontrollable outside forces over which he had little control.

Like his cooperating teacher, Roy Hobbs, Jack believed experience was a problem of already possessing knowledge, not the process by which this knowledge is constructed, interpreted, and transformed. Jack could not conceive of how one comes to know. So while he maintained that experience makes the teacher, he could not account for how that process occurs or how knowledge positions experience. The problem was that Jack had borrowed a discourse that was incapable of doing anything other than positioning experience as the ground of knowledge. Such a discourse would not help him with the complications he lived. At this point, all Jack was learning from his experience was that simply being there was no guarantee of pedagogy.

Not Really a Teacher

Frustration was the first word that came to Jack's mind when asked to characterize his first ten weeks of student teaching:

> Student teaching can be sometimes frustrating because you're not really a teacher. You're taking over someone else's rules, you're taking over where someone else has already begun, someone else who's established their rules and conduct and expectations and their method of teaching and ways of setting up their class and everything else. Those things aren't always the ways that I would have done them and they're not always set up in the manner I would. I don't always agree with the ways they're set up and sometimes I'm not always exactly sure of how they should be set up. [11-30-83]

What Jack seemed most certain about throughout student teaching was that he was more a follower than an initiator. Because he disagreed with the direction, what he was accomplishing was irrelevant. The experience seemed prefabricated and artificial, something that diminished possibilities and his own potential to realize them. It was almost as if student teaching meant stepping outside one's skin to assume the appearance of another. At times,

Jack felt downright invisible. At other times, he felt like a shadow at dusk, certain in the knowledge that his eventual disappearance was inevitable.

Frustration over the reality Jack confronted led him to question whether teaching could be different from what he observed. Except for Edith Daring, who seemed to offer only meager feedback on Jack's classes despite the fact she remained in the room day after day, Jack observed a tired staff. He attributed their fatigue to a combination of routine and administrative fiat:

> There are probably mandatory departmental requirements and who knows where they came from. They exist but nobody really questions or cares about them. Everybody seems to have their method of teaching down. They start at 1776 and they accept that. Well, that's the way it is. After a few years, they have the routine down and they have their particular points they always make in class. . . . Like Roy has been teaching history before the Civil War to ninth and tenth-graders for seventeen years this whole time. And he has that one class, six times a day with six different groups of tracks. He never teaches anything but that class. . . . One of the things he mentioned one time was when someone was talking in the back of the room. He says, "Please. You don't see a teleprompter in the back. You don't see me having any notes. I'm doing this all from my head. So don't interrupt me." My impression to that was, "Well, why the hell don't you have some notes?" I think you have to take notes. Otherwise you get off the track which he sometimes does. But I suppose he's been repeating himself everyday for seventeen years.

Jack was witness to veteran teachers caught in the treadmill of routine. Here experience did not ensure creativity or freedom as much as isolation, repetition, and disengagement. Teachers appeared to be trapped within a world they had little power to effect.

Jack also perceived teacher routinization as a response to the overwhelmingly inadequate classroom conditions and the diversity of student needs. Although his original intention had been to individualize curriculum, the actual conditions of Greenville classes and the uniformly mandated curriculum pace made individualization highly unlikely. Routinization seemed a proper strategy for dealing with one's own limitations, but not without the emotional consequences. Jack was beginning to catch glimpses of what teaching does to teachers:

> I guess my aspirations for reaching everybody has changed a little bit cause there are some kids that don't want to be and I don't know what you can do about it. I only hope I don't become the kind of

person that will turn that inward like I see some teachers doing. Roy has ulcers and he's a real nervous kind of person. Lights a cigarette and the match in his hand shakes and stuff. I hope that I don't end up being kind of self-destructive in that way.

Confronting his own limitations and the limitations of others was painful. But this pain did not produce a critical moment, if pain is one factor in transforming the self. So while Roy reminded Jack of what he did not want to become, Jack's own process of becoming lent little insight into how to avoid such despair.

The more time Jack spent at Greenville High, the further teacher education receded into memory; after ten weeks of student teaching, his university-based education faded to a vague impression of laudable goals devoid of methodology. Beyond its stress on critical thinking, Jack could not describe specific ways teacher education had shaped his practice or thoughts about it. Besides, in his class and in the classes of others, Jack understood that curriculum content rather than pedagogical theory determined classroom structure. No one's teacher education seemed in evidence. Most apparent was the push and pull of a classroom routine that makes time seem like no time at all:

> There's a big temptation to kind of teach the book and if it's not interesting, what can you do? That's the material. There's a temptation to become just like all the other teachers. But I guess you want to try and fit in with them to some extent. Not to the point where you repeat everything they say.
>
> When I first came on, I had criticism. I could see things and I would say I would not do them that way. I think I'm still going to do things my own way to some extent although my conception of my own way has changed a bit.
>
> I've accepted that you can't reach everybody within these classes and the ways they were set up. But if they were my classes, it wouldn't be set up that way. . . . If you have six classes, a study period, a lunch break of twenty minutes, and forty-five minutes off a day, and you have a family and wife, like Roy does, so he has a life outside the school, and I hope that I have a life outside the school, that's an awful lot of time constraints.

In Jack's mind, his largest concession was in recognizing and accepting how a teacher's realities impinge upon teaching ideals. He felt the pull of conformity and the lure of innovation, but wondered if there was ever enough time to break away from routine.

What seemed most significant to Jack was his recognition and ambivalent acceptance of his limitations. Whether by time, self, other persons, or situations and circumstances, Jack felt constrained in both his present and future roles. Teaching took on the appearance of a series of adaptations. Accepting limitations seemed to be a strategy for gaining control in an environment where Jack observed little control.

Finding Gimmicks

Although Jack could not articulate specific differences between his last week as a student teacher and his early weeks, he seemed to have changed. More relaxed, as if the thought of leaving was somehow comforting, Jack seemed to let go of his frustrations and allow himself the space to identify areas that he wanted to improve.

In both classes, completing material took up Jack's major energies. By this time, students were used to doing study guides and seemed relieved at the specificity and concreteness of the task. Frequently, they asked for specific answers to Jack's questions and wanted class time to complete the guides. Whenever they asked for class time, they phrased their request in terms of "working in groups." They knew Jack preferred small discussion groups and hoped he was flattered when they made this request.

However, student discussion groups continued to mean something different to students: unsupervised time to socialize and have fun. As the end of his time drew near, Jack gave more class time over to the students. The study guides seemed to take over.

> I guess the kids expect that I'm just going to stand in front of the class and transmit the precise answers to their papers. In fact, they said to me a few times, "Why don't you just tell us what it is?" "Why do you have to explain everything? Mr. Hobbs doesn't explain everything." I know he does. They're just giving me a hard time in that respect. All they really want to do, they want me to quickly give them the answers and then give them the rest of the class time to have fun. They call it working in groups. But it just turns into talking about things other than history. I think they figure I'm an easy mark to let them work in groups or something. [12-14-83]

Throughout the semester, students repeatedly attempted to negotiate with Jack over the amount of class work. This occurred so frequently because Jack invited such negotiations by presenting students with choices about their work. The students may have also felt that because they worked on the study guides, they deserved free time. In this sense, the study guides were a bargain chip in a trade. But whereas Jack believed choice and informality allowed for spontaneity—a precondition for exploratory learning—students saw choice and informality as a sign that they could take control. Because the power struggles Jack and his students experienced were not mean-spirited and were more reflective of cajoling than of brute force, Jack had no insight into how his actions framed such struggles.

By his last week, Jack began to understand the problem of engaging students in a new light. Now, he believed the problem of motivating students was a problem of pedagogy, not of obdurate students. As his defenses began to fade, Jack believed that motivating students could be accomplished if he would prepare more for each class. He admitted that his class preparation, especially of late, had been hurried and minimal. In this sense allowing students to complete their study guides was a way to spend classroom time:

> The thought crossed my mind that being a new teacher, a first year teacher, I'll probably get a bunch of classes like the ones I have. I'll probably get lower phase classes, classes that other teachers don't want. And G-d, how am I going to be able to handle that?
>
> But then I was thinking, all it really calls for is a little bit more ingenuity, a little bit more creativity. I'll just have to find ways of making it interesting for them. The fault isn't in the class, it's in me. That I haven't really come up with something. I haven't spent the time to think of some unique way of, some gimmick I guess. I guess I need to have a gimmick with them. Before student teaching, I assumed I had to have something like that.

Based on this new realization, two factors seemed to make for successful teaching. First was a bag of tricks, gimmicks that in some way would capture students' attention and spur motivation. Like a magician's magic hat, Jack assumed he could pull these ideas out from somewhere. They existed, but for the moment eluded him. Time was the second factor; it would somehow provide him with gimmicks. Besides time, something that no one controls, Jack began to think that if he had only put more effort into his classes, hard work would have provided the insight and the strategies he needed to be successful. Most significantly, Jack was beginning to see himself as responsible for his pedagogy. Because finding fault often signifies situating blame, Jack now saw himself as totally responsible for the way things went.

Thus, by the last week, Jack's reasoning had come full circle. First, he felt his role as student teacher constricted his creativity and signaled to students that he was an easy mark. Along with the role limitations was the material itself; it was boring. Then Jack blamed the students. They were apathetic and uncaring. Finally Jack returned to himself; he was the major problem. This belief was congruent with Jack's initial understanding of teachers as self-made beings who must shoulder all responsibility for the way things are, for only they initiate learning.

The problems with this view are that it denies the complexity of human interaction and situational demands, the power struggles implicit in the teaching and learning encounter, and, most importantly, the capacities of students and teachers to construct rather than receive knowledge. To begin with a view of these complex dynamics would also mean considering responsibility as a relationship.

I Was Kind of Sad When I Cleaned Out My Desk

A week after Jack completed his student teaching, we met for our final interview. For two hours Jack reflected on his recent experience, primarily viewing it as positive. As in other discussions, Jack looked forward to the time when he would be a "real" teacher:

> I had a very good, positive experience at Greenville High. . . . Things went exceptionally well, I thought. So I was kind of sad when I cleaned out my desk. [But] there is a sense of relief that it's over with. I've been getting kind of impatient, wanting things to be done, wanting to get everything over with. I still have another semester [of course work]. . . . I wish I could get all my course work out of the way and my experience out of the way so that I can do the things I want to do. [12-30-83]

Hindsight, it seemed, gave Jack permission to forget his difficulties. He tended to accept Roy Hobbs's depiction of student teaching as a "honeymoon," a sweet transition between glimpsing the teacher's world and actually living there. On the other hand, Jack also saw student teaching as a holding pen, a waiting time that prevented him from doing what he wanted to do. In his view, course work and experience were mere hurdles to overcome, not an integral part of his process of becoming.

The push and pull of conformity, routinization, and blaming students for their lack of engagement still concerned Jack. He realized, for example, that Roy's plight reflected his attitude as much as his situation. The subjective acceptance of routine can dull creativity as much as bureaucratic pressure to conform. In Jack's mind, Roy's acceptance of the routine also led to his bitterness. Why teachers develop this attitude Jack understood. How they let it happen was still not clear. For Jack, the condition was contagious; like a disease, it must be fought.

The attitude that teachers have in general, something I hope I don't get, is the attitude, well, they have their jungle classes, their lower level classes. That's the phrase Roy likes to use, with kids who are mainlined, mainstreamed from special education. . . . It's a problem with the administration, he puts the blame on everyplace but he doesn't try to deal with the problem.

I would rather try to work. I mean, whatever situation you find yourself in, you can either work or try to make it a better situation, or you can deal with it the way he does. . . . So I hope I would bring in more variety and bring in a lot of new things. I think it's as boring as you make it.

But the actual conditions of "real" teaching—what teachers actually do to make pedagogy meaningful—continued to elude Jack. Catching glimpses of what teaching does to teachers did not show him what to expect or how to work with inherited constraints:

Inside those constraints I'm going to have to develop my own cur- riculum, or my own ideas of what to teach from whatever. That's one of the questions I asked someone. How do you devise, design a meaningful class out of everything that's available today? Everything that's available to you, books, magazines? Everything you can think of? It seems like an overwhelming responsibility to have to do this.

I guess one thought that strikes me that I didn't think I'd hear myself say was that maybe I didn't have enough education courses. . . . And you know, the classes were boring and I thought I had enough of them but maybe in a sense, there are some other topics, some other things that would be real nice to know that we didn't get, or maybe there could be more education courses designed. . . . I would have to say some of the education courses I had I think were pretty valuable. I didn't have a good grasp of what they were trying to say. But getting us to realize that there's such a thing as ideology, that there's a dominant ideology in this country and it pervades every- thing. And we as educators can either, you know, do our share of rowing or something, do our share of promoting that, or we can work around it. It struck me as strange to hear myself say that maybe I could use some other education courses.

That something seemed missing in his own university education was more evident to Jack than what that something might be. Whatever it was, Jack felt it could be received from additional course work in education. Yet such an admission seemed to startle Jack for he also believed that no one could teach him how to teach. These contradictory desires—between going it alone and wanting guidance, and between receiving help and not under-standing—bothered Jack's formulation about experience.

Jack appreciated critical thinking but had no idea, beyond lecturing stu-dents about its value, how to enable others to develop it. At the same time, Jack was beginning to wonder if there was such a thing as the "nuts and bolts" of teaching. He still struggled with the idea that teachers were self-made rather than university-educated, and maintained that since teaching was more an art than a science, there seemed nothing concrete to learn. And while he felt responsible for knowing the facts, teaching was not at all like learning the chronology of United States history:

> I didn't have much of a background in history and felt just a few pages ahead of the students. So in a sense, it was kind of strange to be put into a position, where I'm supposed to know something to teach people and I don't know it myself and I have to hurry up and learn it so I could teach them. . . . But I guess you learn not to say, "I don't know."

Jack's newly formed relationship to history did affect how he understood pedagogy. In both knowledge and pedagogy, Jack was indeed "just a few pages ahead" of his classes. And this harried position lessened his capacity to reflect upon and theorize about his progress in the critical ways he desired. More-over, because Jack felt the push of being certain, of not admitting his own struggles and having no arena to do so, he viewed his struggles to teach as a problem of acquiring experience. The problem was both Jack's dismissal of the experience he was acquiring, for he believed "real" experience would in-deed be instructive, and the way in which Jack conceptually organized his lived experience. Jack's fantasy, that you learned to teach by experience, or-dered his construction of meanings. Like most commonsense knowledge, assumptions leave no trace. Yet some very significant assumptions disturb these formulations. Diana Fuss is quite clear on this point:

> The problem with positing the category of experience as the basis of . . . pedagogy is that the very object of our inquiry . . . is never unified, as knowable, as universal, and as stable as we presume it to be. . . . The appeal to experience, as the ultimate test of all knowl-edge, merely substends the subject in its fantasy of autonomy and control. Belief in the truth of Experience is as much an ideological production as belief in the experience of Truth.[12]

And these beliefs were the props for Jack's denial.

Throughout his teaching, Jack maintained a series of assumptions about teaching and the work of learning to teach that thwarted his own process of coming to know and was a significant effect of the organization of his education. First, Jack believed experience produced teachers. The process of acquiring and interpreting experience was not as significant as already possessing it. Moreover, if experience was problematic, as in Jack's case, it did not count as "real" experience. For Jack, real experience provided a composite of skills and directives; it guaranteed access to "the truth" because in this view experience is unitary, certain, stable, and self-evident. Second, Jack took up the myth that "real" teachers are self-made. This myth shut out the social basis of teaching as well as thwarted his understanding of how personal development is an effect of social forces and interactions. It also prevented Jack from actively searching for outside support. That teachers are self-made meant that answers must come only from within and if they do not, then it is an individual problem. Such a subjectivist perspective can only result in isolation and in self-blame. Third, by the end of his teaching experience, Jack maintained that everything depends on the teacher. It was almost as if teachers single-handedly created learning. The problem with this assumption is twofold: students are viewed as passive recipients of the teacher's knowledge and the teacher becomes instilled with impossible notions of control. In such a discourse, learning can only be conceived as unidirectional, flowing down from the teacher to the students, and power cannot be uncoupled from imposition.

Significantly, this discourse was largely unchallenged by those who surrounded Jack. It might even be more accurate to think about how Jack became an effect of normative discourses. Indeed, one of the ironies of Jack's experience was his inability to critically locate his own subjectivity or theorize about how the normative values of the profession impinged upon him. On the other hand, the discourse of critical thinking is not enough to guarantee either the critical practices or the discursive strategies that might have moved Jack beyond the tautologies of experience. Throughout student teaching, Jack was aware of the limitations of traditional approaches to history and attempted to correct its many omissions by bringing in outside sources. However, Jack had neither the theories nor the support to examine critically how the residue of ideology could be traced to his own subjectivity and the subjectivities of his students. In Jack's mind, ideology resided more in textbooks than in persons. Without the discursive practices necessary for self-reflection, Jack's own inability to self-examine delayed his understanding of how to teach critical thinking skills, or indeed, apply these skills to his own situation.

Most significantly, there was the situation of student teaching, a circumstance so immediate in its demands and so isolating by design that Jack was

never really challenged to participate in or value his own struggle for meaning, and hence attend to his struggle for voice. And thus many of Jack's
dilemmas were an effect of not just the structure of student teaching and
teacher education, and the discourses made available there, but of the economic retrenchment that structured Greenville's curriculum in such a way
that Jack would never have the opportunity to teach a subject area he knew.
This last dilemma underlined Jack's struggles.

5

Discourses of the Real in Teacher Education
Stories from Significant Others[1]

In the early 1980s, during the time of this study, a purview of discourses about the quality of public education vied for dominance. Urgent questions were raised about the goals of educational reform, the quality of present and future teachers, the capabilities and nature of youth, the relationships between school and society, and the potential of educational interventions to affect such discursive fields as nationhood, commerce, family, and subjectivity.[2] Then, as now, struggles ensued over the nature of knowledge, power, and authority, and over what designs, orientations, and inclinations should mobilize the meaning of educational life.

During the first term of Ronald Reagan's presidency, federal funding for public education was dramatically curtailed and reductions were made in student aid for higher education, federally funded school-based programs serving students at poverty-level incomes, and innovative work-study and job training programs for students placed at risk. Along with local tax revolts, massive teacher layoffs, personnel hiring freezes, and increased student-to-teacher classroom ratios, the economic retrenchment of public education provided the backdrop for a polyphony of discourses that attempted to mobilize popular sentiments and to suppress, as well, their antagonistic meanings.

This chapter is concerned with those meanings that refuse to be stabilized, the clashes between authoritative and internally persuasive discourses, and the constructed stories that are produced, embraced, and rejected as the real and the imaginary. Two dimensions of institutional narratives, discussed in chapter 2, will be analyzed: the official perspectives that attempt to represent institutional ideas, and the everyday perspectives of those who hold varying

175

degrees of institutional power. A central question, then, is: What ranges of discourse articulate the spectrum of fear and desire in the field of teacher education? This requires comparison of the official and everyday understandings of what it means to educate and be educated.

In 1983, the last year of Ronald Reagan's first term as president of the United States, the National Commission on Excellence in Education released its alarming report on the status of public education: *A Nation at Risk*. Heralding a spree of governmental and corporate supported reports that pronounced the demise of the liberal agenda in education, the commission, created by the secretary of education T. H. Bell, and chaired by David Gardner, a former Army intelligence officer and president-elect of the University of California, included only one classroom teacher.[3] Evidently the judgments of those who worked in schools were not to be trusted.

A Nation at Risk is characterized by military metaphors, catastrophic warnings, and managerial solutions. The second paragraph, perhaps its most quoted, represents the geography of education as "being eroded by a rising tide of mediocrity":

> If an unfriendly foreign power had attempted to impose on America the mediocre educational performance that exists today, we might well have viewed it as an act of war. As it stands, we have allowed this to happen to ourselves. . . . We have, in effect, been committing an act of unthinking, unilateral educational disarmament.[4]

The "we" of this report, however, implicates more than unanimity. It asserts the "we" of corporate and military interests in opposition to the "they" of other nations threatening to out-compete the United States. There is also an implied "you": the students and teachers who have failed. This report rescripted the crisis of education from one of schools' failing students to one of student and teacher underachievement and mediocrity. It ignored the political location of schools and how this position—as the site of mediation among the tensions of federal, state, and community interests—inscribes the meanings of schooling. Continuing in the tradition that maintains that the interests of business and education are identical, *The Nation at Risk* launched the motives of authoritative discourse as though on behalf of a concerned citizenry. This report was directly released to the media and individual citizens, thereby absolving congress and other federal agencies from taking political responsibility.[5]

A Nation at Risk received so much publicity that in the fifteenth annual Gallup poll on public opinion about public education taken a few weeks after the report was released, George Gallup concluded, "at the time of the survey, the report had reached an audience of approximately one person in five in the

U.S. adult population."[6] Four major problems were highlighted in this poll: lack of discipline, use of drugs, poor curriculum/poor standards, and lack of proper financial support. None of these could be blamed on mediocre teachers. Respondents alluded more to the malfunction of society than of teachers. For example, they blamed lack of discipline on the home and on the absence of respect for law and authority. While the "we" of the *Nation at Risk* positions schools as the failure, public response holds a different interpretation.[7] Whatever phantoms are seen when persons speak about the problems of education, for those who responded to this survey, the undesirable working conditions of teachers loomed largest. Solutions prescribed by the official discourse, however, ignored the everyday, and instead proposed directions meant to strengthen the marketplace, corporate interests, and the centralization of knowledge.[8]

Barbara Finkelstein characterizes the early 1980s' official reform movements, launched by *A Nation at Risk*, as a retreat from democracy. Social and economic justice are not a part of this normalizing discourse. While vague pronouncements of "a shared vision for America," "some common understandings on complex issues," and "a coherent continuum of learning" punctuate *A Nation at Risk*, actually they signal the desire for uniformity, standardization, and adherence to the values of competition, domination, and mastery. The problem is that such desires repress differences, tensions, and values that oppose this particular view of progress. As the authoritative discourse, it functions to authorize what sort of talk and which talkers will be taken seriously:

> Contemporary calls for reform reflect a retreat from historic visions of public education as an instrument of political democracy, a vehicle of social mobility, a center for the reconstruction of conmunity life. . . . Rather, the educational visions of contemporary reformers evoke historic specters of public schools, as crucibles in which to forge uniform Americans and disciplined industrial laborers. They echo traditional commitments to public schools as agents of cultural imposition and economic regulation.[9]

In the governmental reports released, there is a singularity of meaning to academic achievement, success, and excellence, one that links the values of possessive individualism to economic expansion and cultural domination. Such forces of normalization silence concerns for equity, the social distribution of power and wealth, and the politics of difference and diversity. At the same time, dominant meanings of achievement organize popular fears around what it means to be educated and what it means to be prepared for the world beyond schools. Michael Apple summarizes such accomplishments as:

a successful translation of an economic doctrine into the language of experience, moral imperative, and common sense. The free market ethic has been combined with a populist politics. This has meant blending together a "rich mix" of themes that have had a long history—nation, family, duty, authority, standards, and traditionalism— and other thematic elements that have also struck a resonant chord during a time of crisis.[10]

These themes are always a subtext of education, but they can never signify unitary and fixed meanings. *A Nation At Risk,* however, recasts these themes into normative terms and conceives of the work of teachers as asserting instrumentalist values of authority, power, and knowledge.

If teachers are to reassert conservative values, official reports argue, their own education and the education of their students must be made uniform. The high school curriculum must be tailored to the demands of the "new basics," and should be organized to assert the authority of classical texts, objective examinations, and intensified homework. Supposedly, through technologies of control, authoritative discourse can prevail.

As for teacher education, *A Nation at Risk* offers two images of the teaching force. According to the first, the low pay of the profession affects who is willing to become a teacher. This implies that only the incompetent will accept low rates. More significantly, it erases the historic struggles of teacher unions over wages and improved working conditions. According to the second, teachers are identified as academically incompetent and remain so largely because they are required to take too many education courses. This poses a schism between academic content and knowledge of the pedagogical process and eliminates the ambiguous play between how one comes to know and what is to be known. The attempt is to suppress knowledge as a social construction and position it as a neutral mirror reflecting an unchanging reality. Concurrently, pedagogy becomes viewed as synonymous with pregiven techniques that are best learned on the job.

The commission offers administrative gatekeeping solutions to the problems it defined: the testing of teachers to ensure adherence to uniform standards, the establishment of career ladders to promote internal policing of teacher productivity, and the creation of alternative routes to teacher certification that eliminate university interventions. The perspectives of students and teachers, their interests, desires, and affective investments are all ignored. Instead, teaching and learning are to be stabilized by being equated solely with the measurable productivity and the surveillance techniques necessary to control the work of teachers and students.

Against this discourse of crisis, I interviewed public school teachers, school administrators, and teacher educators. They were all affected by what

Ira Shor calls "the conservative restoration,"[11] but in ways unaccounted for in such reports as *A Nation at Risk*. When these professionals spoke of what it means to learn to teach, they were compelled to speak to the quality of their own working lives, of what seemed possible ten years earlier and what now seems impossible. The tensions of their own practices were articulated too: poor working conditions, lack of support, autonomy, and collegiality, feelings of isolation, and contradictions between the demands of contentious interests and their own sense of reality. Yet such a list cannot capture the digressions of these professionals. Like a discordant Greek chorus, each professional's narrative stance contradicts the rest. And while common agreement about what it takes to be a teacher was desired by all, contesting orientations to the practical, the theoretical, and the political made their shared context seem like different worlds.

The perspectives of significant others must be included in any discussion of learning to teach. This is because these persons attempt to shape the everyday identities, investments, and practices of the student teacher; they offer their own lived experiences as sources of emulation and reaccentuate the dominate discourse of teacher reform with their own inflections. However, as we will see in this chapter, the images of teachers and the practices they embody are always in an uneasy dialogue with the contexts and circumstances that these professionals hope to stabilize. They offer student teachers contradictory orientations to philosophy, theory, knowledge, and pedagogy. And within such contradictions inhere the antagonisms between the hopes and desires of the newly arrived and the expectations and deep investments of those already there.

To enter this world is to encounter the contradictions that constitute it. There has never been a common agreement as to how one becomes a teacher. Teaching and learning have never been stabilized by a unitary meaning. The problem is that any movement toward single-minded definitions of learning and teaching works against recognition of the dialogic relations that constitute them. In reality, those who surround student teachers in school contexts bring to their advisory role contradictory feelings about the experience of their own teacher education: what they take to be a betrayal of theory; the refusal of university-based professionals to value their work and judgments; and the failure of teacher educators to recognize their own constraints and what they see as school reality. And while venerating the professional value of finding one's own way, school-based professionals recognize, as well, the need to guide the newly arrived in ways not imagined by the university. The perspectives of teacher educators reverse such concerns. They believe teachers have forgotten their own process of learning to teach and hence lack the patience to work with student teachers. They have observed practitioners' resistances to the student teachers' attempts at pedagogic experimentation.

They point to the regime of the practical as a force that refuses to admit theory. Consequently, for some teacher educators, the university must undo what student teachers learn in school contexts. At the same time, all professionals realize the nature of this dependency—between student teachers and those who seek to influence them—as riddled with contradictions because there is no simple correspondence between what any professional thinks should happen during student teaching, what exactly the student teacher should do to realize these ideas, and what actually occurs.

This chapter analyzes the problems of significant others who, in whatever ways, attempt to act upon the actions of the student teacher. We meet cooperating teachers who take on a student teacher as their classroom apprentice, school administrators who allow student teachers into their schools, and teacher educators who work with student teachers either before or during their internship. Each participant was interviewed and audiotaped for approximately one hour. During our time together, we did not speak of individual student teachers. Instead, I tried to grasp how each professional understood the conditions and circumstances of student teaching, what learning to teach meant to them, and in my narrating of these views, I discuss the contradictory discourses working through such perspectives.

Because all these persons were currently teaching, or had taught sometime in their professional lives, they possessed strong views on how one learns to teach. Their views were based on a combination of common sense, lived experience, authoritative and internally persuasive discourses, and the practical knowledge built from the subjective in their teaching lives. In talking about the experiences of becoming a teacher, they rehearsed and generalized as inevitable their own educational biographies. And while everyone agreed that change was needed, each disparaged the present structure of teacher education in very different ways. Most notable was that each of their attempts to unify conceptions of reality parallelled those of *A Nation at Risk*.

My own questions and the theoretical orientations described in chapter 1 determined the ways I worked upon the following narratives. Each professional's account, in dialogue with my own, constitutes a separate section. At times, my ethnographic voice shifts to critique as I render problematic the voices of others in an attempt to identify what it is that structures the desirable, the undesirable, and the outright destructive in the discourses of teacher education. Categories of professionals are then set in dynamic tension. Finally, key themes are analyzed in the last section of this chapter. The questions I brought to make sense of these narratives include the following: What informs the professional's notion of guidance when essentialist values of common sense, personality, and intuition subvert their efforts to advise? What sense of reality do these professionals construct to legitimate their own efforts? What images of knowledge, experience, and authority work through their practices in and beliefs about learning to teach? How do the effects of their own professional formation organize the ways they work with and describe newcomers? Finally, since one cannot talk about teaching without suggesting a theory of learning, how do these professionals talk about student teachers as learners?

COOPERATING TEACHERS

Roy Hobbs: Social Studies Teacher

Historical circumstances rather than personal desire determined Roy Hobbs's decision to become a teacher. He came of age during the Vietnam war and, like other white males of his generation, avoided the draft by enrolling in college and then graduate school, and subsequently earned a deferment for the choice of teaching as a career. Roy's experience became a statistic in a census bureau government study, "Educational Attainment in the United States."[12] This study found that white males who came of age during the Vietnam war accumulated more college education than those men maturing either before or since:

> I was in that Vietnam generation. If you had the money, if you had the brains, you'd stay in school, stay out of the army. That was me....I never wanted to become a teacher, alright. I also never wanted to become a statistic in Vietnam. So I went to school, had real good grades, went to graduate school, had real good grades, got to graduate school and stayed. Then I got this job [at Greenville High] because my draft board, even at the midst of the height of the war, was not bothering graduate students or teachers.

Bitter about his own teacher education, Roy believed if his program had done its work correctly, he should have been steered away from the teaching profession. Likening his own student teaching experience to that of a war, Roy was forced to confront his own ill-preparedness and what he took as the incompetencies of those who surrounded him:

> My cooperating teacher was awful. He had no insight into the process, into the kids he was teaching, no insight into the environment in which he was teaching. He never mentioned Vietnam. I mean the country was falling apart all around him and there was no mention of it. It was as though what he was doing was real and all this other stuff was unreal.

In addition to that, my internship wasn't an internship. It was like an eight week experience, two of which I spent observing him, six of which I spent teaching. . . . And that was it. Hippity, hop, and you're a teacher. Once I walked in, he walked out. I never saw him. He wrote me a wonderful recommendation on the basis of no frame of reference.

And my university supervisor from college [was] an elementary teacher in a suburb. . . . Never taught in a secondary school, certainly never taught in the atmosphere that existed in the late Sixties in a secondary school. And she was my supervisor, telling me how to go about handling classes, this classroom where these two rows were white, these two rows were Black and the middle row was empty. I didn't make that seating plan. That's how they sat. I felt like a referee in a hockey game. The tension was so incredible you could feel it and you could feel how it eroded the effectiveness of whatever I did. And whatever I did was totally ineffective. Not just because of that but because I knew so little of what I was getting into.

My internship was not even a taste of honey. I had no idea at all of what the job was like, and whether or not I really wanted to do it. And ultimately, what I found out was, given the person that I am, I really didn't want to do it.

It is no wonder that Roy felt abandoned by those who were supposed to advise. They could not, or would not, help him come to terms with the reality of racism, historical dislocation, and resistance. Yet Roy, too, was astonished by this reality for it disrupted what he thought should be his "taste of honey," a time when hope and desire could be both valued and realized. He found it incredible that reality could be so slippery and lack any referentiality. What Roy learned from his own student teaching—and what has stayed with him to the present—is that teaching is an exhausting impossibility. And just as Roy waited out the Vietnam war, seemingly, he waits out his own time as a teacher.

Working with student teachers was the only aspect of teaching that Roy enjoyed:

I don't like what I do, other than dealing with interns. I love that. It's the best part of this job. 'Cause you can see, almost on a daily basis, some sort of tangible result of your having been alive. And I don't think that's necessarily true in teaching.

Throughout his teaching years, student teachers seemed to be the only validation of Roy's self as a teacher. With them, unlike in his own classroom, he could observe his immediate influence, meet his desire for effectiveness, and establish the personal relationships that were otherwise lacking. And on a practical level, by relieving him of his classroom duties, student teachers allowed Roy what he craved: privacy and peace.

However, with or without student teachers, the quality of Roy's teaching life was depressing. And while adamantly condemning the conditions that defined his work—being underpaid, overworked, and ill-prepared for impossible tasks—Roy also attributed his own personality as an effect of his bitter experiences. Roy identified as an introvert, someone who is best left alone; he was bothered by the sociality of school, and with what he conceived of as the equation of teaching with putting on a performance. Roy concluded that extroverts make the best teachers:

> I'm not the kind of teacher who deals well with static. Primarily because I'm that introvert and I have to expend an incredible amount of energy concentrating on what I'm supposed to do. I don't work with notes, I don't work with a video prompter, I teach what I know because I've taught the same thing for seventeen years and it's about time I knew it. I just teach, alright! And because of the amount of energy I have to expend to concentrate, forcing myself to do what I don't want to be doing, at the end of the day, I'm gone. I go home. And my wife complains, "You never talk to me." I'm all done in. I don't have anything left.

Ironically, the dual meaning of static in Roy's narrative disrupts his own claim: he cannot work with the static of students but desires knowledge to remain static, unyielding, and timeless. This desire is impossible, for as much as he might attempt to create a static-free environment, the classroom is already charged by the lived lives of those who are forced to be there. But Roy's investment in viewing pedagogy as synonymous with textbook material, prevented him from understanding students either as introspectively capable or as sources of knowledge. Only Roy could possess static knowledge, and consequently teaching, for him, was like a series of repeat and monological performances where lines are memorized and delivered to an audience of students. Because Roy's image of teaching was anchored in essentialist images of knowing, he could imagine teachers only as essentially constructed. That is, if teachers were born and not made, pedagogy could only be a product of one's personality.

Roy's teaching experience was a testimony to the underside of teaching, a world where teachers have little control over their working conditions and instead attempt to make do with the way things are. But despite his perception that the world of teaching was made from the stuff of deadening routine,

Roy would like to rescue student teachers. He did not want his own student teaching to be repeated and was adamant that cooperating teachers not abandon them:

> The student teacher doesn't see teaching as a grind. Only vicariously do they see it. I think they see it in us, but they don't understand until they get into it. I think student teaching is just like a taste of honey.
>
> The people who handle the experience, who supervise and govern the experience for these interns should be very carefully selected. They should know their subject matter. In my case, they should be people who are relatively sensitive to individuals, people who know their stuff. And they should be people who are required to stick with that kid. To be in the back of the classroom. To be there to direct and guide. . . . [Student teachers] should never have to go through anything quite as painful as an internship can be if you're doing it by yourself. It happens all the time.
>
> And you have all kinds of situations and forces in your classroom over which you have absolutely no control. And you're frequently set up to fail by the system. And the interns don't know that. You got to stick with them. . . . And that doesn't happen a lot because the damn teacher who becomes a supervisor, because of the negligence of the university, uses an intern as a free period.

In viewing student teaching as "a taste of honey," Roy rehearsed its superficiality. In his perceived world, student teachers are gullible and unsophisticated, unable to determine reality, because they are intoxicated by their own fantasies of what it means to teach. Therefore they need to be awakened by their cooperating teacher because everything else puts them to sleep.

Yet Roy's depiction of student teaching was as contradictory as his own experience. When asked to reflect about what student teachers learn during their internship, Roy valorized the introspective knowledge and the relationship to content that defined his own identity as a teacher:

> I think they learn a great deal about what they don't know. They learn that they don't know a great deal about the subject matter they thought they did know. They learn about the great variety of very serious and complicated social problems that schools are unfairly asked to deal with, because schools are incompetent to deal with most of these problems. I think that kids learn about themselves. You're under the gun. And when you're under the gun, you learn a

lot about yourself, a lot about your subject matter. The most important thing is they learn a lot about themselves.

For Roy, student teaching was simultaneously "a taste of honey" and an
experience of being "under the gun," a time when desire and coercion become
entangled. Within such dissonance, one learns what is lacking in the self and
in the way of content knowledge. As for being under the gun, Roy's ideal
cooperating teacher is a protector, for he perceived the school as a hostile
environment, made so because the schools inherited social problems that sour
what could have been "a taste of honey."

Roy Hobbs's understanding of teaching was an effect of his own conceptual ordering of experience. Because he performed daily in a role he disliked,
teaching became coupled with acting. Like an actor, he struggled for command of his audience. But being an actor also meant being someone other
than yourself. And the self-knowledge Roy made from teaching was that he
was not meant to be a teacher. The irony is that while Roy could become
himself when working with student teachers, for this relationship seemed to
validate his experience in ways that classroom teaching did not, Roy did not
believe such relationships could be made with his own classroom students.
This was because his students had become social problems, threatening to rip
open the seamless narrative of history.

Edith Daring: Social Studies Teacher

Edith Daring entered the teaching profession through the back door. Her
college degree was in the fine arts. In the course of her thirty years in education, she had operated a girl's boarding school in Europe, worked in a social
service agency, and, for the last fifteen years, taught in various academic
departments, including her present social studies position at Greenville High.
Originally hired as a fine arts teacher, Edith's previous work experience waived
all educational course requirements and she was granted teacher certification
under the "grandfather" clause:[13]

> I came under the grandfather clause. I never student taught. I think
> you learn to be a teacher from doing. I guess it comes down to
> teachers don't teach anything, they help students learn.
>
> I don't think you gain the eyes of a teacher for the first five
> years. I find that anytime I do a new course, the first year is a
> learning experience for the teacher as well as the kids. I don't care
> how much you've prepared. Because I'm preparing a new course for

next year. And that's a lot of heavy slugging. So it takes three years to get a course where you want to go, in the direction that you think is good and meaningful and the kids are interested in. And I think it takes five years to perfect it. So you don't make a teacher in one year or three years. I think it takes longer than that. That doesn't mean they can't have empathy with kids or they don't know the subject matter. But to make a good, creative, happy person who is teaching, takes more than three years of course work and teaching a course.

Practice, time, dialogue, and creativity are the ingredients for becoming a teacher and the sources of revitalization for remaining one. Edith's narrative highlights the process of teaching, where practice makes practice and where the shape of content is determined during the pedagogical encounter. When Edith spoke of teaching, she juxtaposed it with learning, and in doing so, always considered her students as partners in pedagogy.

Just as creativity was the measure by which she judged herself and others, it was also the primary reason Edith worked as a cooperating teacher:

I like taking student teachers, although there are times when I'm not that happy with it, because I always hope I can learn something. I think student teachers can bring a variety of things to the cooperating teacher. I think it's a two way street.

But the one thing that bothers me about student teachers is they don't seem to be very creative people. Maybe that's unfair. Maybe you acquire creativity as you get older. But I just get the feeling that they're not. Most of them have a reasonable subject matter background with poor ways of, I guess, getting it across. It may not be just the intern, it may be the lack of experience. It may be that you need more in order to become more creative in your techniques.

You get occasional good interns. I had a teacher as an intern who showed all kinds of creativity and was hired a couple of years later at this school, and lost most of that. He always had good rapport with the kids and kept it. But the creativity he had when he became a part of the system, he lost. And that disturbs me.

And I just get the feeling, if you're going to do teacher training, that you should be offering it in the field. You don't teach English the way you teach social studies. And what are the greatest variety that kids could do work, do the things and enjoy learning to some extent? I don't see them coming in with those kinds of things. And I have to assume, unfortunately, that what we perpetuate is replicas of what we learned from. And I'm not sure I see the school of education breaking that pattern. That's a treadmill that people don't seem to get off from.

The meaning of creativity is bound to reflexiveness; the desire to dialogue with a range of perspectives, to see things as if they could be otherwise, and to take up, as well as encourage, the interpretive risks that learning demands. Yet Edith recognized the institutional subversion of these goals, how the university context and schools work to maintain the status quo.

Edith perceived three competing sources as effecting the replication of past teaching models: teacher education, the student teacher's own educational biography, and the institutionalized power of the cooperating teacher:

> Unfortunately, I think student teachers feel, "I want to pass this course so therefore I'm going to do what the cooperating teachers tend to do." For example, one of the kids of mine who student taught left with a very bad and very bitter feeling. She got an "A." She did exactly as she was told and when she was told to do it. And she didn't like it. Enough so she's not teaching. She's an accountant. And I think that's bad news. I would hope the interns can pick and choose the things that suit them. But I'm also hoping that student teachers will pick and choose some things from inside themselves.
>
> And I'm not sure that the cooperating teachers are well chosen. I think it's whoever is willing. And that doesn't always make the best experience. Consequently, if you get somebody who only lectures and gives tests, because you want to pass the course and want good references, that's what you do. Because that's how the game is played. It's not played on growth.

In some ways, Edith perceived student teaching as more like a ritual with survival dependent on how one plays the game. For Edith, the educational game did not stop at student teaching, but continued, throughout one's career, to impinge upon the creativity of teachers. Refusing to play this game, Edith developed her own survival strategies meant to nurture creativity. As a self-described rugged individual, dependent more on her own resources than on those of her peers, Edith believed her peers had nothing to offer. And so, she kept to herself:

> I never take my work home with me. I stay until it's done. I try very hard never to talk about school with friends, because they usually don't understand. I don't talk with teachers because I don't want to hear their sob stories. And I feel I am responsible for my own behavior. Therefore I am responsible for what goes on in my class.

And if things continually are bad, then I need to look at what I am doing.

What you're asking is why am I not burned out. I'm too busy doing other things, I guess, to have time to be burned out. I put a lot of time in. I seldom leave school before 4:00 P.M. and usually not till 4:45. But when I get home, my house is mine, my garden is mine. I can do and forget.

And you know, I'm not sure I learned that right away. 'Cause I worked as a therapist in a mental health center and I learned that when you walk out, you can't take people's problems with you or get too burned out. You just have to be able to pull that curtain down. And I just have developed that very neatly.

You know, I'm fifty years old. I expect that when I retire I may still be in the department. I own a house and have an elderly parent to support, so I am no longer free to roam like I used to. I think if I were totally single, I would consider selling the house and roaming and doing some other things. But it doesn't prey on me at all. I like teaching. Occasionally I wish for a snow day, but not very often.

Well aware of the problems of school life, this teacher refused to succumb to fatigue, blame others for her fate, or waste her time exchanging war stories. In one sense, Edith Daring was self-made because she refused to compromise and support the status quo. Yet in another sense, her own trajectory encouraged her to think of things as if they could be otherwise. Edith played by her own rules and created spaces where she thrived as a teacher and as a person.

Discourses of the Self

When discussing their views on student teaching, both cooperating teachers recounted their own lived experiences. Perhaps because these teachers believed that student teaching, at best, offered mere glimpses into the real work of teachers and did not validate their own process of coming to know, such recollections served as a reminder that theirs was the reality. Yet Roy Hobbs and Edith Daring, in what each chose to reveal, are striking in their differences: each professed antithetical values about pedagogy, knowledge, and authority. The ways each coped with institutional constraints and the strategies each employed to perform as teachers, afford insight into what each make of her or his efforts.

These narratives offer contrasting discourses on pedagogy and the work of teaching. Whereas, for Roy Hobbs, content determined the teacher's work, Edith Daring gave priority to the process of helping students learn. For Edith, content was only the raw material of the teacher's work; organizing it in meaningful ways, attending to the diversity of student interests, drawing upon the creative capacity of students, and orchestrating a pedagogy that encouraged insight into the material were all a part of the construction of knowledge. This process is internally persuasive: students extend their own knowledge in the process of coming to know. For Roy, knowledge was already realized and students were not perceived as sources of knowledge. Nor did Roy view students as appreciating what he took as the self-referentiality of knowledge. In Roy's classroom, there was a strict division of labor: students were required to absorb the predetermined facts that he dispensed. In such a classroom, the voices of the students were expected to intone authoritative discourse. Each pedagogical approach, then, results in relations of power and definitions of knowledge that either attempt to work in spite of students or value students as agents in their own learning.

Within each teacher's definition of knowledge is an implicit theory of how human beings learn. Edith Daring was articulate about the process of learning because her introspection was not fixated on what she lacked. Edith was concerned with relationships that inspire pedagogy. She exemplified affective investment, the desire to learn by doing and to reflect upon the consequences of one's practice. At its best, teacher education might begin this process, but ultimately, in Edith's theory, to approach pedagogy in wonderment, the individual must assume responsibility. The self-knowledge garnered through teaching, then, is the knowledge of how to effect creative change. Roy, however, absolved himself from responsibility because he was convinced that he should never have been a teacher in the first place. Consequently, he did not question the process of how one learns to teach, because his identity as a teacher was, in essence, a mistake.

Both teachers remained highly suspicious of teacher education. This suspicion was partly rooted in their own biographies. Roy felt abandoned by the university; he saw it as an ivory tower, incapable of addressing the harsh reality of school. Edith escaped teacher education and thus viewed it as unnecessary and even harmful. In her mind, the university failed to help its students understand the relationship between pedagogy and content. Nor did it foster the kind of creativity necessary to help student teachers help their students to learn. But whereas Roy was stuck in a dualistic notion of reality, Edith's critique of teacher education emerged from her own hopes and desires of what education should be. Still, both views remained private: neither sought to change the existing structure, nor were they approached by the university-based program for their views.

SCHOOL ADMINISTRATORS[14]

Erma Tough: Chairperson of the Social Studies at Smithville High

Throughout her twenty-six years in education, Erma Tough has watched student teachers come and go. Her concerns about teacher education have shifted with the times and with the dictates of the Smithville community. In 1976 Erma became the first woman chair of the social studies, presiding over a largely male-dominated department and interacting with predominantly male administrators. She admitted this promotion took longer than it should and was well aware that upon entering, what she called, "the men's club," her battles to be seen as capable must be continually fought.

At the time of this study, Erma's social studies administrative duties determined her relations with student teachers. As an administrator, she walked a thin line between community pressures, pedagogical policies, and administrative controls. The place of controversy in the social studies curriculum was one of the major issues. In her mind, student teachers were poorly trained to understand the complex issues surrounding controversial subjects; they lacked practice in working with controversy and seemed insensitive to the values and conservative ethos of the Smithville community:

> Universities should prepare student teachers for how one might deal with controversial issues in the classroom. People who are at the university level, even those teaching at the university, probably don't fully appreciate the fact that you can't deal with controversial issues as openly or offer an opinion, although you would like to, because, first of all, they fail to realize you are dealing with adolescents. That although you're teaching social studies, you're also dealing with kids in very formative years and you have to probably deal more with decision making, with a process, and teach kids process rather than inflicting particular opinions and views. You also have the problems, if you're in psychology and you're talking about sexual issues and you're in public school, you can't be totally open, or allow kids to be totally open in a discussion because of the fact that you are responsible to a community. It's not the freedom of a university.
>
> This school has to reflect the community in a sense. I mean if they don't want that type of thing discussed, you better know that. You have to tread on water, you have to walk on egg shells. You have to make common sense decisions. Probably in that respect, secondary teachers appear to be a lot more conservative. But it's out of necessity. It doesn't mean their views are conservative. Probably social studies teachers are the most liberal in high schools of any department.

But you do have to curb that impulse to run out and say to kids, "You damn fool! Why are you saying that!" And you're dealing with kids who are very opinionated and the best you could do is teach them to stand back and realize there are other points of view.

Social studies is grounded in the dynamics of society and culture; it is necessarily made from the stuff of controversy, antagonistic discourses that push and pull at our sensibilities, our deep investments, and our desires and fears. Controversy is always emotive, threatening to disorganize social convention and individual preconceptions. Erma Tough was well aware of its dangers and thus defined the work of the social studies teachers as keeping the lid on an already boiling caldron. And while she might desire balanced perspectives, there is still the messy issue of how to consider the cacophony of discourses that endow an idea, event, or relationship with controversial meanings.

Erma, however, did not trust that student teachers were mature enough to mediate social antagonisms. Indeed, she positioned student teachers as under the sway of their own antagonisms, as impulsively inflicting their own views on innocent adolescents. At the same time, Erma admitted that adolescents have already made up their own minds. And herein lies the pedagogical controversy: If students already possess their opinions, how does the student teacher invite them to consider different perspectives and reflect on their own process of how they come to know? How can students make decisions without being aware of different opinions? Why is the dialogic process such a threat? Perhaps Erma cannot see controversy in the pedagogical terms in which she sees decision-making, because controversy always disorganizes the emotions and never offers the clear resolutions of making a decision. Perhaps her own location in the school hierarchy positions her fears. In actuality, it seems Erma was afraid of controversy in the classroom, primarily because she did not want to create controversy in the community or in administrative circles. Such caution, however, does not reflect how adolescents learn, and hence lacks pedagogical purpose.

Current news events shape the nature of controversy in the social studies classroom. In mid-November of 1983, for example, the Smithville school superintendent decided that the television movie about life after a nuclear war, *The Day After*, had to be handled with kid gloves, for the town was divided deeply over the issue of nuclear disarmament. He settled the issue by circulating, through word-of-mouth, the policy that teachers could answer any student-initiated question about the film, but classroom discussions should be avoided. Erma was caught in the middle and had to implement a policy that contradicted her own personal political views:

In the meantime, I am apt to have people visiting me, like the Social Workers for Nuclear Responsibility, saying, "Here's great curriculum material, why don't you use them," and this is what they show. And I look at them and I have this impulse to say, "Jeeze, that's great and I'd love to use that." And I have to stand back and go through that and say, "Yeah, I could use that, but I'd better not use this," and really analyze the material much more carefully when it surrounds an issue like that. That might be my view but that might not be my principal's view. He might not feel I should be in the classroom talking about nuclear disarmament or showing materials prepared by groups who obviously are for that. And I have to sit there and say, "Which of these would be acceptable to most people?"

So you have to find that middle statement of, nobody could be against this, or this wouldn't be controversial. Other than that, probably if kids were interested in that issue, you'd tell them to form a discussion group outside of the classroom so that all students wouldn't be a captive audience to exchanging views of that type.

I just get back to my first contention that in the social studies department, a social studies teacher has to display a lot of common sense where those types of issues are concerned. And you hope someone coming off a college campus, where they have been very free to discuss these issues and to make their views known, will realize they can't necessarily work in a public school system and do the same thing. I think there's always a tendency for younger teachers, and I'm sure I was the same way, to charge in, both barrels, and begin to save America.

Much of Erma's work, then, concerned policing the potential and actual crises of controversy. She maintained that student teachers are ill-prepared and perhaps unwilling to homogenize issues to their least offensive denominator. However, not to take up controversial issues does not mean that the classroom is empty of controversy. Moreover, such avoidance does not create an ideologically neutral classroom. Rather, it reproduces the dominant ideology as the desirable ideology. And herein lies the myth and deconstructive moment of Erma and the administrators: the avoidance of controversy cannot prevent the swaying of the classroom students' own ideology. Curricular silences can be as telling as that which is said. The problem is dual: dissent is recast as being insensitive to dominant values, and the avoidance of controversy is in actuality an avoidance of the pedagogy of controversy. Evidently, Erma expected the university to give student teachers pointers on how to teach controversial subjects in noncontroversial ways. Such a desire glosses over the pedagogy of controversy.

Erma Tough entered teaching from the back door, during the late 1950s when school systems recruited secondary teachers directly from university departments. She was granted emergency teacher certification with her first teaching job and, consequently, believed she learned to teach on her own:

> Back then, I didn't have to do an internship. My first day of teaching was when I walked into the classroom. I don't think you can teach someone to teach. I think it's all instinct. Someone makes a noise somewhere and at that moment you decide how to handle it. I know I sound cynical and believe you can't teach somebody to teach. Teaching is just common sense.

Erma's sense of practical knowledge remained unchallenged by the advanced degree course work taken over the years. Dissatisfied with the quality of her continuing education, she summed up her experiences there: "I don't think the professors know a whole lot about what's going on in the high schools. They just look at theory and don't spend much time on how to apply it." At the same time, Erma remained convinced that intuition and common sense were the best guarantees of instruction. And in this way, because for Erma common sense comes from within, she maintained that teachers were self-made, not university-produced.

Of all the components of teacher education, Erma valorized student teaching; for her, public schools rather than universities are the real grounds in education. So when asked what student teachers learned during their internship, Erma Tough rehearsed their newfound appreciation for the work of teaching:

> I think student teachers probably walk away realizing that teaching is a lot bigger job than they might have surmised. They usually end up responsible for one or two classes, maybe three at the most. And they often comment, "How do you have five classes and do all that work and get all that preparation done, and in the meantime, walk in all excited about what you propose to do and have the kids say, 'Ugh!'"
>
> But it's like, suddenly you find out what the real world is about when you walk into it. And you know, we all walk into things with ideals and lofty ideas about what we'd like to accomplish. I think student teachers learn how much work teaching really is.

In Erma's view, student teachers must be initiated into the frustrations; they should adjust to the constraints, demands, and expectations of school life. For her, the internship should be a time when the student teacher's idealism metamorphoses into a cautious practicality and where common sense and intuition, tempered by the exigencies of community values, determine conduct.

In the hierarchy of school administration, Erma worked to mediate community values, administrative policies, and faculty activity. In actuality, mediation meant keeping the lid on, since for Erma, community values are obdurate, without antagonisms of their own, and schools are not the site of social change. Part of Erma Tough's critical posture toward university-based teacher education, then, may be rooted in her bureaucratic mandate to depoliticize social studies education. Potentially, student teachers can subvert this work. As a result, she viewed them as accidents waiting to happen. The assumption within the discourse of accidents is that there exists an order to be protected. That Erma Tough must continually defer her own sense of meaningful education in order to reassert the dominant values—as interpreted by the principal and administrators—was rarely appreciated. That she must undo the university's mistakes and secure the status quo was also misunderstood. And this troubled Erma, for although she carried out conservative policies, she identified as a liberal. Indeed, she herself voices the tensions engendered by such a split.

Thomas Maxwellhouse: Principal of Smithville High

Dr. Thomas Maxwellhouse was in the business of education. As principal of Smithville High, he perceived his main responsibility as that of manager, seeing to it that this high school ran efficiently. Indeed, one of his most recent accomplishments was the computerization of Smithville's record system. With the flick of a switch and the correct code, Thomas had any pertinent statistic at his fingertips. And in this way, the official story of school life was under his constant surveillance.

The principal's office, with its thick red carpeting, dark paneled walls, and heavy oak office furniture, appears regal in comparison with the sparsely decorated main office. His secretary greets and screens all visitors and announces their presence by phone. From his well-appointed office he receives guests, speaks to staff and students, and administers the school. His authority was signified by all that surrounded him.

This principal had a great deal to say about the official story of student teaching. In fact, he let it be known that he had written a chapter in a book that addresses the administrator's role in it. He believed every professional involved must take student teaching seriously, for all student teachers were "future fellows in the profession." While his relations to student teachers varied over the years, Thomas had made it his business to greet each student teacher at the start of her or his internship:

> I have lots of comments about the role of the principal in the student teacher's world because I think the experience of student teach-

ing ought to be as real as such a thing can be. Now, one of the pluses in making a student teacher's experience more realistic is the fact that they can stay in school for eight to sixteen weeks, where, in the past, in my day, I was two weeks here, two weeks there. And if they can stay longer, then I see a lot that the principal can do for the student teacher.

First of all, I like to meet the student teacher before they come into the building and whenever possible, have some kind of interview process that makes them realize that if it looks like they're really qualified, they get the job. And if not, they don't. Frequently, of course, that administrative component sometimes has to be the department chairman. . . . But if the chairman has a reservation, it will always end up on the principal's desk. I think that's a significant part of the beginning of student teaching.

Then I see the administrator as kind of a drawing together person. In another school system, I had the opportunity to bring student teachers together a little more easily. I would sit around the table and I would give them a few pointers, of course, and some ideas that would help them in the school, from a principal's viewpoint, which they have to hear. They should hear an administrator's viewpoint, after all.

So there's little things and there's big things, the curriculum things and the instruction things, the preparation things, that we have to monitor very closely.

We might wonder how seriously Thomas takes student teachers when he viewed the experience as not quite real and when reality was measured by length of stay. Moreover, given that Thomas does not actually do what he would like to do, how pertinent is such advice? After all, greeting student teachers at the door takes only a few minutes. These "big and little things" are without referents but they do position student teachers as uninformed, naive, and in need of pointers.

Although his own student teaching experience told him otherwise, Thomas had high hopes that student teaching could be a time of professional formation. Like other professionals, he supposed student teaching to be a time of discovery and assimilation:

After sixteen weeks, I would hope that they have a pretty good insight into the whole picture, from the administrative things that they should learn to do, from taking a homeroom and study hall, to the extra curricular. And my feeling is, and I didn't experience this, so I'm guessing, that after sixteen weeks, if you don't go out of here with a fairly good idea of what you are about, you haven't done anything yourself. If you go into school for a day as a substitute, you could walk out and never want to return ever. And there's not a man walking on earth who wouldn't blame you. If you go into a school, as a sixteen week intern, and you don't come out knowing where you'll fit into the profession, you just haven't done your thing.

Thomas Maxwellhouse valued student teaching above all educational course work. He identified two factors, neither of which were in his control, that most influence the student teacher's performance: the use of trial and error as a primary learning strategy, and the "native talent" a student teacher brings to the classroom. Theoretical considerations were secondary and made sense only after years of practice. The best that teacher education could provide, according to Thomas, were "tricks of the trade," a familiarity with teaching techniques that work. The rest depended upon the individual because for Thomas, teachers were self-made, not university-produced:

> If it was one word, it would have to be experience. Yes, much of the course work at times in our lives seems much too theoretical than practical.
>
> I do believe there is a native talent to a school teacher. I have to tell you that. Some people are brilliant actors and have the right voices just to sing the perfect note. And there are Pablo Picassos and all sorts of people who have the genius and just seem to fall into line and they're talented and it just blossoms. And many school teachers have this.
>
> I don't negate the college work because there are tricks of the trade, there are tools, there are the broadening of the mind type of things that tell you teach it this way. There are ways of teaching people to evaluate what's going on in their rooms while they're doing their thing to assess themselves, because you have to learn how to do that, because if you're not checking on what you think you're doing, you might not be doing it.
>
> I also felt that the practical experience of the classroom topped me more than the preparation did. I put the two together, but I learned far more on the job. It only makes sense that you learn on your feet. What your student teachers should be told is that student teaching never ends.

What is behind the "things" alluded to in Thomas's verbiage? Practical experience meets native talent, an occasional technique is applied, and these ingredients "top" the teacher. Such an explanation extinguishes the relation-

ships supposed by pedagogy, the knowledges that are produced, and the changes
pedagogy can create within teachers and students.

For Thomas Maxwellhouse, the separation of educational theory from
practice was best bridged with the activity of teaching, something only schools
provide. In his mind, the root of this separation began with the distance
between schools and the university. Their limited contact has led Thomas to
conclude that each institution has very separate functions. Public schools hold
their end of the bargain, but the university, in Thomas's view, falls short.
When I asked about the problems of student teaching, Thomas immediately
replied, "From whose point of view, ours or theirs?" He continued this thought,
implying that these two points of views were diametrically opposed and that
produced the problem. Yet Thomas also admitted larger social forces at work
within the school context: insufficient salaries and fiscal crises:

> If you do your work and I do my work and the teachers do their
> work, a lot of things can be avoided. Problems usually arise from
> both sides after you think you've done your best with all the prelimi-
> nary placements.
>
> I don't think that the teaching profession is attractive right now
> in our area. Eight thousand teachers [in this state] have been fired
> within three years, which isn't good P.R. There's not good money
> like there's been in industry. And pay is important.
>
> I think there's a lot of things that make me very nervous about
> the kinds of people you are going to be producing. I hope it doesn't
> mean that the standards will just, you know, go way down to keep
> the school of education open. And then we'll get those dregs of
> people who couldn't do anything else on campus getting into edu-
> cation and then coming here. That would be a terrible time.
>
> Other problems that I haven't had recently but that I have en-
> countered with certain areas and was very upset about where the
> university didn't come and observe. And I was saying to my teachers,
> "You do your thing." And I was keeping my ear to the rail. And
> nobody would show up from the university and I'd get very, very
> angry.
>
> And I usually say to people the first time I meet them, "I expect
> if we're doing our part, you'll do your part." It's very important.
> Because you people are going to be signing a piece of paper. If the
> bottom line in education doesn't make that a meaningful document,
> then what are we doing?

In some ways, Thomas's discourse mirrors that of *A Nation at Risk*. Its
tautology argues that low pay makes teaching unattractive and hence only

mediocre persons enter the profession. Schools of education are not places of competency or quality, and they are to blame for accepting mediocre persons. Such theories of attribution confuse effects as causes, and social problems become individual failings. Most striking is Thomas's lack of referentiality: his preoccupation is with the surface of "things." Unprepared to view student teaching in dialogic terms, he is obsessed with the finished product.

Things Gone Awry

Each of these administrators possess advanced education degrees. It is, however, their discourse of school reality that informs their perspectives. Such a discourse is charged by an excessive practicality, one that privileges the need to adjust to the way things are, protect the status quo, and subscribe to the prevailing order. It is a discourse that prescribes conduct and inscribes subjectivity. As Richard Smith and Anna Zantiotis explain: "An important effect of discourse about the real is the differentiation between appropriate and inappropriate conceptions of teaching that seems obvious on the basis of an appeal to the 'truth' and the credibility of practicality."[15] Practical experience, as a guarantee of truth, is valorized because of its synchronicity with the exigencies of the real. However, suppressed in this discourse is how the real becomes established, produced, and legitimized in practice. Instead, the practical is filtered through common sense, joining conduct with affect. Supposedly, one intuits activity from experience.

From the perspectives of these administrators, tricks of the trade and educational innovations come and go. The material that constructs the teacher, however, is made from the stuff of intuition, native talent, and the personality traits one brings to the profession. In this way, teachers are thought to be self-made, unaffected by the techniques they employ. However, as discussed in chapter 2, common sense is already conditioned by dominant values, structures, and discourses. In the case of Erma Tough, the noise she heard at the back of the classroom was already laden with institutional meanings. Her response may have seemed to emerge spontaneously, but Erma's recollections do not explain how institutional constraints become lived practices. In the discourse of practicality, institutional constraints are simply given. As long as these administrators define the problem of learning to teach as one of learning to work within given constraints, the naturalizations they construct will continue to position their sense of the real and of the appropriate as synonymous with existing practices.

Their views of pedagogy compel these administrators to define the student teacher as naive, inept, inexperienced, and unprepared. According to this view, the problem is caused by the dualism between the real world of schools and the imaginary world of the university. Student teachers are disasters waiting to happen and the work of administrators is to dispense triage. They do this by reducing the work of the teacher to its most normalizing moment: as dispenser of neutral information and as follower of school policy. In such a scenario, theory is already redundant.

There is a rupture between the administrators' premise that teachers are self-made and their view that experience makes the teacher. On the one hand, the notion of being self-made constructs subjectivity as natural and unaffected by the social. On the other hand, subjectivity must be harnessed by practical experience, which ostensibly "tells" the student teacher how to teach. Erma Tough was being more than cynical when she commented: "You can't teach someone to teach." Like Thomas Maxwellhouse, she was not concerned with the contradictions of development. The concern was with stability. Consequently, the experience of learning to teach and learning itself was understood at its most concrete moment: as a time that endows the student teacher with the skills offered by the school. As long as these administrators defined their work in terms of stable results, their purpose would continue to be smoothing out what they perceived as the rough surfaces of student teachers.

TEACHER EDUCATORS

Alberta Peach: University Supervisor

At State University, supervision is the work of graduate students. In the early 1980s the school of education decreased graduate funding, and fewer supervisors had to supervise more student teachers. Supervisory responsibilities, on top of teaching, far exceeds their contractual agreement to work for twenty hours. And although the graduate students believe they are gaining valuable professional experience—since entry level jobs in teacher education require supervisory experience—the poor pay and demanding work are demoralizing. The stress of the job emerges, too, from the supervisor's role as a buffer between the university and school setting, between the cooperating teacher and the student teacher, and between the university program and the student teacher. Tensions in these relationships are inevitable, and it is the work of the supervisor to mediate each particular and conflicting interest while attending to the professional development of the student teacher.

Alberta Peach, an experienced teacher in rural and urban settings, was immersed simultaneously in graduate school and student teacher supervision when she entered State University in the fall 1983 as a doctoral student in reading education. Her warmth and experienced perspectives on teacher education stand out as first impressions. She took a no-nonsense approach to both her job and her position as a graduate student. With the start of her first graduate semester, Alberta applied for the position of supervisor of secondary student teachers:

> I applied for a supervisory assistantship in secondary education. They were interested in my teaching experience and how I could handle certain situations about discipline. I had taught in a hard core inner city school, so I had plenty of experience with that. They were questioning me about what I would do in certain situations, which I'm sure would lead to how do you advise a student teacher who might have that problem.

Alberta stepped into her newly acquired supervisor's role knowing little about the secondary teacher certification program. She was simply given the required supervision forms, a part-time caseload of four social studies student teachers already placed in four different high schools and sent out into the field. No program orientation for university supervisors was held; she was forced to learn about the program's expectations on her own:

> I think the university specializes in keeping you in darkness, or they assume you know everything. It's the end of my supervision semester, and I now have a handle on what I'm expected to do and none of that was made clear to me in the beginning.

Hard work characterized Alberta's first semester at State University. In addition to taking on a full-time graduate course load, Alberta maintained two part-time assistantships: student teacher supervision and work with the reading department. Her days were split between course work, supervision duties, reading department duties, and attending to her family. She noted that supervision responsibilities far exceeded her ten-hour wage:

> I've been supervising four student teachers since September. I have seen each one of them six times. Three are required, the secondary program requires you see them five times. Two of the high schools are twenty-five miles away from my house. The extra times were with two student teachers because I felt they needed it.

Alberta recalled her first problem as a supervisor: challenging student teachers' perceptions about her work as a supervisor and their work as student teachers. During her first meeting with student teachers, Alberta asked each of them to think back to when they were in school and the teacher introduced the newly arrived student teacher. Their response was laughter; all agreed that classroom students do attempt to manipulate their student teachers. Gently, Alberta reminded them not to take the student teacher's role so personally; images of the student teacher preceded them. The student teacher's images of the supervisor, however, could not be laughed away; fear inscribed both the image and the relationship. They saw supervision as akin to police work and the supervisor more as a judge than an advocate. They anticipated chastisement for any error and expected the iteration of their own powerlessness.

As part of her practice, Alberta struggled to challenge these negative images. Her philosophy of supervision and how she interpreted her past experience as a student teacher told her that supervision could be, in her words, "a helping relationship." Readily, she conceded that her philosophy was not the rule, because development was not an automatic value in the structure of student teaching:

> In the beginning, supervision bothered me 'cause so many of them have the impression that, you know, here was this supervisor with a black book, coming to give me check marks. I was trying to figure out where this comes from. Does it come the semester before? The student teaching experience, I think, becomes very fearful. They feel they have a lot of pressure on them. This is a one shot, and they have to be really successful. I think in the beginning it's really difficult to be real successful. The first thing they have to strive for is just to be comfortable in front of the class.
>
> I sat down with them the first time I met them and told them I was going to be there to help, that I didn't want them to look at me as terrible. And in the end, I thought all of them, maybe with the exception of one who, no matter what I did, would have thought of me as a real supervisor. And the other three really thought of me as someone they could talk to, someone who they could look to for advice, guidance, and just rehash what was going on in their classrooms.
>
> And I was going back to my own student teaching. The guy who I had was great. He was someone I could talk to, I didn't have to put on a show for him. I didn't have to worry when he was coming. But a lot of my colleagues did not have that situation. It was like they were ready to have a mental breakdown when they knew their supervisor was coming.
>
> It's funny because one of them had said to me the first time I met him: "You know, the first day I saw the supervisors I was kind of summing up which one of them am I getting, which one was going to be the nicest one?" It's funny because he is a male. I find him a little bit sexist. When we sat down and talked, he was really

looking for a woman rather than a man because he felt the woman would be more considerate and more sensitive to his needs.

The stereotypes Alberta attempted to break down are inscribed by power relations and lived as relations of gender. Each stereotypical image positioned the identity of the supervisor as contained by stereotypes; observation was equated with surveillance, while the gaze of the supervisor was the gaze of the terrible authority. It was, in a sense, an arbitrary authority, for without agreed-upon goals, the student teacher was powerless to determine the criteria of criticism. For one student teacher, gender constructed this relationship because he equated womanhood with sensitivity. It seems as though for this male student a woman supervisor might be more like a wife than a police officer. Aware, and a bit surprised by these dynamics, much of Alberta's work concerned challenging students to rethink their conceptions of supervision, and in some cases, their investments in gendered relations of power.

Along with reconstructing the supervisor's image, Alberta contended with student teachers' expectations of their supervisory sessions. Because student teaching is so immediate in its demands, students believed there was little time for self-reflection and initially resisted this work. They desired specific acknowledgment from Alberta and did not value dialogue about the complex issues raised by the teaching and learning encounter. Instead, they asked Alberta to limit discussion to what was "right and wrong" about their teaching and give them specific instructional techniques:

> The first time I went out supervising, I realized that they wanted real concrete things. I had watched the class and just took notes. But I had seen they were looking for real specifics. And I really didn't know what I was going to do 'cause I didn't know what I could give them.
>
> So I talked to two other supervisors and they came up with this type of note-taking method where I basically did an ethnographic study of what they were doing during the forty-five minutes I saw them. So I put down the time, what the students were doing, what the teacher was saying, got down as much as I could. And this was a whole guideline of behaviors, completely go through everything that happened in their class and talk about the positive things and the not so positive things. They enjoyed it and looked forward to seeing the notes.
>
> But they wanted me to show them. Show me. Tell me. Show me. And they wanted visual things they could look at and say, "Oh." Maybe it's because the kids are really hung up on getting grades and maybe this type of stimulation is what they need.

Despite Alberta's good intentions, the supervisory relationship was already overpopulated with the intentions, fears, and desires of others. It was oddly reminiscent of how we are educated as children and then, how these memories work as anxiety. The students wanted "concrete things" and judgments, because they believed Alberta was the expert. And in working with ethnographic notes, Alberta endeavored to provide a context that might help students theorize about the concrete. But while Alberta's practice challenged student teachers to theorize about their lived experience and develop pedagogy that extended their beliefs to the realm of practice, those supervisory encounters continued to be haunted by institutional imperatives to stay on track, cover the material, assert the teacher's authority, and appear as if the students were under the teacher's control.

The immediacy of student teaching often subverted Alberta's goal of helping students to reflect upon the underlying values, beliefs, and ideas that propelled their pedagogy. While she tried to convince them to appreciate student teaching as a time of experimentation and development, they were obsessed both with the need for techniques of classroom management and with their own desire to be experts. As a result, issues of control positioned how teaching and learning were understood:

> A lot of them were concerned with their lack of knowledge in their area. And what I tried to explain to them is their cooperating teachers have been teaching for years, have probably been using the text for at least four years, and are totally familiar with it, have gone through it from cover to cover. And these student teachers are seeing it for the first time. So they couldn't be expected to know every single minute detail and how to go through every single book and get all the information that they absolutely needed to present a group lecture.
>
> Another thing they were concerned about, two of them referred to it as the ability to think on their feet. What they found was happening to them was that they'd stand in front of a classroom and they could not think of the correct word, no matter how hard they tried. They just couldn't pull it out of their heads. I had witnessed one student teacher do this and I originally thought it was because of my presence that was making him this way. You could tell he was just struggling for words. But he wasn't comfortable with the material because it was very theoretical.
>
> I think they believe from the beginning that a teacher is supposed to know everything there is to know on the subject. And I sit back and say, "Look. You're lecturing high school kids. You're not

lecturing a college class." I think it comes from the cooperating teachers. Oftentimes the cooperating teacher thinks when they get a student teacher that they are superior-minded. I think cooperating teachers forget that they once were beginning teachers. And they forget what student teaching is like.

I tell them this is the only experience you're ever going to have where you can blow it and no one's going to be on your back. If you have a regular teaching job and you do a miserable job, and the superintendent and principal come in and evaluate you, they're not going to sit down and say, "It didn't go well today. You can try this." They're going to write on their little papers and say, "Do not recommend for tenure or reappointment." I think it's the university's philosophy to get them to go out into the field and try all different types of teaching methods to find out which ones they're comfortable with and to be as creative as possible.

Odd contradictions compose Alberta's narrative. Her goal is to "cure" the interns of their obsession with immediate expertise by emphasizing that expertise requires familiarity, something they will acquire over time. Such comforting words leave unchallenged the concept of expertise and the images of knowledge—both possible and given—that position the power of the expert. These interns assumed that their classroom authority could be built from their control over content. Yet classroom students are significantly missing from this depiction of what it means to know. There is also the assumption that familiarity of the material will somehow lead to good teaching. While there are important relations between understanding the shape of content and the ability to construct meaningful pedagogy, what is oddly absent is the issue of meaningful pedagogy: how to engage students.

A second problem emerges between the experimentation of student teaching and the certainty of teaching. The problem is that Alberta's desire for supervision as a helping relationship was not extended into the world beyond student teaching. There, mistakes have dire consequences and teachers have no redress. The one-shot experience of student teacher thus became a metaphor of the profession, implying that student teachers would need to be certain once they stepped into a real position.

Although Alberta stressed that student teaching should be a creative time, she realized that stressing creativity without providing a range of creative practices was useless. Alberta knew that university course work ignored creative practices and was critical of the assumption that students would receive these methods "on the job." Indeed, the practices she observed in school contexts revealed more about the dynamics of social control than about the dynamics of creative pedagogy:

I don't think that there has been very much in their university training that has prepared them for student teaching. Much of it has
been all theoretical. And I think when they get into that classroom
for the first couple of weeks, they die.

I had one kid who the first week he was there, has started
watching a study hall. And a kid drank ink out of his pen. And he
was like, "What am I supposed to do? My university notebook never
told me what to do in a case like this." And he handled it very well,
strictly on intuition.

I think they've only written one unit prior to going out into the
classroom. I don't think they have any conception of how to apply
a unit, they have no idea, it comes from experience. But they can't
even judge how long how much material you can cover in one class.
I think they need to have long term goals. They just can't plan day
to day.

Their courses are all theory. I think they really need concrete
"how to" type things. And I don't think they're getting that. I don't
think the course outlines at the university have it in their curriculum
at all. I think these professors have been in their ivory tower too
goddamn long.

Implied in this supervisor's narrative are grand questions: How do student teachers come to know the everyday of classroom life and not be subsumed by the immediate? How might university course work address the
everyday, the idiosyncratic, the emotive, and the anxieties that constitute lived
lives? How might theory be useful? Yet in rendering theory and practice as
dichotomous, the practical appears as separate from the values, theories, orientations, and investments that mark a technique, stance, or action as practical in the first place. The practical, as Madeleine Grumet points out, is
"dependent upon our expectations and the questions we ask of it for its
quality and value, and consequently, to study the practical is also to study the
ways in which we contribute to what we see when we look."[16] Our understanding of the practical, then, is always filtered through the lens of the
theoretical.

Problems arise, as discussed in chapter 2, when the practical and the
theoretical are uncoupled, as they are, in different ways, in the university and
in the school. The point is that those preparing to teach must have opportunities for theorizing about their practices. They must also be able to learn
before they understand, make and survive mistakes, and even have a bad day.
As it stands, neither setting accomplishes this. Instead, the anxieties of student teachers are either reduced to problems of technique or ignored as
atheoretical phantoms. Alberta was caught in this dichotomy and was forced

to focus on the remedial skills of getting student teachers through their internship. Working to help them reflect upon what they already know was also important but often lost because of a certain desperation that conditions learning to teach.

Joe Probe: Professor of Social Studies Education

For the last fifty-odd years, Professor Joe Probe has been involved in education. Most of his experience was rooted in the university, for there value was placed on the ideas that were so important to his own development. Joe felt close to his past. He spoke adamantly of historical events as the catalyst for his philosophic perspectives, affective investments, and disappointments. Such events continued to affect his life commitment of critically analyzing the world around him. In reconstructing his biography, inevitably Joe rehearsed his present. Saddened by his awareness that students barely understood his own historical antecedents, Joe Probe supposed that these students were without their own:

> Unlike many people, I think people do get wiser with experience, if they are capable of growing. But, at the same time, things that highly excite me, my biography, isn't necessarily a part of the life history and concerns of people today.
>
> I'm out of the Nazi regime. I'm out of totalitarianism and communism and so forth, the fascism and hostility to that, and McCarthyism. There were the big bugaboos, the things that oriented the liberal mind. And I've been liberal right up through John Kennedy. His death is a mortal blow to me.
>
> More recently, I think, this thing has lost its vitality and significance. The premise of liberalism has not been realized. For myself, I see more promise in terms of critical analysis, the willingness to reexamine the fundamentals of the society and its orientations.

Joe's narration resides between the promise of liberalism and the effects of social engineering. He suggested such breaks might be repaired by future critics, persons willing and able to distance themselves from social imprintations and all the imaginary relations they presuppose. For Joe, critical analysis was the new promise and the key to transcendence.

At State University, Joe Probe's work in social studies education consisted primarily of teaching required education courses. Although his course titles have changed with state mandates, the underlying theme stayed the same: that social studies teachers have a moral imperative to help students critically consider their role in society. So Joe attempted to effect this goal by convinc-

ing education majors to develop their individual critical capacities. His un-
even attempts were a consequence of the tension between instilling critical
thought and transposing this process into specific pedagogies. Not satisfied
with prepackaged solutions, Joe Probe struggled with the larger goal of preparing critics who would then devise their own pedagogy:

> This is something that's puzzled me for a long time. At one time,
> I even believed it was a matter of learning certain techniques, a series
> of steps or logical skills. And I think this is probably a necessary
> ingredient, but it isn't the complete thing. The longer I've been at it,
> the less I've been enamored at logic and types of critical thinking
> skills. But getting students aware and getting under their skin, making
> them aware of the inconsistencies in life, the unfairness of life, the
> discontinuities in society. Because I think you have to be debugged
> on things yourself, be concerned before you can start the process of
> critical thinking.
>
> My frustration with the kids is that they've been in a cocoon
> here for four years. Many of their courses haven't been taught from
> a problematic point of view and they haven't had enough time or
> experience to distance themselves from their work and see how it
> relates to life. I know if I were a student now, I probably wouldn't
> understand myself.
>
> But I still think that what I've been doing this year, adding more
> and more, is to emphasize the sad state of knowledge in the field of
> social studies, the questionable nature of all knowledge claims, in
> history or psychology, that the jury is out on everything.
>
> In quieter times, as the Fifties, say, when things were getting
> better and more people were involved in sharing the wealth, you
> probably had better excuses saying everything was good. But it's a
> different ball game now.

Joe posed the problem of consciousness as one of deprograming others
from the prevailing ideology in order to accept the uncertainties masked by
knowledge. Complacency, satisfaction, and a sense of unity were sources of
resistance to the critical and Joe attempted to "get under the students' skins."
Yet his attempts to bother students was lonely work, limited by lack of shared
commitment from his colleagues, resisted by the students who did not want
to be bothered, and delayed by the students' inexperience with taking on the
perspectives of the critic. In this way, Joe's efforts risked being reduced to the
idiosyncracy of the lone individual.

Education students of the day were as problematic to Joe as the concept
of critical thought. He supposed their insulated life experiences and their

proximity to privilege endorsed their resistance to being "debugged" and prevented them from viewing their lives with suspicion. Yet because Joe believed
the process of becoming critical to be a deeply personal one, much of his work
endeavored to convince individual students to assume the responsibility of a
critical stance:

> Unless social studies teachers, one of the few agents of society, lead
> students to distance themselves from the social reality out there, and
> become critical of it, that's their function.
>
> The only thing I can come up with is critical thinking, or more
> recently, emancipatory thinking, transcending the realities of every-
> day life. But I know this, from my own experience, from my own
> biography, and I'm committed to it. Transmitting it to young people
> is quite another thing.
>
> I still think, even though they don't internally understand it, you
> have to put a bee in their bonnet, you have to start someplace. You
> have to make them a little bit aware that the fit between themselves
> and their jobs shouldn't be too easy, they shouldn't settle in too soon.
> And they should be struggling against the realities and habitual
> practices all around them. They should be adversarial toward things.
>
> And the trouble with these kids is that they're so much a part
> of American society, they're so much a part of their recent experi-
> ence that everything's looking up for them. And it's hard for them
> to see this. That's why so few of them are experientially and mature-
> wise really equipped to teach social studies.

Joe's dilemma, as he himself posed it, was that while social studies teachers should lead their students to transcend the realities of everyday life, those
preparing for such work were incapable of transcendence. What Joe did not
admit is that transcendence is an impossible goal. No one stands outside the
fray, outside history. Nor can knowledge exist outside the interests that produce it in the first place. Insofar as Joe emphasized the distancing of students
from the social reality "out there," he assumed the individual as autonomous
in the sense of being able to choose to transcend the effects of the social
world. But it may be too much to demand of beginners.

Behind Joe's version of the critic is an autonomous individual. Such a
notion is problematic. As Peter Griffins reasons: "the notion of autonomous
individuals making free and unconstrained choices assumes that those individuals existed as individuals before the moment of choice."[17] Individuality is always
a historical construct, not an essential quality. Individuals, however, because
they must use language to express their individuality, do not merely speak for
themselves. Nor can they choose to speak without the help of ideology.

Joe desired a teacher education that could reaffirm his own biography. His ideal, rooted in the classical liberal education tradition, contended that teacher education should begin at the graduate level, after the student has acquired a strong grounding in an academic discipline and, presumably, has achieved greater maturity. Such an enterprise would be concerned with how knowledge is used and scholars would do battle with epistemological and ontological dragons. When Joe rehearsed his desires, he contrasted them with his present circumstances as a teacher educator:

> We had a department of education when I first came here and then it became a school. And like all bureaucracies, it knows no bounds in terms of expansion and development. We've taken our part of the pious methods of techniques, which is very unfortunate. There's nothing in methods courses, there's nothing. It all goes back to the way people's intellectual processes operate.
>
> We leave subject matter and mastery to other departments and then we train kids who have a certain orientation and then try to humanize their knowledge and make them aware of the differences between adolescents as a captive audience and college students with their maturity and motivation. We try to ease the transition into the real world here, but most of the action is in the substantive fields. And I don't think you get in the history department someone who's vitally interested in the values of education. They're telling their story in a very specialized way.
>
> I think that if the School of Education is willing to address this problem, it would really have to do it other than in strictly methodological ways. I think we've exaggerated techniques and method far beyond what it's capable of doing. Somewhere along the line, values and morality have to be brought back into the educational process. Subject matter will not do it by itself.
>
> The School of Education should be a force that reinserts values. It would probably be a graduate level enterprise where you'd have college scholars from the various disciplines who were fundamentally teachers and concerned with the meaning and use of knowledge.
>
> It's astonishing, in the size of the school we have, so few people are critical of the organization, are remotely aware of the technological, quantitative biases that prevail in the educational world. We're all going down the accustomed routine, repeating our own socialization and passing this uncritically on to future practitioners.

In Joe's ideal teacher education, the problem of learning to teach was never addressed. Dismissing techniques and methods to make room for values and ideas does not solve the problem. Rather it sets up another kind of dualism, between philosophy and practice. While rightly Joe criticized the methods-as-an-end approach designed to ease the transition between the university and the school, what he sought to insert was a values-as-an-end approach. These adversarial values, however, in privileging critique over pedagogy, assume that dissatisfaction leads to good pedagogy. Again, a sense of transcendence underlies Joe's advocacy; it is as if schools of education can be immunized against technocratic values, that ideas and values can somehow supplant or transcend technologies of control. But the problem is that ideas are already discursive social practices in that they hold normative commitments and standards of valuation, and they organize relations of power. The unasked question—can we teach people about knowledge in ways that refuse to position dominant and subordinate relations—requires a discourse of pedagogy that considers the problem of how knowledge becomes critical.

Joe did not take up, in explicit terms, the dilemma of how one transforms practice when the contexts of practice resist transformation. Instead, he prescribed an adversary stance. His investment was in helping student teachers understand the tensions between the university and school as productive, that such tensions could serve critical awareness. Evidently, if student teachers understood the normalizing pull of conformity, they might be better able to resist its lure. And within this power struggle, Joe wished the university to be the vanguard:

> I don't think the school of education becomes servants of the public schools. I don't think they're in the job to ease the adjustment, the transition. Because then you merely perpetuate the idiosyncracies of the traditional practice.
>
> I've always felt more of an adversarial role toward the school, but do it in a gentle way, not attacking personalities, or individual schools, but try to instill an impatience, I suppose, or an adversarial attitude toward existing arrangements. But I also said I would never teach in the public schools right now. I couldn't teach. I'd have a heart attack the second day, I think. The tasks are unrealistic.
>
> I'm not interested in training technicians or skilled transmitters, or masters of the latest technology in education. They'll adapt to that naturally. I'm trying to woo them away from that, indoctrinating them in the other direction, so to say. The best you can do is give them, put a bee in their bonnet, as it were, to create a certain amount of tension between their expectations and the job realities, so they won't adapt too easily in the long term.
>
> But I don't know whether it's right or wrong to turn someone's horizon upside down before student teaching. But if all I did was

make people feel good about themselves, and they go out and perpetuate the inane, then I wouldn't be doing my job. Teachers must be moral people and be able to become outraged against society.

Joe's visions of what happens in schools is contradictory. He would like his students to be adversarial, but understands how the work of the teacher is structured by values of conformity. He would like to exploit the tensions between the university and the school, but is cognizant of the massive tensions already structuring the teacher's work. Admittedly, in such a context, Joe would not survive. The existing arrangements are not comfortable. In such a contradictory place, what are the sources of outrage? Can moral outrage be taught? Whose outrage would be privileged? And how does one transform outrage into pedagogy?

Joe did not look to pedagogy as both a problematic and a means to understand the dilemma of cultivating critical thought. Joe depended mainly upon the Socratic method of dialogue where he raised the questions and students responded. The problem is not the methodology itself, but that his students never had opportunities to rehearse the possibilities this specific methodology might offer. And herein may lie the primary contradiction of his courses.

Although Joe attempted to provide an intellectual framework for his students, his own pedagogy does not advance the epistemological issues he takes up. The unasked question is: How will such a framework, like critical awareness, inform his student's pedagogical decisions? Simply telling students of the facts of oppression is insufficient. They need opportunities with what Ann Berlack describes as "the social-psychological connections between experience and consciousness."[18] Without an inquiry into how significance is made and broken, the perceived distance between academic knowledge and social experience will remain undisturbed, and students will continue to have difficulties understanding how the political becomes personal.

Joe's students may very well leave his course with a vague feeling that all is not well in the schools. These students, however, are now confronted with yet another level of problems, unaddressed in Joe's methods courses: What do they do with these values? How do values guide pedagogical practice? What does it mean to be a critic in a context that always already authorizes the push toward normalization? The philosophical problems Joe raises are the problems of individual consciousness yet to become pedagogical practice. Once confronted with the realities of school life, students may have a nagging notion that critical awareness is essential, but possess no clue as to its integration into classroom life, except for discussing it in the manner of their professor. In this way, the import of Joe's classes must quickly fade as the more immediate problems of school life take hold. The irony is that Joe and his students share some of the same difficulties: the students of Joe's students also have the knotty problem of distancing themselves from their biographies. But without a persistent dialogue on the problems of changing persons and on changing circumstances, without experiences with the discursive practices that challenge persons to think and act as if things can be otherwise, and without an analysis of why critical thought is resisted in schools, the messenger is reduced to one who delivers only bad news.

What appeared to be a generation gap—that the lived experiences of Joe are quite different from those of his students—is really about the tensions between the past and the present, between what is interesting then and now, and how one's present reorients one's understanding of the past. Joe Probe was not an avid scholar of popular culture. He had no insight into what mattered to his students, or why, beyond their relationship to privilege, many resisted his message. Had Joe been able to connect the deep investments of his students with their teaching desires and needs, he might have been able to transcend the dualism of youth and experience. His students are not "raw material" but persons who, like Joe, bring their own deep investments to teacher education. Had Joe explored these subjective dimensions and what it was that structured them, he might have challenged his own discursive practices and repositioned the social relationships so necessary to any meaningful change.[19]

The narrative of Joe Probe suggests many of the tensions of teacher educators, between the schools and the university, between theory and practice, between knowledge and experience, and between the real and the ideal. At the time of this study, teacher education was besieged by criticism, from the federal government, the corporate world, the schools, and the teachers. Professors are not immune to these tensions and the problem for everyone involved is one of how social change comes about in obdurate institutions. Yet the emphasis on critical thought and the dualism Joe positioned between critique and technique did not lead to what Joe called "emancipatory thinking." Such a dualism can only privilege one type of activity over another. For emancipatory thought must become embodied in practices that permit one to draw upon and extend one's own deep investments, desires, and lived experiences, and connect these dynamics to one's present circumstances. Joe was hard pressed to make these connections because he saw his work as that of advocacy: while the message was in place, the work of the student teacher was to carry it out. Such transference, as Joe admitted, seemed as impossible as teaching.

Adverse Moments

University-based teacher education is not a monolith. It produces contradictions that, if unaddressed, work to sustain the very schisms teacher educators attempt to close. So while some teacher educators may encourage skepticism, as the correct approach to interpreting educational life, missing is the pedagogy for enacting change. Without any meaningful pedagogy and without a range of discursive practices, skepticism as a stance can easily give way to cynicism. Given this dilemma, students hopeful of enacting change and of viewing their teaching as transformative practice, must, in a sense, turn to the system itself. Their newly acquired skepticism is thus turned inward. Student teachers learn that the intent to change neither brings about effective transformative practice nor allows them unilaterally to take up the existing practices. On the one hand, if they take up existing practices, they are critical of this capitulation. On the other hand, if they attempt transformative practices, they may fail. What tends to happen is that student teachers are left with a vague feeling of discontent and hence their need for concrete advice.

The discomfort, then, that Joe Probe the professor desires, and that Alberta Peach the university supervisor must assuage, is an effect of the contradictions of teacher education. These teacher educators, however, understand the meaning of discomfort differently. Alberta Peach, for example, perceived excessively theoretical knowledge as the source of discomfort, while Joe maintained that the tyranny of methods contributes to the theoretical aimlessness of the discipline. Such perceptions organize how each professional works with those preparing to teach. Part of the tension was that, at best, Joe had minimal contact with the schools. His understanding of school life was abstract yet informed by a fearfulness that teaching, as it is lived, is impossible. Alberta, on the other hand, recognized the possibilities of teaching, but viewed her practice as thwarted by the remedial work she was forced to assume. She expected university course work to ease the transition between the university and the school, while Joe anticipated such dissonance as a source of transformation. The division of labor in teacher education—where methods instructors teach without a context and where supervision is overdetermined by context—prevented each professional from attending to the multiple meanings of dissonance.

These professionals may serve a common program but their approaches, hopes, and frustrations work against each other. Imagine being a student in this program. Course work may seem intellectually rich but applications become an individual dilemma. The professors profess values that make sense in the university classroom, but seem an impossibility in school contexts. Those methods encountered during university course work are foreign to the university supervisor, and the grand plan of making a difference becomes subsumed by the everyday. In such a scenario, what hopes for experimentation can be realized? The need is not for programs to devise unitary philosophies, but for programs—in conjunction with schools—to create multiple opportunities for the newly arrived to practice in meaningful ways. As it stands, the structure of teacher education works to disrupt the fledgling confidence of the newly developing teacher.

ANTAGONISTIC DISCOURSES

The voices of those who surround student teachers speak common words, such as experience, maturity, knowledge, and theory. The irony is that while common words are there, their connotations and inflections collide. These words are slippery, overburdened by contesting theories of the real, and tensions among what should count, what should be discounted, and what is unaccounted. When it comes to learning to teach, there is no single-minded conception of success, of competence, of conduct, or of survival. There are no common agreements as to the desirable teacher's stance, the constitution of good pedagogy, or the relationship between theory and practice. This instability is not the problem. It becomes so only when multiplicity is denied and the pretense is that it does not exist. When multiplicity is suppressed, so too is the struggle of student teachers to deal with, articulate, and transform their circumstances—and all the vulnerabilities this entails—into meaningful learning. If student teaching is characterized by multiplicity, then the professional's discourse of certainty will not be able to assist the student teacher's potential to respond creatively to such difference. In such turbulence, where certainty is sought and eludes, and where the real is unfastened by relations of power, what kinds of tensions work against multiple understandings of teaching and learning?

One way to interpret the stories of student teaching, as told by significant others, is to consider how the broad questions of place, knowledge, and pedagogy are addressed in their respective discourses and to examine as well how these discourses become positioned as common sense. For many of these professionals, experience is viewed as already possessing a dynamic power; it is approached as if it was the source of knowledge and pedagogy, and as if it was delineated space. For example, practicing pedagogy in schools is thought to be educative, while learning about teaching in university settings is not. Yet this dualism that positions schools as the real and the university as the fiction cannot account for the fact that although these professionals desired student teaching to be meaningful, few trusted the student teacher's capacity to construct meaning. Hence the power of experience supplants the struggle to know. To understand how the student teacher becomes constructed in this discourse of the real, it is necessary to deconstruct the underlying assumption that real experience can somehow bestow appropriate meanings upon the student teacher. This requires an exploration of the effects of the discourse of the real and how it works to define knowledge, pedagogy, and place.

Central to each of the above tensions is the myth that experience maps meaning by organizing perceptions. This valorization of experience fails to ask what it is that structures social expression and how the dynamics of social expression produce our understandings of experience in the first place. The contradiction is that experience can take on meaning only after it is lived. As James Donald explains:

> In a common sense way we often take experience to mean simply what happens to us—the *lived experience* . . . But that *lived* already implies the ambiguity of the term—it hints at a process whereby we attribute meaning to what happens to us. Our cultural identities are formed as the experiences of our biographies accumulate: we become *experienced*. And that entails the conceptual ordering of what happens to us within consciousness.[20]

Such conceptual orderings are an uneasy combination of authoritative and internally persuasive discourses, a dialogic play that can naturalize experience as already containing essential meanings, or construct understandings of experience from the multiplicity of meanings that are accessible through a range of other discourses. The problem is to distinguish how we come to know what we know, what it is that structures what we know, and how our knowledge of the world works to position experience as lived. Philip Corrigan states the problem this way: "We need to shift our images of education and pedagogy in at least three ways: to widen our understanding of how we are taught, and how we learn, and how we know, noting that none of these is the same."[21] The discourse of common sense is incapable of addressing and distinguishing these dynamics.

In the discourse of common sense, the value of experience is delineated by space. The student teacher must negotiate the meanings of two placements: that of the university and that of the school. Each place appears to haunt the other with contesting values, investments, and performative practices. In the dominant mythology of teacher education, the sole work of the university is to prepare student teachers for classroom practice. The problem is that the meanings of classroom practice are neither unitary nor static. Rather, classroom practices are produced, interpreted, and acted upon in multiple and contradictory ways.

Erma Tough and Thomas Maxwellhouse, for example, desire classroom practice to maintain the continuity of existing school policies. For Alberta Peach and Edith Daring, classroom practices are creative. Joe Probe wants the teacher's work to be antagonistic to the status quo, a kind of anti-practice, whereas Roy Hobbs desires a hermetically sealed practice, free from disruptions. Each image of classroom practice is a combination of how common sense, institutional imperatives, techniques, private hopes, and theoretical orientations are read. Each asserts its own sense of what is critical and its own conceptions of power and knowledge. Contained within the lived experience of classroom practices, then, are the push and pull of multiple and contradictory discourses. The point is how to help student teachers understand what it takes to act as subjects in contexts that they themselves did not set up. In refocusing our attentions, the value of experience becomes uncoupled from place and instead depends upon the ways in which we construct experience as lived, and whether such constructions permit the agency of the knower and access new discursive practices.

Similarly, the ways that each professional defines knowledge resist any unitary meaning. As expressed by these narrators, knowledge is bound by conflicting notions of utility, each signifying antagonistic combinations of the practical, the instrumental, and the transformative. They also assert criteria for judging competence and conduct. For example, Roy Hobbs and Erma Tough, for different reasons, privilege knowledge as instrumental, something to be dispensed without disrupting the information or the people to be informed. In this model of transmission, the competence of the teacher is measured by the students' ability to reproduce received forms of knowledge. Useful knowledge, for Joe Probe, is transformational: knowledge should bother, disrupt, and provoke the learner. The teacher's ability to instill moral outrage indicates the extent of competence. Joe's vision of knowledge, however, still depends upon transmission, because there is an assumption that moral outrage can be received rather than constructed and produced through exchange. Alberta Peach and Edith Daring are interested in personal and practical transformations; a competent teacher integrates the what and the how of knowing and creatively guides students in the construction of their own knowledge. Theirs is a more dialogical model, one that views teaching as a place of departure.

Each version of knowledge suggests images of authority, expertise, and power, and thus is understood as mimetic and received, and as constructed and interpreted. Each discourse portends forms of practice, measures of success, and sets the conditions of its production. Thus, to know the material cannot be reduced to one universal meaning. Nor should it be. Indeed, to know the material necessitates the repression and the extension of the subjectivities of teachers and students. Always supposed in any conception of knowledge is what is to be expressed and how such expressions are produced in understanding. The point is to theorize about such dynamics and to construct views of knowledge that permit reflection upon how it is constructed and interpreted.

The majority of these narratives are oddly silent about what pedagogy can mean. Complex relations among the student, the teacher, and the text are suggested, however, by Edith Daring. This teacher approached the difficult problem of "how to get the material across" by rehearsing how she comes to know through practice. Roy Hobbs obscured such complexity when he described his work as "just teaching," or as amplifying prefabricated knowledge in order to cover the text. In different ways, the "tricky things" alluded to by Thomas Maxwellhouse, and the useless techniques disdained by Job Probe evoke the problem of divorcing knowledge from how one comes to know. Such problems are not solved merely by invoking common sense or by inserting moral values. Neither of these dynamics can ever stand outside particular discourses. Alberta Peach grappled with such an issue but with her focus on familiarity and experience she omitted how meanings shift as experience becomes lived. For Thomas Maxwellhouse, Erma Tough, and Alberta Peach, theory is the culprit that disrupts intuitive knowledge. They valorize common sense without concern for the social forces that call it into being.

The transmission model of theory and of pedagogy, and the assumption that practice either follows theory or is atheoretical, obscure the potential dialogic relations that can produce transformations within the knower and over what is to be known. To move beyond such dualisms, however, teachers, students, and researchers must develop what David Lusted calls "a pedagogy of theory":

> A more transactional model whereby knowledge is produced not just at the researchers' desk nor at the lectern but in the *consciousness*, through the process of thought, discussion, writing, debate, exchange; in the social and internal, collective and isolated struggle for control of understanding; from engagement in the unfamiliar idea, the difficult formulation pressed at the limit of comprehension or energy; in the meeting of the deeply held with the casually dismissed; in the dramatic moment of realization that scarcely regarded concern, an unarticulated desire, the barely assimilated, can come alive, make for a new sense of self, change commitments and activity.[22]

This approach to theory is attentive to the multiple and often contradictory ways one comes to know as knowledge is produced and understood. Lived experience rather than the phenomenon of experience itself becomes the concern. When the problem of transformation is coupled with pedagogy, our sources of theory can be extended beyond the taken-for-granted dualism of academic content and pedagogical process.

The question of how teachers learn to teach, intrinsic to the workings of teacher education, is not easily answered in these reconstructed narratives. The one word Maxwellhouse offers, "experience," may seem as simple as common sense yet the propensity for experience, as we have seen, never guarantees access to a particular meaning, competency, truth, or a particular form of conduct. There is a prevailing myth of experience as telling but what each narrator reveals is the fact that experience can be known only after we express what happens. And although what gets said is determined by our relation to the material world, our power to authorize particular versions of the real, and what we do not say, the terms of our understandings depend upon the discourses we take up.

The work of V. N. Volosinov is helpful in challenging the orthodoxy that experience contains an objective lesson. Volosinov argues that consciousness and experience have no independent reality outside how our cultural codes deploy knowledge. "We do not," Volosinov writes, "see or feel an experience— we understand it. This means that in the process of introspection we engage our experience into a context made up of other signs we understand."[23] Consequently, experience is not instructive in and of itself. This means that our work is to consider how we perceive the world through particular epistemological commitments and symbolic systems, and how our meanings are organized, disorganized, and produced within the multiple positions we inhabit. The point is to reflect, in critical ways, upon the processes and forces that structure experience as meaningful, useless, or even mysterious. Such reflections can help us theorize pedagogically about the antagonistic discourses that position our sense of the practical, the real, and the necessary.

The narratives of significant others suggest the complicated dualisms that are produced when experience is presented as if it were the sole arbitrator of practice, knowledge, and space, and when theory is understood as capable of existence only outside practice. Such views are not very different from the normative discourse of teacher education discussed in the first part of this chapter. Working through both the reports and these narrations are relations of power and repressive myths that, if unarticulated, serve to act upon the actions of student teachers in ways that perpetuate and render natural the schisms that constrain what is possible during the teaching internship. In both the reports and these narratives, university-based teacher education is positioned as the problem and the student teacher is sometimes blamed for this circumstance. What is ignored in both contexts, however, is the fact that teacher education must be conceived as more than a technocratic problem of training. Indeed, the problem is with this reduction.

Throughout this chapter, I have argued that to understand the dynamics of teacher education, we must analyze its discourses. Consideration must be given to the views of those who seek to influence what is taken as the most real moment in teacher education—the internship—and those views must be located in relation to the authoritative and internally persuasive discourses that infuse such views with mythic powers. Such dynamics are explored in chapter 6. The official and practical orientations of those who oversee student teachers are significant in that they work to inform, position, and fashion student teachers and their "teaching" in both practice and theory. They do this by valuing particular practices as desirable and necessary, and by glossing over the deep vulnerabilities engendered by educating others while being educated.

What is at risk in our educational formation is not our ability, as the official reports urge, to compete with other nations. That goal can only assert adherence to particular notions of economic development. What is at risk is our ability to reflect upon what we take for granted and determine how such meanings repress the potential in Maxine Greene's words to "make present what is absent, to summon up a condition that is not yet."[24]

6

Practice Makes Practice

The Given and the Possible in Teacher Education

Learning to teach, like teaching itself, is a time when desires are rehearsed, refashioned, and refused. The construction of the real, the necessary, and the imaginary are constantly shifting as student teachers set about to accentuate the identities of their teaching selves in contexts that are already overpopulated with the identities and discursive practices of others. Theirs is a vulnerable position; the borders of borrowing and owning are not easily discernable, and the advice, support, and guidance of others expresses an odd combination of authoritative and internally persuasive discourses.

Within such contexts, where desires are assigned and fashioned, student teachers strive to make sense and act as agents in the teacher's world. Indeed, much of their time is taken up with negotiating, constructing, and consenting to their identity as a teacher. This process, however, is problematic because particular orientations to autonomy, authority, certainty, and order, taken up by those already there, work to dismantle this negotiatory stance and threaten to make *student teacher* an oxymoron.

As I have argued throughout this study, to consider what it is that structures the discursive practices of those learning to teach requires a double consciousness of persons, structures, and of the discourses that join them, and an acknowledgment of how the inadequacies of the present structure work through the practices of newcomers. The structure of learning to teach is fundamentally flawed.

To view the problem of learning to teach as simply one of preparedness and ill-preparedness does not allow for the contradictory realities that

221

individuals confront. That judgment can neither illumine the turmoil of learning to teach nor assuage the deeply personal dissonance engendered by the circumstances of being there. The commonsense formula of preparedness or ill-preparedness rooted in the normative discourse of teacher education cannot explain what it is that structures the practices and subjectivities of individuals and why certain practices dominate and persist over others. The fact is, to place student teachers in compulsory school settings and to expect them to act as if they have entered a neutral zone where they can single-handedly fashion it into places of learning sets them up for the discursive practice of self-blame. Such a typical scenario makes the student teacher the site of conflict, and in doing so, inhibits the development of practices that could be internally persuasive.

This chapter is concerned with the given and possible realities of learning to teach. In working through the practices of Jamie Owl and Jack August, I offer a discourse that can reconceptualize these practices in ways that might aid in the rethinking, and I hope, in transforming the ways people learn to teach. Part one of this chapter deconstructs the values, beliefs, and orientations—the cultural myths—that magnetize Jamie and Jack.[1] In the second part of the chapter, I focus on the dialogic possibilities of teacher education and what this can offer to those learning to teach.

Throughout my analysis, I have borrowed from Walter Benjamin's cultural criticism. Like Benjamin, I argue that there are always two simultaneous dimensions of social life: the given and the possible. These dimensions become accessible to us when specific events, circumstances, and dilemmas are viewed from a different perspective. Here, I have extended metaphorically Walter Benjamin's description of photographic technique to my work as an ethnographer: "The enlargement of the snapshot does not simply render more precise what in any case was visible, though unclear: it reveals entirely new structural formations of the subject."[2] So too with critical ethnographic work: we can construct new understandings of the formation of the subject if we can extend what is given into a theory of the possible.

THE GIVEN POSITIONS: DISCOURSE AND IDEOLOGY

As described in chapter 1, cultural myths provide a set of ideal images, definitions, justifications, and measures for thought, feelings, and agency that work to render as unitary and certain the reality it seeks to produce. Myths provide a semblance of order, control, and certainty in the face of the uncertainty and vulnerability of the teacher's world. Given the emphasis on social control in the school context, order and certainty are constructed as significant psychological and institutional needs. In the case of student teachers, cultural myths structure a particular discourse about power, authority, and knowledge that heightens individual effort as it trivializes school structure and the agency of students. The problem is that when the power of individual effort becomes abstracted from the dynamics of the social, student teachers cannot effectively intervene in the complex conditions that push them to take up the normative practices that discourage their desires for change.

Cultural myths are persuasive because they reorganize contradictory elements of authoritative and internally persuasive discourse. They perform the work of discourse: communities are counted and discounted; particular orientations to authority, power, and knowledge are offered; discursive practices are made available; and persons are constructed or "interpellated" as noncontradictory subjects.

The idea of interpellation, borrowed from the work of Louis Althusser,[3] signifies the complex process whereby persons choose to identify with the ideologies that "summon" them; in turn they understand themselves to be the source rather than the effect of that summons. As Stuart Hall explains:

> Ideological discourses themselves constitute us as subjects for discourse. . . . [Interpellation] suggests that we are hailed or summoned by the ideologies which recruit us as their "authors," their essential subject.[4]

Student teachers are "summoned" by cultural myths—a language for describing who they might become and what they should desire—and through these myths, they recognize themselves as a teacher or feel as if they do not possess what it takes to become one. The real tension these myths attempt to dismiss is that there is nothing essential about who a teacher is or becomes. It is only through particular discourses that teachers can become viewed as possessing essential qualities. Other discourses offer different meanings. And there are always antagonistic discourses that urge particular dispositions at the cost of others. Consequently, no teaching identity is ever singular or without contradictions; the teacher's identity expresses a cacophony of calls.

The cultural myths, described below, contain such contradictions: they beckon and repel, promote and dispute, particular meanings about the work and the identity of the teacher. Three myths are examined below: everything depends upon the teacher; the teacher is the expert; and teachers are self-made. Each myth authorizes a discourse on power, knowledge, and the self that works to promote the impossible desire of assuming the self to be capable of embodying a noncontradictory subjectivity and capable of asserting a form of control that depends upon the individual's unambivalent acceptance of authoritative discourse. Such a desire makes no room for the complications we live.

Everything Depends on the Teacher

Implicitly, both teachers and students understand two rules governing the cultural tensions of life in compulsory education: unless the teacher establishes control, there will be no learning; and, if the teacher does not control the students, the students will control the teacher. This power struggle, predicated upon the institutional expectation that teachers individually control their classes, constructs learning as synonymous with control. Additionally, outside aid in controlling the class is perceived as a sign of professional incompetency.[5] Teachers tend to judge themselves, and others tend to judge them, on the basis of their success with this individual struggle. Everything—student learning, the presentation of curriculum, and social control—is held to be within the teacher's domain, while the teacher's isolated classroom existence is accepted as the norm. Isolation thus creates a strong pressure to recognize the learning of students as a product of social control. This pressure is especially problematic for the student teacher, who is, in actuality, engaged in her or his own process of learning while coming to terms with the contradictory effects of social control.

The conditions of spontaneity and the unexpected disrupt any attempt to predict the effects of teaching. But while they are significant features of the student teacher's lived experiences, the institutional push to present a stable appearance tends to make the student teacher perceive the unexpected as a "bind" rather than an opportunity. Consider, again, the voices of Jack August and Jamie Owl:

> Today was the day when I really didn't know what to expect. It *seems* as a teacher, you're going to have to react then and there. [Jack August]

> Quick thinking . . . getting myself out of the bind I'm in *seems* like a requirement in teaching. To be able to know, what next, what next. If something isn't working, or to make those transitions really fast to avoid unpleasant silences. [Jamie Owl]

Both Jack and Jamie invest in the belief that they must master the art of premonition and instantaneous response—both of which depend upon the teacher's ability to anticipate and contain the unexpected—to ensure control as a prerequisite for student learning. The problem is that within the push to control learning, the student teacher must devalue her or his own power to explore with students the dangerous territory of the unknown. At the same time, an essentialist view of the teacher is constructed:

Natural teachers apparently include those whose enthusiasm enables them to muddle through in spite of mistakes, and those who, by virtue of ballast and inhibitions, make no mistakes.[6]

Such a construct positions uncertainty as both a character flaw and a problem of management that can be solved by what inheres in the person. In either case, there is an attempt to evade the complicated uncertainty that realizes learning in the first place.

The pressure to control learning, however, affects more than the student teacher's practices. It also constructs views about knowledge and the knower. When the double pressures of isolation and institutional mandates to control force teachers to equate learning with social control, pedagogy is reduced to instilling knowledge rather than coming to terms with the practices that construct both knowledge and our relationships to it. Such pressures deny the webs of mutual dependency and the power relationships that shape classroom life. Consequently, the subtext of classroom life remains "unread" when the student teacher feels compelled to predict, contain, and thus control what is to be learned. Implicit in this stance is a mimetic theory of learning and of knowledge; students absorb the singular meanings of a work. Intertextuality, or the knowledge of other contexts and texts one brings to any new understanding, is unaccounted.

At the same time, this commonsense theory is continually disrupted by the complexity of classroom life. Students are never simply learners; they arrive in their classrooms already knowledgeable. And this knowledge never merely reflects a reality out there. Rather the knowledge of students always mediates how they understand the work of learning. The fact is, not everything depends upon the teacher, and when the teaching stance is constructed as if it did, the teacher's work becomes confined to controlling classroom life and exerting institutional authority as if it were pedagogical. The problem is that although both Jamie and Jack desired to be different and to construct themselves as nonauthoritarian in order to relate to their students as persons who are also struggling and learning, these student teachers felt the push toward asserting themselves as if they could be certain about the unknown and as if they had nothing to learn. Their attempt to take up such certainty limited their visions of the possible and made them feel like frauds.

Because Jack and Jamie defined as rigid the complex tensions embodied in the imperatives of social control, they constructed the teacher's identity as either tyrant or comrade. Each end of this spectrum of fear and desire is problematic: the tyrant imposes an autocratic rule, while the comrade discards all explicit rules. By rendering the teacher's identity dichotomous and by defining either end of this spectrum as unitary and noncontradictory, they could not consider the multiplicity of identities that they in fact embodied and that the contexts elicited. Nor could they come to terms with the fact that teachers already possess the power to authorize discourse. This prevented them from analyzing their own contradictory selves in ways that could work though such a dualist identity in order to consider the multiple choices that contradictions offer. Instead, they individualized these contradictions to a problem of ambivalence, not as a structurally induced dilemma. Ambivalence as a discursive process is not so much descriptive as conscriptive; to name a phenomenon ambivalent compels one to render practice into dichotomous categories and then view such categories as inevitable rather than understand them as the social constructions that they are.

In moments of ambivalence, Jack and Jamie vacillated between these two possible identities, and found that neither produced the intended results. Jack, for example, gave pop quizzes but allowed students to speak without raising their hands. Jamie gave tests, but refused to police them. Neither identity, however, could be embodied without contradictions. Nor were they sufficient for constructing creative, participatory, and relevant pedagogy, because such identities are only capable of defining students in terms of what they lack— authority or freedom—and of defining the teacher as the sole agent in the classroom. What Jack and Jamie were constituting was an unbearable pressure to perform as if teaching was a unitary and noncontradictory activity, and everything depended upon the presentation of a unitary self. And this desire, rooted in authoritative discourse, is impossible.

Their understanding of the teacher's identity also affected their relationships with students. Both student teachers desired to create a classroom that valued student participation. This was missing in their own education, and indeed each desired to return to their students what neither possessed. However, when Jack and Jamie responded to their students' concerns, desires, and investments, they did so on a deeply personal level and then vacillated between the incredulity that can accompany the unexpected and the despair that can shadow the unknown. Such oscillation became a part of their pedagogy.

For example, Jack and Jamie expected their students to act as they would act. This expectation framed their perceptions of classroom life. So when the students raised their own concerns, Jack and Jamie could only read them as the student's rejection—or acceptance—of what they saw as the teacher's humanity. The responses they offered to students could not get them beyond consideration of their own individuality. These student teachers were unable to render meaningful the multiple meanings and tensions that were already circulating in their classrooms. This was because Jack and Jamie were not provided the discursive practices that could ground their responses pedagogically. The myth that everything depends upon the teacher provokes this retreat into the self.

Moreover, the immediacy of classroom life and their valorization of the teacher's ability to respond in instantaneous ways inhibited Jamie and Jack's reflections on student participation. Participatory learning was within their reach but neither student teacher was encouraged to develop the research skills and pedagogical strategies required for cooperative learning. So despite their shared desire for their students to take responsibility and call out their own ideas, neither student teacher could consider the kinds of authorization and structure that sustains such a vision. Their dualistic constructions of the teacher's identity—as either tyrant or comrade—thwarted reflection into how their pedagogy worked to sustain a teacher-centered classroom despite their intentions to do otherwise.

For these student teachers, the sources of pedagogy either resided in the essential, noncontradictory self—built from the common sense that emerges from experience—or inhered in the curriculum, the work they could either dispute or promote. But because they took up the myth that everything depends upon the teacher, when things went awry, all they could do was blame themselves rather than reflect upon the complexity of pedagogical encounters.

The Teacher as Expert

One of the most commonly expressed fears of prospective teachers is that they will never know enough to teach. Two fears are collapsed into one: knowing how to teach and knowing everything there is to know about the material. The fear and anxiety rooted in not knowing what to do force the student teacher to look to teaching methods as the source rather than the effect of pedagogy. The "methods-as-an-end" discourse, discussed in chapter 2, attempts to objectify, as a technical problem, these subjective fears and thereby to render the unknown familiar by positioning pedagogy as the acquisition of "tricks of the trade" and suppressing the political commitments that structure every methodology. There is that socialized expectation that methods can be applied like recipes and somehow remain unencumbered by the specificity of the pedagogical act. The anxiety born from authoritative discourse pushes one to take up such meanings in unitary terms. However, this approach to practice cannot accommodate the fact that methodology always means more than mere application; there are effects—both intentional and unintentional—that require consideration of *how* something partially, contradictorily, and incompletely works. That is, these student teachers needed ways to understand how methodology can work against itself.[7]

The second fear, never knowing enough to teach, expresses the larger cultural expectation that teachers be certain in their knowledge and, that knowledge express certainty. Clearly teachers and their students must be able to work with meanings and construct sophisticated epistemological relationships. But this myth works to reduce knowledge to an immediate problem of knowing the answers.

The identity of the teacher as expert is problematic because student teachers dwell in two uncertain worlds: they are being educated as a student while educating others as a teacher. This doubling of identity works against the fact that both positions should be marked by the ability to be open to the unknown and a readiness to engage in interpretation as a precondition to knowledge. Recall the voices of Jamie Owl and Jack August:

> The pressure is there to know, whether it's from yourself, or the students, or other teachers. I mean there's a category on the teacher certification evaluation form: Is this person knowledgeable in her field? But when you're in the classroom, initially you're trying to prove yourself, and you want to know. Then someone asks a question. There is that tug. "Gee, why don't I know? I should know that." [Jamie Owl]

> I didn't have much of a background in history and felt just a few pages ahead of the students. It was kind of strange to be put into a position where I'm supposed to know something to teach people and I don't know it myself and I have to hurry up and learn it so I could teach them. [Jack August]

While these student teachers felt the pressure to know and the corresponding guilt in not knowing, in taking up normative discourses of classroom performance, they were prevented from attending to the deeper epistemological issues—about the construction of knowledge and the values and interests that inhere in knowledge. Instead, knowledge was reduced to a set of discrete and isolated units to be acquired, while not knowing, and indeed, any condition of uncertainty, became a threat to the teacher's authority. Such a vision does not show how the uncertain can open pedagogic opportunities.

Having been students themselves, teachers have taken up a view of knowledge overdetermined by classroom life and governed by the compartmentalization of curriculum. The combined effects of compulsory school—and university—education have naturalized the construct of the teacher as expert. Knowing answers appears to demonstrate the teacher's ability to "think on one's feet," seemingly a significant ingredient in the making of a teacher. Yet the valorization of thinking on one's feet can serve as a compensation for not being prepared enough. And a "command" of the material also becomes a powerful indicator of competency and skill. Thus student teachers look toward a future of certainty measured largely according to the "mastery" of content. So while, from the student teacher's standpoint, the veteran teacher appears to know the material backward and forward, knowledge, in this construct, is confined to the iteration of the textbook content, familiar because of years of use.

Many student teachers and the professionals who surround them, then, approach the problem of knowing not as an intellectual, emotional, and esthetic challenge, but as a function of accumulating classroom experience. The theory of knowledge asserted here depends upon stasis; knowledge is understood as unencumbered by values, interests, and ideology, and is handled as if it were transcendent. Acquiring classroom experience and therefore becoming an expert becomes the key to controlling knowledge and imposing it on students as a means of control. Yet as we have seen throughout this study, such rigid formulas do not work in practice; life intervenes.

The construct of the teacher as expert also tends to produce the image of the teacher as an autonomous and unitary individual and as the source of knowledge. From this standpoint, teachers seem to have learned everything and consequently have nothing to learn. As a possession, knowledge also implies territorial rights that become naturalized by the compartmentalization of curriculum. When knowledge is coupled with private property its alterity, the relations between the said and the unsaid and the relations between the self and the other, cannot be acknowledged. The irony is that such a construct sustains the discourse of common sense, where the tyranny of the obvious cannot call on itself to demonstrate its own contradictions. But any practice, as Catherine Belsey argues, is always theoretical:

> There is no practice without theory, however much that theory is suppressed, unformulated or perceived as "obvious." What we do . . . however "natural" it seems, presupposes a whole theoretical discourse, even if unspoken, about language and about meaning, about the relationships between meaning and the world, meaning and people, and finally about people themselves and their place in the world.[8]

The teacher as expert, then, is in actuality a normalizing fiction that serves to protect the status quo, heighten the power of knowledge to normalize, and deny the more significant problems of how we come to know, how we learn, and how we are taught.[9] The understanding that all knowledge is a construct and can thus be deconstructed and transformed by the knower is also disregarded. However, recognizing that knowledge can only take the form of a construction can open us to the dialogic, a discursive practice that can produce knowledge capable of deconstructing the discourse of common sense. Students can learn how social and historical practices produce and shape what is taken and refused as knowledge.

Teachers are Self-Made

The third cultural myth, that teachers are self-made, serves contradictory functions, for it supports the conflicting views that teachers form themselves and are "born" into the profession. This myth provides a commonsense explanation to the complicated problem of how teachers are made. It is a highly individualistic explanation that produces the construct of "the natural teacher." This natural teacher somehow possesses talent, intuition, and common sense, all essential features that combine to construct a knower as subjectivist. The valorization of these qualities diminishes reflection on how we come to know and on what it is we draw upon and shut out in the practice of pedagogy. In such an essentialist discourse, the historical forces and institutional structures that naturalize this particular brand of subjectivity are denied.

More than any other myth, the dominant belief that teachers "make" themselves functions to devalue any meaningful attempt to make relevant teacher education, educational theory, and the social process of acknowledging the values and interests one brings to and constructs because of the educational encounter. When applied to the struggles of the student teacher, the discourse of this particular myth appropriates the Christian symbolism, "baptism by fire." The circumstance of student teaching is thus viewed as a tortuous moment that tests the inner strength of the novice. A kind of social Darwinism is also sustained, where only the strong survive. But left out of this symbolism are the social forces that birth such a terrible context. While covering its own theoretical tracks, the myth that teachers are self-made structures a suspicion of theory, and encourages the stance of anti-intellectualism. And while this myth may be a contradictory response to teachers' real alienation from their firsthand experience with the decontextualized theory so often dispensed in teacher education programs, a larger consequence concerns the rejection of any concept of theory and the valorization of an essentialized self as the sole source of knowledge.

Instead of the effort to critique, produce, and ground theories, there is a pervasive expectation that the individual exhales everything that makes a teacher. For example, Jack August remarked:

> I think teaching is something that I'm going to learn how to do myself. Nobody is going to be able to teach me. You have to rely on your own experience. I think you have to do it and develop your own style.

But what does it mean to rely upon one's own experience? For Jack, as well as for many of the professionals who surrounded him, experience was viewed as the guarantee of meaning, and these meanings were thought to exist prior to their articulation. The problem is that experience becomes meaningful only after it is thought about, and after, as Stuart Hall explains, we reexamine it:

> It is in and through the systems of representation of culture that we "experience" the world: experience is the product of our codes of intelligibility, our schemas of interpretation. Consequently, there is no experiencing *outside* of the categories of representation. The notion that our heads are full of false ideas which can, however, be totally dispersed when we throw ourselves open to "the real" as a moment of absolute authentication, is probably the most ideological conception of all.[10]

In other words, Jack's reliance on experience is, in actuality, a reliance upon a particular discourse of experience that works to cover its own narrative tracks by valorizing what is constructed as authentic. For Jack, however, his experience seemed marked by obfuscation and consequently, because it was not transparent and telling, was discounted as inauthentic. Such logic is tricky in that it sustains itself even when it does not deliver what it promises: unmediated knowledge. While Jamie, on the other hand, understood the treachery of experience—the instability of meanings that work to decenter any unitary truth—her investment in teaching herself to teach also constructed the teacher as self-made.

In the supposedly self-made world of the teacher, pedagogy is positioned as a product of one's personality and therefore is replaced by teaching style. This teaching style, viewed as an extension of one's personality, functions to distinguish one teacher from the next and is valued as an important source of one's individuality.[11] Indeed, many in the field of teacher education promote the view that teaching style cannot be taught, but is considered a self-constructed product, mediated only by personal choice. The mistaken assumption is that somehow, teaching style metamorphoses into knowledge. In this discourse, teaching style becomes like a costume: one tries on different personae until the right one is found. Such a metaphor reduces pedagogy to its most mechanical moment. In the case of the student teacher, the problem is not so much that teaching style can reflect something about the individual as it is the mystification of the process whereby teaching style develops.

The professional legitimation of teaching style over pedagogy ignores both the social basis of pedagogy and the institutional pressure for teachers to exert social control. In reality, every pedagogy is influenced by the complex social relations among teachers, students, school culture, and the larger social world. Within compulsory relationships, contradictions and social dependency are inevitable dynamics, constructing an arena of struggle within which teaching style becomes subject to social negotiation. Teaching style, then, turns out to be not so much an individually determined product as a dialogic dynamic among the teacher, the students, the curriculum, the knowledge constructed in exchange, and the discursive practices that make pedagogy intelligible. Thus the myth that teachers are self-made serves to cloak the social relationships and the context of school structure by exaggerating personal autonomy. Like other myths, this one provides the final brush strokes on the portrait of the teacher as rugged individual: if one cannot make the grade, one is not meant to be a teacher.

The Dynamics of Biography

To understand the process whereby experience becomes meaningful requires that we situate ourselves in history and recognize as critical the relationships and intersections—both given and possible—of biography and social structure. Theorizing about such connections allows individuals a double insight into the meanings of their relationships to individuals, institutions, cultural values, and political events, and into how these relationships interpellate the individual's identity, values, and ideological orientations. This kind of insight can help individuals participate in shaping and responding to the social forces that affect, impinge on, and construct how experience becomes lived.

In the case of student teachers, understanding the contradictory dynamics of their own biography can help them to determine the interventions necessary to move beyond the sway of cultural authority. The concern should be with how we become entangled in and can become disentangled from the dynamics of cultural reproduction. And because education is always about interventions and the struggles of authorization—in the realm of the cognitive, the affective, the esthetic, the social, and the cultural—it behooves those learning to teach and those already teaching to rethink how social forces and dominant categories of meaning intervene in and organize their own lives and the lives of their students.

The exploration of biography, however, cannot be limited to the nostalgia of the personal or the rhapsody of the unique. Attention must be given to the historical contexts of the past and the present, and to the antagonistic discourses that summon and construct what we take to be our subjective selves. We are all situated by race, class, and gender, and without an understanding of the social meanings that overdetermine how we invite and suppress differences, the complexity of biography is reduced either to the dreary essentialism that beneath the skin we are all the same, or to the insistence that difference can be overcome through sheer individual effort. Each case depends upon the denial of history and the suppression of subjectivity. Each orientation is an effect of a discourse that covers its own narrative tracks.

It is significant that with few exceptions, the majority of the persons in this text did not speak about their own race, class, or gender. Indeed, initially, these categories become conscious only when one can situate the feelings of marginality, exclusion, and stigmatization, or the feelings of privilege, entitlement, and safety, as an effect of how race, class, and gender are socially defined and lived. Yet the nonsynchroneity of these social categories worked throughout their practices in ways reminiscent of the silences described in chapter 1. Certain things were not spoken about and these silences are significant. While I will briefly address why race, class, and gender were so absent from their stories, each of these social categories work through individuals in multiple and contradictory ways.

In the situation of race, part of the silence may well be because these persons worked and learned in racially segregated contexts where, as Caucasians, they were the norm, and consequently could not locate themselves as raced. Indeed, race became an issue only during times when individuals felt their own limitations, as in the case of Roy Hobbs during his student teaching. And there, race was constructed only in terms of antagonism, the implication being that in times of peace, race becomes insignificant. The curriculum, as well, contributes to such exclusions. Fitting in with what Ward Churchill calls "white studies,"[12] the hegemonic academic curriculum shuts out consideration of the controversial dynamics of race and racism by either presenting Caucasian views as universal, or obscuring the convoluted dynamics of race with its occasional parade of noncontradictory racial role models. Both directions, criticized elsewhere, either deny difference or position it as something to be overcome.[13]

In the case of class, although the majority of the persons in this study were from the working class, their professional and subjective identification were invested in the construct of individual effort rather than confronting their actual class location. Jamie Owl's burgeoning class consciousness is the exception. She was able to theorize about "the hidden injuries of class."[14] However, Jamie did not receive support in this theorization and consequently was left to vacillate between self-blame and anger. This was because the dominant discourse excludes from its account how the unequal distribution of knowledge and wealth affects educational inequality and the lives of persons and instead emphasizes the individual's power to break away from such constraints or the culpability of the individual who cannot.

While gender was always already a subtext of lived experience, it too seemed obscured by the value set on individual choice, which could apparently transcend the complicated meanings and beckonings of this social category. For example, because Jack August allowed classroom students to sit anywhere they chose, he did not find it significant that without exception the boys "chose" to sit in the front of the classroom, while the girls took seats in the back. Nor did he think it problematic that boys dominated classroom discourse. Instead, he attributed their behavior to individual personality rather than consider the social dynamics at work. In Jack's reasoning, these boys happened to be the ones who like to talk. For the men of this study, gender was not significant. Nor did they perceive the dominant social meanings of masculinity as constraining to them or as oppressive to others. Erma Tough, Edith Daring, and Alberta Peach, on the other hand, did understand sexism and in their respective strategies attempted to dissipate and rearrange the constraints they encountered. Whereas Edith Daring looked to legal redress, Erma Tough and Alberta Peach focused on the interpersonal.

Finally, while everyone in this study had a defined sexual orientation, we can easily surmise the heterosexual participants— those who nonchalantly mentioned their spouses and lovers—then surmise the homosexual and lesbian participants who chose not to make such a mention. A minor point like this is significant because the dominant assumption of heterosexuality works to undermine difference and the ways difference can and cannot be acknowledged. In addition, no one seemed concerned with the sexual politics and struggles of youth. This absence of self and social consciousness does affect the quality of possible interventions: if race, class, and gender do not matter, than racism, classism, sexism, homophobia, and so on, are not recognized as fashioning oppressive spaces that require intervention.

The suppression of the social categories we all embody has particular sources in the field of teaching. Value is set on treating everyone the same and this value works against the idea of differential treatment to redress past and present constraints. At the same time, teachers are also supposed to "shed" their own social casings and personal preferences in order to uphold the discourse of objectivity that beckons individuals as if they could leave behind the social meanings they already embody. This particular brand of "fairness" requires teachers to deny the historic oppressions operating in the larger world and working through their own subjectivity and encounter each student and each other as if they were unraced, unclassed, and ungendered.[15] The problem is that both the physicality of race and gender, and the conditions of class, are already overburdened with meanings that work on an unconscious level. To refuse the effects of such meanings does not banish them from the lived world of the classroom, or from the subjective world of teachers and students. Instead, the repressed always returns: the denial of difference is lived as the suppression of difference.

The cultural myths described above can help explain how difference becomes homogenized and how biography is never challenged. They can be considered as a way to come to terms with both the dissonance engendered by classroom life and the differences teachers attempt to mediate. Cultural myths are not so much mechanical recipes as they are authoritative orientations for interpreting. They work to interpellate the world of teachers and students. There may not be a direct correspondence between each myth and a specific pedagogy, but the underlying values that each myth supports summon us to conform to bureaucratic expectations while obscuring the more complicated process of attempting to live these expectations.

Certainly, cultural myths promote a view of the teacher as rugged individual, an identity that bestows valor on the lonely process of becoming a teacher, but at the same time suppresses the social meanings and forces that beckon the subject as a rugged individual. While individual effort is, of course, a necessary condition in learning to teach, so too are social negotiation, interaction, and social dependence. Yet the normative discourse of teacher education masks such complexity both by positioning the process of learning to teach as "sink or swim," and stigmatizing negotiation. Social interdependency is thus understood as a weakness, while a particular brand of autonomy becomes a strength.

The discourse of the rugged individual represents a familiar and admired legend in the dominant culture, a lesson, so to say, in the possibility of overcoming any inherited circumstance through sheer ingenuity and individual effort. Typically, this lesson rehearses economic success in the individual's ability to rise from "rags to riches," and promotes racelessness and genderlessness in the individual's choice to be viewed as unencumbered by social categories. For the rugged individual, any context—be it history, race, class, gender, or physicality—is positioned as if it were a mere handicap to be individually overcome. In this view, the rugged individual becomes competitive and possessive, uninterested in social change and obsessed with getting ahead. Thus the ideology that supports this construction of the individual as rugged is used to justify success or failure, all on individual terms. In other words, the rugged individual is a transcendental being, able to rise above the disorder of social life and be untouched by its dynamics and its beckonings. Such a construct infuses the individual with both undue power and undue culpability.

William Ryan, in his analysis of how social problems become individualized when social context and history are trivialized, aptly termed this ideology "blaming the victim."[16] Encouraged by the belief that the individual is solely responsible for what is in fact a product of complex social circumstances and forces, the discourse of blaming the victim ignores the ways history deposits its traces as antagonistic meanings. In the case of learning to teach, the cultural myths of the self-made, autonomous, expert teacher supports the ideology of blaming the victim and ultimately promotes a simplistic understanding of the operation of power in educational life.

These dynamics of cultural reproduction are made insidious by its involuntary nature. Student teachers do not set out to collude with authoritarian pedagogy. Nor do they desire to suppress their own subjectivity or those of their students. Just the opposite: they usually begin with intentions of enhancing student potential and find this intention thwarted by socially patterned school routines. As stated earlier, student teachers often describe their involuntary collusion with authoritative pedagogy as "learning what not to do," and hope that when they are the "real" teacher, they can somehow reverse this process because "real" experience will help them transcend past inadequacies. Consequently, Jack August, for example, blamed his lack of effectiveness on the circumstances of student teaching rather than on how structural conditions of the teacher's work compelled him to maintain the status quo. Student teachers thus see no way out of this reproductive cycle while they are student teaching. They possess no comparative perspective and lack both the prior experience in, and institutional support for, challenging the status quo and understanding how institutional constraints become lived practices. The irony of this dynamic is that cultural myths are evoked to serve not only as an "ideological escape," in that they function to preserve a facade of power in a seemingly powerlessness situation, but also serve as an "ideological trap," in that they sustain the teacher's isolation and naturalize the press for social control.

What does it mean to individualize the social process of teaching? Teaching is fundamentally a dialogic relation, characterized by mutual dependency, social interaction and engagement, and attention to the multiple exigencies of the unknown and the unknowable.[17] Individualizing the social basis of teaching dissolves the social context and dismisses the social meanings that constitute experience as lived. These forces are displaced by the supposed autonomy and very real isolation of the teacher in the current school structure. Once student teachers are severed from the social context of teaching, the compulsion is to reproduce rather than transform their institutional biography. The values embedded in the institutional biography become sedimented, and serve as the foundation for the uneasy acceptance of cultural myths that legitimize and render as natural hierarchical views of authority, knowledge, and power. Each of these dynamics works to normalize the institutional push for social control. The value of individualism, inhering in each myth, requires an overreliance on the self, which in actuality mandates an overdependence on one's institutional biography, since this part of one's biography is most familiar to the school context. Consequently, a significant social outcome of the individualization of learning to teach is the reproduction of school structure through pedagogy and the suppression of any differences that can move one toward a dialogic understanding of pedagogy and the self. A return to the complex forces that subjectively work through biography may well allow prospective teachers different choices in understanding and reconstructing their teaching selves.

POSSIBLE POSITIONS: TOWARD A DIALOGIC UNDERSTANDING OF LEARNING TO TEACH

What might it mean to take up the dialogic in teacher education? At first glance, the dialogic may remind one of the dialogue, the conversations between persons and the shared sense that communication is possible only through exchange. A concern with the dialogic, however, allows us to move beyond the conversation itself to attend to the conditions of its production: the words we choose, the way we reinflect them with past and personal meanings, the style used to position meanings, and the mix of intentions that are inevitable when speakers interact. And when we can consider what it is that conditions conversations, we can move away from the normative view that language is merely neutral and descriptive to the dialogical view of language as ideological and conscriptive. This understanding can help us begin to identify the kinds of discourse that are made available, and decide whether a discourse can provide the practices we desire.

A dialogic understanding, then, acknowledges this multiplicity: the ways talk, practice, and understanding are mediated by difference, history, point of view, and the polyphony of voices possessed by those immediately involved and borrowed from those who become present through language. Thus a dialogic understanding is one that takes into account contingency and simultaneity. For example, our attempt to tell the whole story is qualified by what can be said and the rules that govern the unsaid. The story is also refashioned by listeners who reaccentuate the voices of others with their own values. In this way, the dialogic suggests both simultaneity and difference.

This perspective on the dialogic, drawing upon the work of Mikhail Bakhtin,[18] allows us to move beyond dualistic perspectives and to focus, instead, on the polyphony of forces that interact, challenge, beckon, and rearrange our practices and the positions we take up in teacher education. We are invited to resign ourselves from the imperatives of finality and conformity, and view our practices as process and becoming. To retheorize our practices in teacher education, then, requires that we attend to the double problem of changing ourselves and transforming our circumstances.

Throughout this study, I have juxtaposed two simultaneous discourses in teacher education: the normative and the dialogic. My hope is that this juxtaposition will allow those in teacher education to understand that while the normative discourse is powerfully convincing, it is not immutable. The dualisms of the normative discourse are not the only choices available to those learning to teach and to those teaching teachers. Dialogic discourses can offer different ways to reconceptualize practice and, most significantly, attend to the complex vulnerabilities of lived experience in ways that move beyond essentializing the self and thus abstracting the individual from the social world. Discourses infused with the dialogic may also allow us to consider that the work of critique can encourage ways to construct public spaces that, in the words of Maxine Greene, "provision . . . opportunities for the articulation of multiple perspectives and multiple idioms."[19]

Admittedly, opening our critiques to include "what is not yet" is delicate work. Within the obligation to offer programs of change lurks the technocratic impulse, the desire to simplify the complexity of discursive practices and magnify the application of discrete techniques. The danger is that this impulse displaces the slower work of understanding how the immediate fashions our desires. My study is in the tradition of the slower work of constructing theories, of working through the repressive myths that interpellate subjectivity, and of theorizing what it is that structures discursive practices. At the same time, theories do not preclude consideration for practices. Indeed, the idea that practice makes practice is an argument for understanding the complex dialogue between practice and theory, biography and social structure, knowledge and experience, and difference and commonalities.

To understand the dialogic in teacher education, we must be concerned with the local—what happens in the everyday world of the university and the school—and with the global—the social forces that organize, surround, and summon its institutions. In both contexts, we must examine the discursive practices that sustain its structures in taken-for-granted ways. As I have argued throughout this study, teacher education does not begin and end once students walk into schools of education. There is an attempt at insularity in the university and in the school of education, but such insularity is continually disturbed by the contradictory realities these institutions attempt to stabilize. As we have seen, problems arise when such complexity is ignored or deliberately suppressed. My argument is that significant change in the field of teacher education is dependent upon a simultaneity of changes in the larger culture. Yet at the same time, institutions of teacher education have the potential to arrange their programs in ways that can make a difference in the quality of the everyday lives of students and teachers. There already exists small interventions, small changes, that must be acknowledged.

Toward the end of chapter 2, I introduced schools of educational practice that acknowledge the voices of those learning to teach. One example, the teacher-as-researcher, already provides opportunities and strategies for the newly arrived to reflect upon their teaching dilemmas by constructing and studying their narrative accounts and the narrative accounts of others. Researching our practices can produce knowledge about the specificity and contingency of the stories in educational life. The teacher-as-researcher movement offers the research strategies and the reflexive analytical skills that can encourage the development of sensitive practices. This approach, if situated politically, may also challenge the unhelpful dualism of objectivity and subjectivity as it positions as partners those learning to teach, those already teaching, and those working within teacher education. The intent of such collaborative work is to break down the isolation so endemic to the structure of experience in education and to transform the ways we understand how knowledge is produced. What becomes accessible are examples of how practice makes practice when teachers go about examining the nature of pedagogical knowledge.[20]

Three points are significant here. First, there are particular skills that the newly arrived must learn in order to understand the dynamics of classroom life in complex ways. Skills such as observation, taking on the perspective of others, identifying one's own deep investments in relation to others, analyzing instances of power and pedagogy, raising questions, and working with a range of interpretive strategies can move those learning to teach beyond the sway of institutional biography. Practicing such strategies and skills while researching their dilemmas can aid prospective teachers in their own design of meaningful pedagogy. Second, the identity of the teacher as expert can shift to one of inquirer when the teacher is also a researcher. Methodologies must be further developed to challenge not just the ways in which teachers work with students but the ways in which everyone involved can imagine who they are becoming. Third, when teachers view their work as research, it becomes more difficult to take the dynamics of classroom life for granted. Research does hold the potential to deconstruct the obvious. Yet such an approach to the teacher's work depends upon the search for meanings, an awareness of the politics of interpretation, and styles of theorizing that can open one to the unforeseen. Such directions require, as well, an understanding of the meanings we already hold and the consequences for the positions they inspire. This realization is not yet, however, a major force working through the teacher-as-researcher model. Indeed, the researcher's presence and investments must move from celebrating the unique to critiquing the problematic.

While viewing the teacher as a researcher can offer possibilities for reconceptualizing and acting deliberately in educational life and set up the conditions for discursive practices in the delicate work of extending one's educational voice, this work alone will not suffice. Prospective teachers need different opportunities to consider the perspectives of youth and how these perspectives differ from their own. Those who are learning to teach and those who are teaching teachers must have opportunities to consider the dynamics of education in contexts beyond the classroom. Everyone needs multiple opportunities to understand the contradictory investments, commitments, and styles of youth. Indeed, as long as the education of teachers is defined exclusively in terms of work in individual classrooms, teacher educators and prospective teachers will continue to have difficulties creating relationships between knowledge and experience, between schools and the larger social world. Therefore, programs of teacher education need to reconceptualize and extend the notion of classroom internships to include attention to and experience with youth cultures and the structures that sustain them.[21]

These briefly described interventions can only open opportunities for creative practices if those in teacher education explore simultaneously the dynamics of power and desire in educational life. Throughout this study, I have shown some of the problematic effects when the practice of power is understood solely in terms of individual choice or as an outcome of the social structure. Such a dualism cannot address power as a discursive practice. Biography and social structure are in dialogic tension, and this acknowledgement can begin to attend to the complications already embodied in the teacher's work. Linda Brodkey identifies such complexity: "To teach is to authorize the subject of educational discourse."[22] Brodkey's use of the term "subject" is dual: the subject as knowledge that is produced, and the subject as the author of knowledge.

Teachers possess the power to legitimate or refuse what can be spoken and who can speak. They have the power to authorize discourse as authoritative and internally persuasive. Teachers can work with their students to create an environment that is respectful of difference. How such dynamics act upon the actions of the students and the teacher must become a central concern to those learning to teach and to those who are teaching learners. Practice is productive: it produces and authorizes knowledge, identities, and voices, all of which persuade and are persuaded by relations of power. Thinking about practice and developing sensitive practices that can acknowledge difference and partiality, and extend the kinds of knowledge brought to and produced in educational life, is not beyond the reach of teacher education. Indeed, "to tolerate disruptions of the taken-for-granted," as Maxine Greene argues, is the beginning of education.[23]

These small changes may help make available discursive practices that open the pedagogic imagination. But larger questions must also be asked by those involved in teacher education. What would a utopia of teacher education be like? What kinds of identities might be made available? Would there be a separation between learning to teach and teaching? How would knowledge be organized and understood? Would there be schools? How might we redefine the work of teachers and students? What kinds of knowledge, imagination, and ways of being would be desirable? How might theory and practice be recognized and understood? If we could wake up tomorrow to a radically different structure that helped us throw into question all that we believe, how would we be different?

Everyone in teacher education needs the space and encouragement to raise questions that attend to the possible and acknowledge the uncertainty of our educational lives. For in doing so, we can begin to envision the discourses, voices, and discursive practices that can invite the possible.

7

"The Question of Belief"

The Hidden Chapter of *Practice Makes Practice*

"The things to look at," writes Edward Said, "are styles, figures of speech, setting, narrative devices, historical and social circumstances, *not* the correctness of representation nor its fidelity to some great original."[1] Readers are advised when encountering the texts of culture to consider both the structure of the narration and what it is that structures its modes of intelligibility. They are invited to question their interpretative glance. Such advice may seem strange when the text being examined is an educational ethnography. At first glance, ethnography seems to promise "fidelity to some great original," that is, to the original of culture. For those engaged in the doing and the reading of mainstream educational ethnography, more often than not, it is the "ethno" and not the "graphy" that seems to be the focus of attention. As a genre of research, I would note just three of its attractive and mythic "ethno" qualities. First, ethnography is both a process and a product; there are methods for how to go about narrating culture, and these social strategies promise a text. Second, good ethnographic texts tell stories that invariably embody qualities of a novel. Implicitly, ethnographies promise pleasure or at least new information to the reader. Third, an ethnography takes the reader into an actual world to reveal the cultural knowledge working in a particular place and time as it is lived through the subjectivities of its inhabitants. Easy access persuades readers that they can imaginatively step into this world and act like a native, or, at the very least, understand the imperatives of cultural assimilation. These textualized qualities appear seamless because they blur traditional distinctions among the writer, the reader, the stories, and how the stories are told.

These qualities of narrative are seductive in the power they bestow. There is a belief and expectation that the ethnographer is capable of producing truth from the experience of being there and that the reader is receptive to the truth of the text. In both instances, experience is "the great original." Ethnography assures us that there is both a "there" and "beings" who are there. Indeed, ethnographers claim to transpose their language onto something from "out there." In this way, the ethnographic text intends to translate, even as it is meant to stand in for, social life. The reader learns to expect cultural secrets and may well suppose that outsiders can become vicarious insiders.

An ethnography offers moments of empathetic power in the ways it positions cultural knowledge and in the ways it positions readers of culture. Private moments are rendered public, and the goal of understanding—albeit through secondhand knowledge—is assumed to be within the reach of readers. In this mainstream and modernist version, ethnography depends upon the rationality and stability of writers and readers and upon noncontradictory subjects who say what they mean and mean what they say. This is the straight version of Ethnography 101.

With the advent of poststructuralist theories, the above understandings need to be examined. The ground upon which ethnography is built turns out to be a contested and fictive geography. Those who populate and imagine it (every participant, including the author and the reader) are, in essence, textualized identities. Their voices create a cacophony and dialogic display of contradictory desires, fears, and literary tropes that, if carefully read, suggest just how slippery speaking, writing, reading, and desiring subjectivity really are. In poststructuralist versions, the realism of ethnography is taken as an effect of the discourses of the real; ethnography may construct the very materiality it attempts to represent. Poststructuralist critiques begin with assumptions of historicity and define ethnography as both a set of practices and a set of discourses. As an interpretive disturbance to the promise of representation, poststructuralists read the absent against the present. Thus, the ethnographic promise of a holistic account is betrayed by the slippage born from the partiality of language—of what cannot be said precisely because of what is said, and of the impossible difference within what is said, what is intended, what is signified, what is repressed, what is taken, and what remains. From the unruly perspectives of poststructuralism, ethnography can only summon, in James Clifford's terms, "partial truths" and "fictions."[2] In this ethnographic version, the authority of ethnography, the ethnographer, and the reader is always suspect.

Three kinds of ethnographic authority are being questioned here: the authority of empiricism, the authority of language, and the authority of reading or understanding. In the first case, what does it mean to disrupt what Paul Smith terms the "simple empiricism"[3] of ethnography, that there is a real out there to narrate and to read? When it comes to considering the authority of language and the seeming stability of meaning from which it derives, what happens to writing and to reading if we take as our place of departure T. Minh-ha Trinh's warning about the effects of writing: "Words empty out with age. Die and rise again, accordingly invested with new meanings, and always equipped with a secondhand memory."[4] What happens to the authority of reading—the presumption that there is a direct relationship between the reader's reading and the text's telling—if we begin with Althusser's (cited in Rooney) refusal of textual innocence: "There is no such thing as an innocent reading, we must ask what reading we are guilty of."[5] Can ethnographic writing provoke textual and methodological doubt when, as Paul Atkinson argues: "The ethnographic text depends upon the plausibility of its account?"[6] How does one believe the ethnographer, when, as Peggy Phelan theorizes: "In doubting the authenticity of the image, one questions as well the veracity of she who makes and describes it?"[7] If ethnographic authority depends upon a tacit agreement among the participants, the ethnographer, and the reader (that the story is real, the discourse transparent, and only the names have been changed to protect the innocent) and that agreement is always betrayed, how is the ethnographic pact effectuated? How does one understand plausibility and persuasion? If the relationship between the real and the representational is always in doubt, what is the basis of belief and identification?

These difficult questions surround the doing and the reading of educational ethnography. Today, educational ethnographies and writing about this genre are pushing at normative disciplinary boundaries in terms of what it is that structures methodological imperatives, the ethnographer's stances, and the ethnographic voice; the kinds of theoretical traditions through which data are constructed, represented, and narrated; what are taken to be problems suitable for ethnographic research; and, the problems of how one might read against the ethnographic grain.[8] Questions of subjectivity move beyond the stance of knowing how others make sense and toward a consideration of how reflexivity can be practiced when making sense of oneself is understood as occurring through the construction of the other.[9] Still other questions push against the very concept of reflexivity to consider the constitutive constraints of representation itself.[10] Ethnographic theorizing has become more tentative and less concerned with the old struggles of establishing authority as a way of research; it is more concerned with the archaeology of construction, the sedimentary grounds of ethnographic authority.

Poststructuralist theories raise critical concerns about what it is that structures meanings, practices, and bodies, about why certain practices become intelligible, valorized, or deemed as traditions while other practices become discounted, impossible, or unimaginable. For poststructuralists, representation is always in crisis, knowledge is constitutive of power, and agency is the constitutive effect, and not the originator, of situated practices and histories.[11] While it is beyond this chapter to provide more than a sketchy account of poststructuralism, my purpose is to explore how particular poststructural considerations have challenged me to think differently about pinning "the real" onto the ethnographic account and to theorize, in explicit terms, the politics of recounting and being accountable. While it might be discomforting to leave a sentimental ethnography that desires to represent without looking back, because ethnography is always about a second glance, it is necessary to consider what precisely this second glance might imagine.

Given the ethnographic real as a contested territory, in this chapter, I examine what is at stake in writing and reading this ethnography when one attempts to account for what Phelan terms "the question of belief"[12] in the real and in the representational. Are there ways to think the unthought of ethnographic narratives? That is, is there an ethnographic unconscious that marks its constitutive limits? Is there a knowledge ethnography cannot tolerate knowing? My concern is with what reading with suspicion—for both writers and readers of ethnography—has to do with how one might imagine the construction of ethnographic narrative beyond the naive faith that seeing is believing. Rather than critiquing someone else's study, this chapter is a form of speculative self-critique. I take the odd position of moving behind the scenes of my own ethnographic work to elaborate the theoretical and narrative decisions I made in producing my text. As a hidden chapter in my own ethnographic text, I offer thoughts about the narrative dilemmas unleashed when one attempts to write a poststructuralist ethnography or when one attempts to take seriously the problem of producing an account of social life that bothers the writer's and perhaps the reader's confidence in truth, in the visible, and in the real. While I retain the hope that ethnography can offer education a more complicated version of how life is lived, my concern is with the thorny issues unleashed when representation, however emancipatory, is acknowledged as crisis. Hence, I move back and forth between two related themes: conceptual issues in the study of the meanings of teaching and theoretical issues in the production of narratives structured within poststructuralist perspectives.

Poststructuralist concerns haunt this ethnographic research. With ethnographic data in hand, I decided to study these data (and hence the problem of learning to teach) as if I were reading a novel and, consequently, as if narratives of teaching were primarily a complex of contradictory interpretations and competing regimes of truth. I wondered what would it mean to read student teaching as if it were a text. Looking backward, my narrative desire was to write a Rashomon of student teaching, an ethnographic opera where voices argued, disrupted, and pleaded with one another; where the high drama of misunderstandings, deceit, and the conflicting desires made present and absent through language and through practice confound what is typically taken as the familiar story of learning to teach. I tried to write against the discourses that bind the disagreements, the embarrassments, the unsaid, and the odd moments of uncertainty in contexts overburdened with certain imperatives. I tried to do this by provoking and contradicting multiple voices: the ethnographic voice that promises to narrate experience as it unfolds, the hesitant voices of participants who kept refashioning their identities and investments as they were lived and rearranged in language, and poststructuralist voices that challenge a unitary and coherent narrative about experience.

In studying the lived experience of actual individuals but not wanting to individualize or render as a psychological problem the social disarray these individuals lived, I wanted to move beyond the impulse to represent the real story of learning to teach and attempt to get at how the constraints and frustrations of teaching are produced as the real story. Additionally, while the people in my study were actual persons, my intent was not to represent their actuality. Rather, taking the work of Foucault seriously, I wanted to trace how student teachers became an invention of the educational apparatus. Given the inordinate amount of research about this population, given the way the subject of student teacher is "an incitement to discourse," I became curious about how student teachers became a historical problem for education, how student teachers became constituted as a problem population. My interest, then, was to trace the invention of the student teacher, to explore: how this invention became viewed as synonymous with experience in education; how the subject position of student teacher was lived and fashioned in education; and why certain modes of intelligibility, such as the binary of theory and practice, became a central problem.

The tension I felt given these approaches to the study of teaching was between working with these theories and still writing an ethnography. That is, while educational ethnography promises the narrative cohesiveness of experience and identity and the researcher's skill of representing the subject, poststructuralist theories disrupt any desire for a seamless narrative, a cohesive identity, or a mimetic representation. Poststructuralism disturbs the ethnographer's confidence in knowing experience or in possessing the writerly power to do anything else but borrow discourses and tack them onto other discourses. So the simple fact of "being there" does not guarantee access to truth. Thus, the tradition of ethnographic authority derived from participant observation becomes a site of doubt rather than a confirmation of what exists prior to representation. These positions undermine the ethnographic belief that reality is somehow out there waiting to be captured by language.

In poststructuralist versions, subjects may well be the tellers of experience; but every telling is constrained, partial, and determined by the discourses and histories that prefigure, even as they might promise, representation.

To fashion narration with the imperatives of poststructuralism means that the researcher must become over concerned with experience as a discourse and with competing discourses of experience that traverse and structure any narrative. The ethnographic narrative must somehow acknowledge the differences within and among the stories of experience, how they are told, and what it is that structures the telling and the retelling.[13] Borrowing poststructuralist theories that bothered my ethnographic confidence, then, required that I work with language differently, that I admit how my own telling is partial and governed by the discourses of my time and place. These recountings cannot, however, ease or resolve the contradictions born in language, the discourses that bind and unleash meanings, and the real made present and absent by my efforts. Given these discursive boundaries, my writing could only point to the contradictions that structure the uneasy dialogue between humanism and poststructuralism, between what is taken as lived experience and the afterthought of interpretive efforts, between the real subjects and their textual identities.

I confess that I still have difficulty uncoupling myself from the persuasive promises of ethnography. I desire to construct good stories filled with the stuff of rising and falling action, plots, themes, and denouement. And yet, within the narrative tropes I chose to employ, there is a contradictory point of no return, of having to abandon the impossible desire to portray the study's subjects as they would portray themselves. Thus, I positioned myself behind their backs to point out what they could not see, would not do, and could not have said even as I struggled against such omnipotence. I tried to hold tightly to the ethic of not producing these subjects as persons to blame or as heroes of resistance. Instead, my concern was one of questioning how the categories of blame and resistance became discursively produced and lived. In textualizing their identities, I held on to the hope that readers would be compelled to ask the dangerous questions: What is it that structures my own stories and my own intelligibility? What do my moral imperatives cost?

Here, then, were my contradictory desires: to textualize identities at their most vulnerable moments, to speak about and for individuals by juxtaposing their words with my own, to dramatize the ordinary days that make time seem like no time at all, to *narrate development as a creepy detour*, and to persuade readers of the credibility of my interpretive efforts. I wanted to warn them that all I could offer were partial truths and my own guilty readings of other people's dramas. The space I attempted to open was one where experience could not speak for itself but could be considered as a category that bracketed and even performed certain repetitions, certain problems, certain desires. Within such a space, experience, like representation, was already divided from itself. Much of my work as a reader of what others did, in fact, questioned how that experience was structured, how what was constituted as experience was reminiscent of education's available and normative discourses. I tried to study the cost of experience.

The secondhand stories that I attempted to narrate were grounded in the worlds and the words of those who live in teacher education. My first attempts to build an ethnography were quite traditional. Like the good fieldworker-cum-ethnographer, I followed student teachers throughout their high school internships. Working under the old assumptions of ethnography, I viewed student teaching as ethnographically friendly because it had a beginning, middle, and end, and *that*, I thought, was a significant quality in any ethnographic account. Yet I was naive in constructing such an expectation. It prevented an interested reading of both the competing stories working through and against the narration of experience and the conceptual orderings of everyone involved that seem to position experience as seamless even while it was lived as disorderly, discontinuous, and chaotic.

While student teaching was bounded by a specific commitment, there was no correspondence among how chronology was being constituted by the participants, how I was constituting the ethnographic present, and how everyone involved was fashioning narrative unity. These multiple and simultaneous notions of time fashioned the subject of student teaching in particular ways. That is, neither the idea nor the identity of the student teacher was finished by the conclusion of student teaching. Time did not clarify what it meant to learn to teach. Instead—and this is where poststructuralism allowed me to rethink the very category of time—time itself, had become a discursive site of struggle. There was never enough time to do all that one wanted to do; student teaching went on for too long; it betrayed the promise of effective practices; the chronology of the curriculum could not account for existential time to think things through; and most discounted the time of student teaching as not quite real time. Working against such complexity was the construct of the ethnographic present, a sense of time that is frozen in the immediate and refuses to admit either competing chronologies or even to recognize chronology itself as a normative construct.

Within this twilight zone were the student teachers. A significant amount of interview talk and observational field notes focused their perceptions of their experience as student teachers. But a different sense of time fashioned how they talked about their educational biographies in relation to learning to teach. I came to this study with clear ideas about how educational biography is reproduced in learning to teach but, again, had not considered chronology itself to be problematic. Thus, I could not make sense of the contradictory process whereby the past is reinvented and textualized through the discourses and practices of the present. A linear and literal sense of time could not account for the ways in which student teachers produce their identities. And they do produce them, not as if they moved through an orderly experiential continuum, but as if identities already constituted a cacophony of beckonings and involuntary returns. Could an ethnographic narrative present the "secondhand memories" of student teachers rather than the student teachers themselves as the site of struggle?

My dilemma was how to organize but not normalize the stories of student teaching. In thinking about how to structure their narratives from interviews and field notes, knowing that I learned about their stories week by week, I decided not to mix their sense of time with the unfolding chronology that bound their own narrative truths. Doing so would give me too much power as an ethnographer. These student teachers built and rebuilt their identities with small and contradictory details because they were caught in an oxymoron called *student teacher*. Their first sense of chronology, however secondhand, was significant to them. Working under the old promise of representation, my first drafts of their stories detailed how they saw their world. But these early versions could not read how their very constitution of chronology impeded insight into who they thought they were becoming. The problem was that my first writing attempts represented traditional ethnographic structure, hence a humanistic ethnographic subject. My initial chapter titles said as much: "The Story of Jamie Owl" and "The Story of Jack August." Such phrases promised a unitary narrative, a noncontradictory and stable subject, and, of course, a cohesive account. The problem was that these narratives were traversed by competing story lines, contradictory representations of the meanings of learning to teach, and of subjectivities that refused to stand still. In trying to write a traditional ethnographic narrative, I had affixed "Jack" and "Jamie" to the unified subjects' positions of humanistic discourse despite the fact that they were continually becoming undone by the slippage of this very discourse.

To disrupt my own retelling, I rewrote each chapter, constituting my narrative to form a kind of photographic negative to theirs. I followed the photographic technique of Walter Benjamin: "The enlargement of the snapshot does not simply render more precise what in any case was visible, though unclear: it reveals new structural formations of the subject."[14] The new chapters were retitled: "Narratives of Student Teaching: Stories from Jamie Owl" and "Narratives of Student Teaching: Stories from Jack August." My hope was to reposition the site of struggle from the individual to their narratives and to pluralize their retelling to account for the competing stories, "new structural formations," and the hesitations of chronology that were made present and absent through their language. These contradictions of chronology, knowledge, and identity, as expressed in their words, structured the subheadings of each chapter. They tell the story in miniature. Jamie Owl's subtitles include: "Grand questions," "Should I stay or should I go," "I'm not a teacher," "A world without people," "Taking note," "Being noted," "Give them what they want," "Maybe I should go out in a blaze of glory," and, "School, school, school!" Jack August's subtitles include: "Shouting out ideas," "Keeping them on their toes," "How do you sway people?" "How am I supposed to judge class participation?" "Not really a teacher," "Finding gimmicks," and, "I was kind of sad when I cleaned out my desk." These phrases suggest a tentativeness; they allude to, in ways my own words could not, the uncertainty that cannot be uncoupled from the teacher's identity.

To heighten the detours of experience and hence to gesture toward experience as an unstable construct may well agitate traditional ethnographic notions of agency and voice. One of the values that originally attracted me to ethnographic research was the commitment to the participant as a knowing, intentional being, or, at the very least, to the assumption that cultural knowledge is produced within culture. The method promises to deliver voices that have been previously shut out of normative educational research and to remedy the ways educational research normalizes populations through its imposition of categories that situate individuals as the site of the problem. For many who do ethnographic work in education, there is the political commitment to the right to speak, to represent oneself, however partially; in this version, the ethnographer must be committed to advocating subjugated knowledge. However, these necessary commitments need not preclude an approach to representation that situates narrative efforts, as opposed to the narrators themselves, as a site of crisis.[15] Because representation cannot deliver what it promises, unmediated access to the real, ethnographers must think the categories of agency and voice beyond the humanist assumptions of a self capable of transcending history or a self that can somehow recover his or her authenticity from the unwieldy effects of discursive regimes of power and truth.

Whereas humanistic versions of agency and voice posit the subject as the originator and must, consequently, imagine the social, or the structural, or the historical as that which somehow distorts what should have been there all along, the version of agency and voice that I asserted began with the notion that as constructions these aspects of the self are provisional, contradictory, and ambivalent. Because in this version they are continually being fashioned in practices, agency and voice are the social effects and not the originators of history and of social relations. It is not the ethnographer's work to bestow or to disavow the verisimilitudes of others. Instead, the problem is to theorize the modes of intelligibility that constitute subjects. The problem is not one where the ethnographer authenticates a particular truth. Rather, the ethnographer traces, but not without argument, the circulation of competing regimes of truth.

In poststructuralist narratives, subjects cannot be uncoupled from the conscious and unconscious discourses that fashion how subjects become recognized and misrecognized. Every discourse constitutes, even as it mobilizes and shuts out, imaginary communities, identity investments, and discursive practices. Discourses authorize what can and cannot be said; they produce relations of power and communities of consent and dissent, and thus discursive boundaries are always being redrawn around what constitutes the desirable and the undesirable and around what it is that makes possible particular structures of intelligibility and unintelligibility. Feminist poststructuralist theories have been particularly helpful in describing this drama. They argue that by assuming people to be effects of language, knowledge, power, and history rather than their essential authors, a more provisional, historical, and ethical understanding of agency is possible.[16] The point is that if discourses construct and incite the subject and produce contradictory investments, pleasures, and knowledge, they can also be employed to deconstruct the kinds of naturalization that push one to take up the impossible moral imperatives of policing categories, insuring boundaries, and attempting to live the promises of a noncontradictory, transcendental self. Precisely because one's conceptual ordering of experience structures intelligibility and unintelligibility and because one's conceptual ordering of experience is an effect of discourse, one might also be able to begin to employ more suspicious discourses that exceed practices of normalization.

With these poststructuralist insights, I could position the sign of *student teacher*, as an oxymoron. I did this because those with whom I spoke were caught in a messy process of theorizing whom they were becoming when they were learning to teach. A word such as *teacher* is already overpopulated with other contexts; with other people; with competing forms of knowledge; and with desires, pleasures, and fears. Thus, the word itself constitutes both a set of discourses and a set of practices. Its contradictory meanings cannot be isolated from the speaker, the listener, or the histories and practices that over determine contexts of education and pedagogy. The problem is that, as a discourse and as a practice, the word *teacher* and the subject positions it produces always have the potential of producing disavowal within the subject who lives this discursive category as a crisis of representation.

Such theorizing, after all, may not make sense to the people behind my text. Indeed, there still remains the messy problem of whether the people in my text, if asked, would see themselves as inventions of discourses and as fragmented subjectivities. Most, if not all of my participants, were deeply invested in the humanistic notion of an essential self that had somehow been repressed by some condition, person, idea, or social structure. They all believed there was a real self to possess and to represent and yet, in a general sense, they viewed the context of education as a site that demanded they hold these real selves in abeyance. More particularly, the student teachers and those who surrounded them viewed the condition of student teaching as inhibiting real teaching. Like most people in teacher education, they were deeply invested in the idea that experience is telling, that one learns by experience, by being there, and not by theories. If this were not the case, why have such a long internship? If learning to teach does not come about through practice teaching, if schools are not the best places of teacher education, where does that leave us? I am getting at the inevitable tension, born from the theories that structured my narrations, that my interpretation will agonize what they take as their lived experience. And if ethnography authenticates representation, what does it mean to employ theories that call into question promises of representation and belief?

The only way I know around this teleology of representing "the great original" without falling into arguments regarding true and false consciousness is to revision the project of ethnography beyond the structuring regulations of the true and the false, the objective and the subjective, and the valid and the invalid. At the very least, it means approaching ethnographic writing as an effect of a contest of discourses, even if the ethnographer has the power to suggest what is at stake when identities are at stake.

The question of research as well will need to be rethought. As a sign, it can also be filled with provocations that disturb the impulse to settle meanings. I now think of ethnography as a regulating fiction, as a particular narrative practice that produces textual identities and regimes of truth. Such an approach admits a significant problem ignored by traditional ethnographic narratives, namely the inevitable tensions of knowledge as partial, as interested, and as performative of relations of power. This returns us to the clashing investments in how stories are told and of the impossibility of telling everything. There is that excess, that difference within the story, informing how the story is told, the imperatives produced within its tellings, and the subject positions made possible and impossible there. These signifying spaces must be admitted as central to the structure and regulation of ethnographic work if readers are to participate in exceeding and informing the meanings ethnography might offer. The reason we might read and do ethnography, then, is to think the unthought in more complex ways, to trouble confidence in being able to observe behavior, apply the correct technique, and correct what is taken as a mistake. Ethnographic narratives should trace how power circulates and surprises, theorize how subjects spring from the discourses that incite them, and question the belief in representation even as one must practice representation as a way to intervene critically in the constitutive constraints of discourses.

My guilty readings of the story of learning to teach began when I could admit my constructed categories and render them explicit, thus uncoupling my own voice from those of the participants in my study. Such guilty readings may well open my text to the charge of prescriptiveness, of judging the characters I constructed in ways that do not resonate with their own lived experience. There may be no escaping this charge because my own interested reading began with the belief that learning to teach is not simply about acquiring discrete and neutral skills, of reproducing the gestures of others, or even of developing a teaching style. Rather, the problem of learning to teach, like the problem of education itself, is a problem of which identities, which knowledge, and which practices might be offered and at what cost? The problem of learning to teach is also a problem of narrative and so, of inter- pretation. We can ask, how did things become the way they are? What would it mean to narrate our education as a question rather than a fate?

Writing ethnography as a practice of narration is not about capturing the real already out there. It is about constructing particular versions of truth, questioning how regimes of truth become neutralized as knowledge, and thus pushing the sensibilities of readers in new directions. If ethnography is to provide a critical space to push thought against itself, ethnographers must begin by identifying their own textual strategies and political commitments and pointing out the differences among the stories, the structures of telling, and the structures of belief. Put differently, educational ethnography and the writing of educational narratives might well begin to wander along what Samuel Delany terms as "the margins between claims of truth and the claims of textuality."[17]

These critical practices require something more of readers. Readers of ethnography must also be willing to construct more complicated reading practices that move them beyond the myth of literal representations and the deceptive promise that reality is transparent, stable, and just like the represen- tational. Poststructuralist theories of writing and reading may allow readers to challenge and rearrange what it is that structures the reader's own identity imperatives, the reader's own theory of reading that produces boundaries of the credible and the incredible. One's own structures of intelligibility might become open to readings not yet accounted for, not yet made. Perhaps the power of the writer and the reader can only reside in an awareness of the play of contradictions and the performances of power that both suture and unravel any ethnographic text. As a question of belief, reading and writing ethnog- raphy might provoke a different way of thinking, an ethic that refuses the grounds of subjectification and normalization and that worries about that which is not yet.

Notes

INTRODUCTION

1. For a discussion on the problem of social change and relevancy in teacher education, see Avner Segal, *Disturbing Practice: Reading Teacher Education as Text* (New York: Peter Lang, 2002). For a discussion on the difficulty of change in education, from the vantage of students and teachers, see Dan Yon, *Elusive Culture: Schooling, Race, and Identity in Global Times* (Albany: State University of New York Press, 2000) and for the difficulty of self transformation in learning to teach, see Kate Evans, *Negotiating the Self: Identity, Sexuality, and Emotion in Learning to Teach* (New York: Routledge, 2002). For a discussion on resistance to current events in teacher education, see the special issue of *Journal of Teacher Education,* "Teacher Education at the Turn of the Century: The Profession Responds," 51:3 (May/June 2000).

2. For a history of changing curriculum and the accompanying difficulties change represents, see William Pinar, William Reynolds, Patrick Slatter and Peter Taubman, *Understanding Curriculum: An Introduction to the Study of Historical and Contemporary Curriculum Discourses* (New York: Peter Lang, 1995).

3. Siegfried Bernfeld, *Sisyphus or the Limits of Education,* trans. Frederic Lilge (Berkeley: University of California Press, 1973), 3.

4. William James, *Talks to Teachers on Psychology: and to Students on Some of Life's Ideals* (Cambridge: Harvard University Press, 1983).

5. Ibid., 151.

6. Anna Freud, "Four Lectures on Psychoanalysis for Teachers and Parents (1930)," in *The Writings of Anna Freud, Volume 1 1922–1935* (New York: International Universities Press, 1974), 73–136. I explore the phenomenon of interference in *Lost Subjects, Contested Objects: Toward a Psychoanalytic Inquiry of Learning* (Albany: State University of New York Press, 1998).

7. Immanuel Kant's "Lecture-Notes on Pedagogy," was first edited by one of his students, Friedrich Theodor Rink in 1808. Rink situates Kant's views on education somewhere between anthropology and philosophy. (For Rink's introduction and Kant's lecture notes, see *The Educational Theory of Immanuel Kant,* trans. Edward Franklin Buchner (Philadelphia: J.B. Lippincott Company, 1904), 101. Jean-Jacques Rousseau's

Emile or On Education was published in 1762. See Jean-Jacques Rousseau, *Emile or On Education*, trans. Allan Bloom (New York: Basic Books, 1979), 61.

8. Theodor Adorno, *Critical Models: Interventions and Catchwords*, trans. Henry Pickford (New York: Columbia University Press, 1998).

9. Hannah Arendt, "The Crisis in Education," in *Between Past and Future: Eight Exercises in Political Thought* (New York: Penguin, 1993), 173–196.

10. Ibid., 185.

11. Maxine Greene, "The Matter of Mystification: Teacher Education in Unquiet Times," in *Landscapes of Learning*, 53–73 (New York: Teachers College Press, 1978), 70.

12. Shoshana Felman, "Education and Crisis, Or the Vicissitudes of Teaching," in *Testimony: Crises of Witnessing in Literature, Psychoanalysis, and History*, Shoshana Felman and Dori Laub (New York: Routledge, 1992), 1–56.

13. Ibid., 1.

14. Leo Tolstoy, *Anna Karenina*, trans. Richard Pevear and Larissa Volokhonsky (New York: Viking, 2001), 1.

15. Sigmund Freud, "The Dynamics of Transference (1912)," in *Standard Edition*, vol. 12 (London: Hogarth Press, 1968), 97–108.

16. Paula Treichler, "AIDS, Homophobia, and Biomedical Discourse: An Epidemic of Signification," in *AIDS: Cultural Analysis, Cultural Activism*, ed. Douglas Crimp (Boston: MIT Press, 1988), 31–71.

17. Maxine Greene, *The Public School and the Private Vision: A Search for America in Education and Literature* (New York: Random, 1965), 114.

18. For an excellent study of the fragmentation of curriculum and its epistemological history, see John Willinsky, *Learning to Divide the World: Education at Empire's End* (Minneapolis: University of Minnesota Press, 1998).

19. Julia Kristeva, *Hannah Arendt*, trans. Ross Guberman (New York: Columbia, 2001), 43–45.

CHAPTER ONE

1. Willard Waller, *The Sociology of Teaching* (New York: Russell and Russell, 1961).

2. Walter Benjamin, "Theses on the Philosophy of History," in *Iluminations*, Hannah Arendt, ed. (New York: Schocken Books, 1969), 257.

3. Maxine Greene, "Excellence, Meanings and Multiplicity," *Teachers College Record* 86 (1984): 283.

4. Dan Lortie, *Schoolteacher: A Sociological Study* (Chicago: University of Chicago Press, 1975), 61.

5. Ibid., 62.

6. Robert Everhart, *Reading, Writing and Resistance* (New York: Routledge and Kegan Paul, 1983), 74.

7. For a discussion of personal practical knowledge, see Michael Connelly and D. Jean Clandinin, "Teachers' Personal Practical Knowledge at Bay Street School: Ritual, Personal Philosophy and Image," in *Teacher Thinking: A New Perspective on Persistent Problems in Education*, R. Halkaes and J. K. Olson, eds. (Heirewig, Holland: Swets Publishing Service, 1984), 134–48. Also see D. Jean Clandinin, "Personal Practical Knowledge: A Study of Teachers' Classroom Images," *Curriculum Inquiry* 15:4 (1985): 361–85 and E. Michael Connelly and D. Jean Clandinin, *Teachers as Curriculum Planners: Narratives of Experience* (New York: Teachers College Press, 1988). For a significant critique on personal practical knowledge as a discourse, see John Willinsky, "Getting Personal and Practical with Personal Practical Knowledge," *Curriculum Inquiry* 19:3 (Fall 1989): 247–64.

8. I have encountered these characteristics of style, often attributed to teachers, in my own practice as a public school teacher, and presently as a university professor.

9. By the establishment of the common school movement (1883), women constituted the overwhelming majority of its trainee population and thus the actual teachers. Two related factors are used to explain the number of women who entered teaching through the normal school in the nineteen century: (1) women were a source of cheap labor; and (2) the prevailing ideology of domesticity essentialized women as natural teachers of children because of their biology. It is also noted that although women were the primary teaching labor force, they rarely achieved managerial status. To this date, teaching, for women, constitutes a "universal job ghetto." See Joni Seager and Ann Olson, *Women in the World: An International Atlas* (New York: Simon and Schuster, 1986), 16. For critical analyses of women and teaching, see Sarah Freedman, Jane Jackson, and Katherine Boles, "The Other End of the Corridor: The Effect of Teaching on Teachers," *Radical Teacher* 23 (1982): 2–23, and Madeleine Grumet, "Pedagogy for Patriarchy: The Feminization of Teaching," *Interchange* 12 (1981): 165–84.

10. Waller, *Sociology of Teaching*, 419.

11. For a critical discussion of the contradictory views of professionalism and how these images shape preservice students' responses to collective union activity, see Mark Ginsburg, "Reproduction, Contradiction and Conceptions of Professionalism: The Case of Pre-Service Teachers," in *Critical Studies in Teacher Education: Its Folklore, Theory and Practice*, Thomas Popkewitz, ed. (Philadelphia: Falmer Press, 1987), 86–129.

12. Carolyn Steedman, *The Tidy House: Little Girls' Writing* (London: Virago Press, 1982), 6–7.

13. For a study that illuminates the "category maintenance work" children and adults do to maintain hegemonic notions of gender, see Brownyn Davies, *Frogs and Snails and Feminist Tales: Preschool Children and Gender* (Sydney: Allen and Unwin, 1989).

14. For a discussion of the teacher as transformative intellectual, see Stanley Aronowitz and Henry Giroux, *Education Under Siege: The Conservative, Liberal and Radical Debate over Schooling* (S. Hadley, Mass.: Bergin and Garvey, 1985).

15. Sherry Turkle, *Psychoanalytic Politics: Freud's French Revolution* (New York: Basic Books, 1978), 19.

16. Roland Barthes, "Myth Today," in *Mythologies* (New York: Hill and Wang, 1985), 109–58.

17. Ibid., 117.

18. For a lucid discussion on the discourse of common sense, see Catherine Belsey, *Critical Practice* (New York: Methuen, 1980).

19. James Donald, "Language, Literacy, and Schooling," in *The State and Popular Culture* (Milton Keynes: Open University Press, 1987), 59.

20. Linda Brodkey, *Academic Writing as Social Practice* (Philadelphia: Temple University Press, 1987), 83.

21. Clifford Geertz, *Local Knowledge: Further Essays in Interpretive Anthropology* (New York: Basic Books, 1983), 26.

22. Roger Simon and Donald Dippo, "On Critical Ethnographic Work," *Anthropology and Education Quarterly* 17 (1986): 196.

23. See chapter 7, "Curriculum Theory and the Language of Possibility," in Aronowitz and Giroux, *Education Under Siege*, 139–62. Also see Walter Benjamin, "The Work of Art in the Age of Mechanical Reproduction," in *Illuminations*, 217–52. For a discussion on the mystifying powers of language, see the cultural criticism of Ariel Dorfman, *The Empire's Old Clothes: What the Lone Ranger, Babar, and Other Innocent Heroes Do to Our Minds* (New York: Pantheon Books, 1983).

24. Uma Narayan, "Working Together Across Difference: Some Considerations on Emotions and Political Practice," *Hypatia* 3 (Summer 1988): 38.

25. Raymond Williams, *The Long Revolution: An Analysis of the Democratic, Industrial, and Cultural Changes Transforming Our Society* (New York: Columbia University Press, 1961), 48.

26. Brodkey, *Academic Writing*, 49.

27. The ways in which the ethnographic narrative covers its own narrative tracks is wonderfully analyzed by Mary Louise Pratt, "Scratches on the Face of the Country; or, What Mr. Barrow Saw in the Land of the Bushman," in *"Race," Writing and Difference*, Henry Louis Gates, ed. (Chicago: University of Chicago Press, 1986), 138–62. Also see Trinh T. Minh-ha, *Woman, Native, Other: Writing Postcoloniality and Feminism.* (Bloomington: Indiana University Press, 1989).

28. Turkle, *Psychoanalytic Politics*, 50.

29. Brodkey, *Academic Writing*, 90. For an illuminating discussion of the problematic of ethnography, see Linda Brodkey, chapter 2, *Academic Writing*. There Brodkey identifies one of the most significant tensions of ethnographic work: "The controversy raised by ethnographic narratives is whether the data are interpreted or analyzed, or put another way, whether the researcher or the research methodology is telling the story" (84).

30. For a discussion of the ethics of the researcher's participation in research, see Patti Lather, "Research as Praxis," *Harvard Educational Review* 46 (1986): 257–77, and Mary Savage, "Can Ethnographic Narrative Be a Neighborly Act?" *Anthropology and Education Quarterly* 19 (1988): 3–19. For exemplary examples of the educator's participation in her own research, see D. Jean Clandinin, *Classroom Practices: Teacher Images in Action* (Philadelphia: Falmer Press, 1986), Shirley B. Heath, *Way with Words: Language, Life and Work in Communities and Classrooms* (Cambridge: Cambridge University Press, 1983), and Janet L. Miller, *Creating Spaces and Finding Voices: Teachers Collaborating for Empowerment* (Albany: State University of New York Press, 1990).

31. Linda Alcoff, "Cultural Feminism Versus Poststructuralism: The identity crisis in Feminist theory," *Signs* 13 (1988): 433.

32. Henry Giroux, *Theory and Resistance in Education: A Pedagogy for the Opposition* (S. Hadley, Mass.: Bergin and Garvey, 1983), 172.

33. Michel Foucault, *The History of Sexuality: Volume I* (New York: Vintage, 1980).

34. Ibid., 27.

35. Anthony Giddens, *Central Problems in Social Theory: Action, Structure and Contradictions in Social Analysis* (Berkeley: University of California Press, 1979/1986), 83.

36. Popkewitz, "Ideology and Social Formation in Teacher Education," in *Critical Studies in Teacher Education*, 5.

37. Giddens, *Central Problems in Social Theory*, 91.

38. Ibid., 83.

39. Adrienne Rich, "Foreword: On History, Illiteracy, Passivity, Violence and Women's Culture," in *On Lies, Secrets, and Silence: Selected Prose 1966–1978* (New York: Norton, 1979), 11.

40. Ibid., 11.

41. Tilly Olsen, *Silences* (New York: Dell, 1979), 7.

42. Karl Marx, *The Eighteenth Brumaire of Louis Bonaparte* (New York: International Publishers, 1981), 15.

43. Noelle Bisseret, *Education, Class, Language and Ideology* (London: Routledge and Kegan Paul, 1979), 1.

44. M. M. Bakhtin, "Discourse in the Novel," in *The Dialogical Imagination*, M. Holquist, ed. (Austin: University of Texas Press, 1981), 341–42.

45. Ibid., 344.

46. A rash of national reports on the status of education—such as the National Commission on Excellence in Education, "A Nation at Risk: The Imperative for Educational Reform" (Washington, D.C.: Government Printing Office, 1983)—call for a return to authoritarian forms of education. For a critique of these reports, see

Michael Apple, *Teachers and Texts: A Political Economy of Class and Gender Relations in Education* (New York: Routledge and Kegan Paul, 1986) and Catherine Cornbleth and Ester Gottlieb, "Reform Discourse and Curriculum Reform," *Educational Foundations* 3 (Fall 1989): 63–78. For a discussion of conservative tendencies in education, see Henry Giroux, *Schooling and the Struggle for Public Life: Critical Pedagogy in the Modern Age* (Minneapolis: University of Minnesota Press, 1988).

47. Bakhtin, *Dialogical Imagination,* 342.

48. Ibid., 346.

49. Ibid., 293–94.

50. Wendy Hollway, "Fitting Work: Psychological Assessment in Organizations," in *Changing the Subject: Psychology, Social Regulation and Subjectivity,* Jules Henriques, Wendy Hollway, Cathy Urwin, Couze Venn, and Valerie Walkerdine, eds. (London: Methuen, 1984), 26.

CHAPTER TWO

1. George S. Counts, "Break the Teacher Training Lockstep," *Social Frontier* 1 (June 1935): 6–7. Reprinted in *Teacher Education in America: A Documentary History,* Merle L. Borrowman, ed. (New York: Teachers College Press, 1965), 218–23.

2. Ibid., 221.

3. Cited in Herbert Kliebard, *The Struggle for the American Curriculum, 1893–1958* (Boston: Routlege and Kegan Paul, 1986), 134.

4. Harold Rugg, *The Teacher of Teachers: Frontiers of Theory and Practice in Teacher Education* (Westport, Conn.: Greenwood Press, 1970), 22.

5. Seymour Sarason, K. Davidson, and B. Blatt, *The Preparation of Teachers* (New York: John Wiley, 1962), 7.

6. Hannah Arendt, *The Human Condition* (Chicago: University of Chicago Press, 1958), 41.

7. For a discussion of the vocational roots of teacher education, see Beverly Gordon, "Teaching Teachers: Nation at Risk and the Issue of Knowledge in Teacher Education," *Urban Review* 17 (1985): 33–46, and Merle Borrowman, *The Liberal and the Technical in Teacher Education* (Westport, Conn.: Greenwood Press, 1956).

8. Maxine Greene, "The Matter of Mystification: Teacher Education in Unquiet Times," in *Landscapes of Learning* (New York: Teachers College Press, 1978), 53–73.

9. Thomas Popkewitz, "The Formation of School Subjects and the Political Context of Schooling," in *The Formation of School Subjects: The Struggle for Creating an American Institution* (New York: Falmer Press, 1987), 16.

10. For a detailed discussion of the role of psychology and scientific management in education, see Herbert Kliebard, *The Struggle for the American Curriculum;* Michael Apple, *Ideology and Curriculum* (Boston: Routledge and Kegan Paul, 1979); Barry

Franklin, *Building the American Community: The School Curriculum and the Search for Social Control* (London: Falmer Press, 1986); and Cleo Cherryholmes, *Power and Criticism: Poststructural Investigations in Education* (New York: Teachers College Press, 1988).

11. For a brief discussion of the ideological investments of the Enlightenment, see Jane Flax, "Postmodernism and Gender relations in Feminist Theory," *Signs: Journal of Women in Culture and Society* 12:4 (Summer 1987): 621–43.

12. Kliebard, *The Struggle for the American Curriculum,* 1.

13. Giroux, *Theory and Resistance in Education,* 176–78.

14. Borrowman, *The Liberal and Technical in Teacher Education,* 99.

15. Randall Collins, *The Credential Society: An Historical Sociology of Education and Stratification* (New York: Academic Press, 1979), 129–30.

16. See Apple, *Ideology and Curriculum,* 6.

17. For a discussion of conservative and reconstructionist movements in the education of teachers and students, see chapter 1 in Giroux, *Schooling and the Struggle for Public Life.*

18. John Dewey, *Experience and Education* (New York: Collier Books, 1972), 33.

19. Ibid., 38.

20. Ibid., 39.

21. Greene, *Dialectic of Freedom,* 23.

22. For an illuminating discussion of the discourse of school subjects, see Popkewitz, *The Formation of School Subjects.*

23. Williams, *The Long Revolution,* 53.

24. Philip Wexler, "Structure, Text, and Subject: A Critical Sociology of School Knowledge," in *Cultural and Economic Reproduction in Education: Essays on Class, Ideology and the State,* Michael Apple, ed. (Boston: Routledge and Kegan Paul, 1982), 283.

25. Ibid., 287.

26. James Donald, "Green Paper: Noise of Crises," *Screen Education* 30 (Spring 1979): 17.

27. Popkewitz notes: "By the first two decades of the twentieth century the universities had taken a direct role in the forming of the school curriculum." In *The Formation of School Subjects,* 14.

28. For an insightful discussion of the relationship between fields of knowledge and academic socialization, see Edward Said, "Opponents, Audiences, Constituencies and Community" in *The Anti-Aesthetic: Essays on Postmodern Culture,* Hal Foster, ed. (Port Townsend, Wash.: Bay Press, 1983), 135–59. In this essay Said traces the depoliticalization of academic knowledge and how this process determines compartmentalization. Said is worth quoting on this point:

It is assumed that the skills traditionally associated with modern literary criticism ... are there to be applied to *literary* texts, not, for instance, to a government document, a sociological or ethnological report or a newspaper. This separation of fields, objects, disciplines and foci constitutes an amazingly *rigid* structure which, to my knowledge, is almost never discussed by literary scholars. There seems to be an unconsciously held norm guaranteeing the simple essence of "fields," a word which in turn has acquired the intellectual authority of a natural, objective fact. Separation, simplicity, silent norms of pertinence: this is one depoliticizing strain of considerable force, since it is capitalized on by professions, institutions, discourses and a massively reinforced consistency of specialized fields. [146]

29. For a discussion of the historic development of liberal studies and the schisms between liberal studies and educational studies, see chapters 1 and 2 of Landon Beyer, *Knowing and Acting: Inquiry, Ideology and Educational Studies* (New York: Falmer Press, 1988). Beyer analyzes the disparities between liberal studies and applied studies, and historically traces how educational studies have become subordinated to the goals of liberal learning.

30. David Lusted, "Why Pedagogy?," *Screen* 27 (Sept.–Oct. 1986): 2–3.

31. Mina Shaughnessy, "Diving In: An Introduction to Writing," in *Reclaiming the Classroom: Teacher Research as an Agency for Change,* Dixie Goswami and Peter Stillman, eds. (Upper Montclair, New Jersey: Boyton/Cook Publishers, 1987), 69.

32. Ibid., 70.

33. Barbara Schneider, "Tracing the Provenance of Teacher Education," in *Critical Studies in Teacher Education,* 212.

34. Seager and Olson, *Women in the World,* 33.

35. Henry Giroux and Roger Simon, "Curriculum Study and Cultural Politics," *Journal of Education* 166 (Fall 1984): 231.

36. R. W. Connell, *Teachers' Work* (Sidney, Australia: George Allen and Unwin, 1985), 87.

37. Williams, *The Long Revolution,* 50.

38. Adeline Morris, "Dick, Jane and American Literature: Fighting with Canons," *College English* 47 (Sept. 1985): 467–81.

39. Barbara Herrnstein Smith. "Contingencies of Value," *Critical Inquiry* 10 (1983): 2. For a discussion of how values shift to preserve a particular view of the literary, see Donald Morton and Mas'ud Zavazadeh, "The Cultural Politics of the Fiction Workshop," *Cultural Critique* (Winter 1988–1989): 155–73.

40. Ibid., 26. For a more elaborate discussion, see Barbara Herrnstein Smith, *Contingencies of Value: Alternative Perspectives for Critical Theory* (Cambridge: Harvard University Press, 1988).

41. Manuel Alvarado and Bob Ferguson, "The Curriculum, Media Studies and Discursivity: A Reconsideration of Educational Theory," *Screen* 24 (May–June 1983): 29.

42. Ibid., 29.

43. Geoff Whitty, *Sociology and School Knowledge: Curriculum Theory, Research and Politics* (London: Methuen, 1985), 17.

44. See, for example, Jean Anyon, "Social Class and School Knowledge," *Curriculum Inquiry* 11 (Spring 1981); Apple, *Ideology and Curriculum;* and Giroux, *Theory and Resistance in Education.*

45. These researchers have all suggested school culture as productive. Classroom actors have the creative capacity to produce discourses and practices that are not only other than those anticipated and expected, but are ones that contest modes of domination. This is the productive sense. But school culture is also reproductive in that the dominant meanings and social relationships supportive of the social structure are legitimized and perpetuated by school practice. By considering both movements in dialogic tension, these theorists attempt to move from a simple transmission model of culture to a more complex and contradictory representation. Borrowing from some of the theories of poststructuralism, these researchers also advocate skepticism toward conventional views on the singularity of knowledge, truth, power, and language, and the dismantlement of the stable conceptions of meaning, identity, and subjectivity. See, for example, Peter McLaren, *Schooling as Ritual Performance* (Boston: Routledge and Kegan Paul, 1986); Henry Giroux, *Schooling and the Struggle for Public Life;* Michael Apple, *Teachers and Texts;* Cleo Cherryholmes, *Power and Criticism;* and the collection of articles in *Becoming Feminine: The Politics of Popular Culture,* Leslie Roman, Linda Christian-Smith, and Elizabeth Ellsworth, eds. (New York: Falmer Press, 1988).

46. Wexler, "Structure, Text, and Subject," 286.

47. Linda McNeil, *Contradictions of Control: School Structure and School Knowledge* (New York: Routledge and Kegan Paul, 1986), 191.

48. See, for example, Landon Beyer, "Aesthetic Experience for Teacher Preparation and Social Change," *Educational Theory* 35 (Fall 1985): 385–87; Margaret Buchmann and J. Schwille, "Education: The Overcoming of Experience," *American Journal of Education* 92 (Nov. 1983): 30–51; Martyn Descombe, "The Hidden Pedagogy and Its Implications for Teacher Training," *British Journal of Sociology of Education* 3 (1982): 249–65.

49. Robert Tabachnick, "Intern-Teacher Roles: Illusion, Disillusion and Reality," *Journal of Education* 162 (1980): 122–37.

50. Mark Ginsburg, "Reproduction, Contradictions, and Conceptions of Curriculum in Preservice Teacher Education," *Curriculum Inquiry* 16 (Fall 1986): 287. For an extended discussion of these student teachers and for a thorough analysis of the context of their teacher education and the social contradictions that structure their work, see Mark Ginsburg, *Contradictions in Teacher Education and Society: A Critical Analysis* (New York: Falmer Press, 1988).

51. Ibid., 298.

52. Descombe, "Hidden Pedagogy and Its Implications," 250.

53. See, for example, D. Jean Clandinin, *Classroom Practice;* E. Michael Connelly and D. Jean Clandinin, "Personal Practical Knowledge and the Modes of Knowing: Relevance for Teaching and Learning," in *Learning and Teaching the Ways of Knowing,* Elliott Eisner, ed., 84th Yearbook of the National Society for the Study of Education (Chicago: University of Chicago Press, 1985), 174–98; E. Michael Connelly and D. Jean Clandinin, *Teachers as Curriculum Planners;* and Freema Elbaz, *Teacher Thinking: A Study of Practical Knowledge* (New York: Nichols Publishing, 1983).

54. Connelly and Clandinin, "Personal Practical Knowledge and the Modes of Knowing," in Eisner, *Learning and Teaching the Ways of Knowing.*

55. Clandinin, "Personal Practical Knowledge," 361.

56. Ibid., 362.

57. Peter Woods, "Life Histories and Teacher Knowledge," in *Educating Teachers: Changing the Nature of Pedagogical Knowledge,* John Smyth, ed. (London: Falmer Press, 1987), 122.

58. See C. Wright Mills, chapter 2, "Grand Theory," in *The Sociological Imagination* (New York: Oxford University Press, 1968), 25–49.

59. Richard Butt, "Arguments for Using Biography in Understanding Teacher Thinking," in Halkaes, *Teacher Thinking,* 100.

60. For a fascinating example of Grumet's methodology in the study of teaching and gender, see Madeleine Grumet, *Bitter Milk: Women and Teaching* (Amherst: University of Massachusetts Press, 1988).

61. Madeleine Grumet, "Supervision and Situation: A Methodology of Self Report for Teacher Education," *Journal of Curriculum Theorizing* 1 (1979): 207.

62. Ibid., 234.

63. Briefly, the method of currere is composed of four temporal stages: regressive, progressive, analytic, and synthetic. The regressive stage explores one's educational past in relationship to one's present. The progressive stage is projective: one imagines the future, or as Pinar wrote, "what is not the case, what is not present." The analytic stage returns to the present to consider the interrelationships among ideas, people, contexts, and emotional states. This analytic photograph is then studied in relation to prior stages. At the synthetic stage, an integration of the self-knowledge bracketed from the past, present, and future is attempted. For a more through description, see William Pinar, "The Method," in *Toward a Poor Curriculum,* William Pinar and Madeleine Grumet (Dubuque, Iowa: Kendall/Hunt, 1974), 58.

64. Ibid., 52.

65. William Pinar, "The Voyage Out: Curriculum as the Relation Between the Knower and the Known," *Journal of Curriculum Theorizing* 2 (Winter 1980): 73.

66. Peter Woods, "Conversation with Teachers: Some Aspects of Life History Method," *British Educational Research Journal* 11 (1985): 17.

67. Cameron McCarthy and Michael Apple, "Race, Class, and Gender in American Educational Research: Toward a Nonsynchronous Parallelist Position," in *Class,*

Race, and Gender in American Education, Lois Weis, ed. (Albany: State University of New York Press, 1988), 30.

68. Willinsky, "Getting Personal and Practical with Personal Practical Knowledge," 249. The study of personal practical knowledge as discourse represents a new direction in this field. Willinsky's critique of the narrative accounts that support the notion of personal practical knowledge suggest that such a research direction assumes subjectivity to be noncontradictory and unitary, and thus cannot examine the power relations among the researcher, the researched, and the discourses that work through their meanings.

69. See Patti Lather, "Critical Theory, Curricular Transformation and Feminist Mainstreaming," *Journal of Education* 166 (March 1984): 49–62; Aronowitz and Giroux, *Education Under Siege;* and Kathleen Weiler, *Women Teaching for Change: Gender, Class and Power* (S. Hadley, Mass.: Bergin and Garvey, 1988).

70. Carl Boggs, *Gramsci's Marxism* (London: Pluto Press, 1978), 71.

71. Antonio Gramsci, *Selections from the Prison Notebooks,* Quintin Hoare and Geoffrey Nowell Smith, eds. (New York: International Publishers, 1976): 330–31.

72. Lortie, *Schoolteacher: A Sociological Study,* 61.

73. James Clifford, "Introduction: Partial Truths," in *Writing Culture: The Poetics and Politics of Ethnography,* James Clifford and George Marcus, eds. (Berkeley: University of California Press, 1986), 19.

74. Henriques, *Changing the Subject,* 3.

75. My theorizing of subjectivity has been influenced by the work of Roger Simon, "Work Experience," in *Critical Pedagogy and Cultural Power,* David Livingstone, ed. (S. Hadley, Mass.: Bergin and Garvey, 1987): 155–78; Chris Weedon, *Feminist Practice and Poststructuralist Theory* (New York: Basil and Blackwell, 1987); and Henriques, *Changing the Subject.*

76. Paul Willis, *Learning to Labour: How Working Class Kids get Working Class Jobs* (Westmead, England: Saxon House, 1977), 177–78.

77. Sara Freedman, "The Other End of the Corridor," 3.

CHAPTER THREE

1. Cortney Cazden, "Four Comments," in *Children In and Out of School,* Perry Gilmore and Alan Glatthorn, eds. (Washington, D.C.: Center for Applied Linguistics, 1982), 224.

2. Jamie Owl's story is composed from our ex post facto interviews. The interview transcripts, totaling 167 handwritten pages, represent twelve weekly interviews. Each audiotaped interview lasted between two and three hours, and was conducted in Jamie Owl's apartment. While the interviews were open-ended, and typically explored Jamie's weekly classroom experiences, the first interview was autobiographical, focusing

on Jamie's understanding of how she came to teacher education. The last interview, occurring a few days after Jamie completed her student teaching, concerned what student teaching presently meant to her life.

3. Upon completion of the interviews, I constructed a chronological case study grounded in Jamie's narrative and qualified by my reinterpretation of it. Part of my interpretation was shaped by one of Jamie's key themes: the clash between the subjective meanings constructed from Jamie's experience and the objective conditions of existence Jamie encountered. Specifically, I was interested in how Jamie's lived experiences addressed the following questions: How does the experience of learning to teach shape knowledge about pedagogy and the teacher's identity? How does perception shape our understanding of experience?

While Jamie's experience was far from compartmentalized, in that simple categories hardly do justice to the entanglements woven by our understandings of experience, I have organized Jamie's narration chronologically, with the use of headings. To achieve what Peter Woods (1985) terms "subjective depth" (p. 13), I have worked with the methodology of life history. (See for example, Woods, "Conversations with Teachers"; idem, "Life Histories and Teacher Knowledge"; and Richard Butt, "Arguments for Using Biography in Understanding Teacher Thinking."

Another part of my interpretation depended upon talk with colleagues, my own knowledge and experience in teacher education, the theoretical framework discussed in chapter 1 and 2, and Jamie's comments on the first draft of her story.

4. The reader is reminded that although Jamie Owl is real, her name and the names of persons and places have all been changed in order to preserve her privacy and the anonymity of other persons and settings.

5. The date of each particular interview woven throughout each section is noted at the beginning of each section. A change of date signifies a new interview.

6. In parts of this section, I have drawn upon and revised parts of my articles, "Who Has the Floor?: Curriculum, Teaching, and the English Student Teacher's Struggle for Voice," *Curriculum Inquiry* 19:2 (Summer 1989): 143–62 and "The Terrible Problem of Knowing Thyself: Towards a Poststructuralist Approach to Teacher Identity," *Journal of Curriculum Theorizing* 9 (Fall 1990).

7. Margaret Mathieson, *Preachers of Culture: A Study of English and its Teachers* (Totowa, New Jersey: Rowman and Littlefield, 1975), 201.

8. Harold Rosen, "The Autobiographical Impulse," in *Linguistics in Context: Connecting Observation with Understanding,* Deborah Tannen, ed. (Norwood, New Jersey: Ablex Publishing, 1988), 69–88.

9. Freema Elbaz and Robert Elbaz, "Curriculum and Textuality," *Journal of Curriculum Theorizing* 8:2 (Summer 1988): 108.

10. McNeil, *Contradictions of Control.*

11. Paulo Freire, *Pedagogy of the Oppressed* (New York: Herder and Herder, 1971), 35.

12. Rosen, "Autobiographical Impulse," 82.

CHAPTER FOUR

1. Weedon, *Feminist Practice and Poststructuralist Theory*, 79–80.

2. Lusted, "Why Pedagogy?," p. 13–14.

3. These three in-depth interviews coincided roughly with the beginning, middle, and end of his student teaching experience. The first in-depth interview concerned Jack's autobiography, how he came to the field of education. The second focused on his daily understandings of teaching, what it was like for him to teach. Finally, Jack's reflections on the meanings of teaching and learning to teach constituted the last in-depth interview.

4. In these transcripts of classroom discourse, student names were used only if Jack addressed students by name. Otherwise, to distinguish unnamed students, I identified the students by gender. As with all other names in this study, the students' names are fictitious.

5. Jack did not read any drafts of his case study. Eight months had passed between my time with Jack and the first writing of his story, and Jack had left the area. Consequently, my representation of Jack's struggles does not reflect Jack's comments. It does, however, reflect the comments of Jack's supervisor, Alberta Peach, who felt my rendition was accurate and compelling.

6. My entrance into Greenville High was surprisingly smooth; this high school seemed isolated from State University by distance and by design. But Professor Joe Probe of the school of education suggested I contact his student of twenty-two years ago, currently the chairperson of social studies at Greenville High. I contacted Burt Rerun by telephone and was relieved to hear a friendly and receptive voice. Upon meeting, Burt Rerun secured all permission for my weekly school visits as well as the permission of Jack's cooperating teachers. Both cooperating teachers were open to my presence and at the conclusion of Jack's student teaching were interviewed about their general perceptions of the student teaching experience. (See chapter 5, below.)

7. The reader is reminded that although Jack August is real, as are the persons who populate his story, his name and the names of all persons and places have been changed to preserve privacy and to ensure anonymity.

8. As in Jamie Owl's story, the dates of each interview and observations appear with the first blocked quotations of each section. The reader is reminded that unless a new date is noted, each beginning date includes the succeeding data of that subsection.

9. A few days before Jack assumed responsibility for his second history class, United States armed forces, under executive order from the Reagan administration, invaded the socialist country of Grenada. The popular mass media, although banned from observing this military invasion, presented it as necessary to saving the lives of a small population of United States citizens attending a Grenada medical school. These students were depicted as being threatened by an apparent Cuban military buildup. In addition, a Cuban-built airport was initially described as a military landing base. Later, investigation into the invasion of Grenada revealed another story. The

airport's structure, begun by the Cubans but completed by the United States, was not for military purposes. Although Grenada was indeed preparing for a United States invasion, its preparation was obviously warranted. However, the United States government continued to stand behind its "official" story and, one year later, celebrated "the liberation of Grenada day," inviting the rescued medical students to a Rose Garden ceremony. Maurice Bishop, the president of Grenada, was killed during the invasion.

For a good discussion of the Grenada revolution that draws on interviews with Caribbean writers and Grenadians, see Chris Searle, *Words Unchained: Language and Revolution in Grenada* (London: Zed Books, 1984).

10. Todd Gitlin termed made-for-television movies like *The Day After* the network executives' attempts to turn toward relevance. Indeed, since the proliferation of nuclear arms throughout the world, the international antinuclear peace movement had become a popular theme for television to exploit. It was inevitable, then, that a major network would attempt to encapsulate the consequences of nuclear war in its own special way.

As a competitive industry, networks have more than the public interest in mind. Network executives' primary concern are their ratings and the profit that high ratings generate. In 1982, for example, the National Broadcasting Company (NBC) telecast a two-night miniseries entitled *World War III*. Building on hourly suspense, this four-hour movie chronicled the tensions between the Soviet Union and the United States. By the third hour, the KGB had tricked a future United States president into launching the first nuclear strike. With the third hour, the subject of thermonuclear war had become game for the little screen. The NBC ratings soared, for its film had touched on such popular sentiments as the cold war, romance in dangerous times, and a probable United States military victory should diplomacy fail.

Not to be outdone, ABC began producing a made-for-television film about the consequences of nuclear war. What was particularly striking about this film was its focus on specific families in middle America. After establishing viewer sympathy for its characters by revealing their hopes for the future, a camera shot took the viewers to a corn field surrounded by silos. There children watched openmouthed as Soviet missiles sailed overhead.

By the next commercial, Kansas City was wiped off the map. For the next eighty minutes, the film focused on the aftermath of nuclear war.

In the original script, there were no survivors. However, the ABC politically conservative executive order transformed this final version. The new version, sanctioned by the Reagan administration, reiterated Reagan's position that a limited nuclear war is possible. This version, complete with survivors, was put on the air. Once again, popular media played out its role as a supporter of the status quo. More significantly, ABC swept the Nielsen ratings for the month. That in itself became a media event.

For a more thorough discussion, see Todd Gitlin, *Inside Prime Time* (New York: Pantheon Books, 1983), 157–204.

11. For a discussion of gender differences in moral development, see Carol Gilligan, *In a Different Voice: Psychology and Women's Development* (Cambridge: Harvard University Press, 1982).

12. Diana Fuss, *Essentially Speaking: Feminism, Nature, and Difference* (New York: Routledge, 1989), 114.

CHAPTER FIVE

1. The term "significant others" is borrowed from the research literature on student teacher socialization. I use the term to categorize the professionals who, in some way, have structural power to affect the conditions of student teaching. These persons include cooperating teachers, university professors and supervisors, departmental chairpersons, and school administrators. Classroom students and student teachers, while possessing power to affect the conditions of student teaching, are not included in this definition since their power is largely informal rather than structural.

2. For an excellent discussion of Reaganism and the construction of youth, see Lawrence Grossberg, "Rockin' with Reagan, or the Mainstreaming of Postmodernity," *Cultural Critique* 10 (Fall 1988): 123–50.

3. There were four major reports published in 1983, the year this study began: (1) National Commission on Excellence in Education, *A Nation at Risk;* (2) College Board, *Academic Preparation for College: What Students Need to Know and Be Able to Do* (New York: College Entrance Examination Board, 1983); (3) Twentieth-Century Fund Task Force on Federal Elementary and Secondary Education Policy, *Making the Grade* (New York: Twentieth-Century Fund, 1983); and (4) Task Force on Education for Economic Growth, *Action for Excellence: A Comprehensive Plan to Improve Our Nation's Schools* (Denver: Education Commission of the States, 1983).

4. National Commission on Excellence in Education, *A Nation at Risk,* 5.

5. For a discussion of how the commission's report was presented, see Gail Kelly, "Setting the Boundaries of Debate about Education," in *Excellence in Education: Perspectives on Policy and Practice,* Philip Altback, Gail Kelly, and Lois Weis, eds. (Buffalo: Prometheus Books, 1985), 31–42.

6. George Gallup, "The 15th Annual Gallup Poll of the Public's Attitudes Toward the Public Schools," *Phi Delta Kappen* (September 1983): 34.

7. Not surprisingly, forty-five percent of these respondents, as opposed to twenty-five percent in 1969, would *not* want a child of theirs to take up the career of teaching in the public schools. Of those who dismissed this profession, reasons listed in frequency of mention are: 1) low pay; 2) discipline problems; 3) unrewarding, thankless work; and 4) the low prestige of the teaching profession. See George Gallup, n. 6, above.

8. For an illuminating analysis of the politics of the 1983 reform reports, see Beverly Gordon, "Teaching Teachers," 33–46; H. Svi Shapiro, "Capitalism at Risk: The Political Economy of the Educational Reports of 1983," *Educational Theory* 35 (Winter 1985): 57–85; chapter 4 of Ira Shor, *Culture Wars: School and Society in the Conservative Restoration* (Boston: Routledge and Kegan Paul, 1986); Michael Apple, "Redefining Equity: Authoritarian Populism and the Conservative Restoration," *Teachers*

College Record 90 (Winter 1988): 167–84; the collection of articles in Philip Altback, ed., *Excellence in Education;* and the poststructuralist analysis of Cornbleth and Gottlieb, "Reform Discourse and Curricular Reform."

9. Barbara Finkelstein, "Education and the Retreat from Democracy in the United States, 1979–198?," *Teachers College Record* 86 (Winter 1984): 277.

10. Apple, "Redefining Equity," 173.

11. Shor, *Culture Wars.*

12. "College Linked to Vietnam War," *New York Times,* September 2, 1984, 24.

13. The grandfather clause is an alternative means for acquiring teacher certification. Although no longer in operation, it was actively invoked during teacher shortages during the years 1950–1982. This clause recognized practical experience as a substitute for educational course work and student teaching. In addition, it permitted states to award additional teacher and administrative certification with minimal educational course work in order to meet the personnel demands of school systems. In the state in which this study was carried out, the grandfather clause expired in 1982.

14. The administrators interviewed in this section worked at Smithville High School, a site used for State University student teachers. During fieldwork for this study, I visited Smithville weekly to observe a secondary social studies student teacher not included in this study.

15. Richard Smith and Anna Zantiotis, "Practical Teacher Education and the Avant Garde," in *Critical Pedagogy, the State, and Cultural Struggle,* Henry Giroux and Peter McLaren, eds. (Albany: State University of New York Press, 1989), 112.

16. Madeleine Grumet, "Supervision and Situation," 191–92.

17. Peter Griffin, *Literary Theory and English Teaching* (Philadelphia: Open University Press, 1987), 58.

18. Ann Berlack, "Teaching for Outrage and Empathy in the Liberal Arts," *Educational Foundations* 3 (Summer 1989): 78.

19. For a discussion about the relationships between popular culture and schooling, see Henry Giroux and Roger Simon, eds. *Popular Culture: Schooling and Everyday Life* (S. Hadley, Mass.: Bergin and Garvey, 1989); and Cary Nelson, ed. *Theory in the Classroom* (Chicago: University of Illinois Press, 1986).

20. James Donald, "Language, Literacy and Schooling," in *State and Popular Culture,* 59.

21. Philip Corrigan, "Playing . . . Contra/Dictions, Empowerment and Embodiment: Punk, Pedagogy, and Popular Cultural Forms (on Ethnography and Education)," in *Popular Culture: Schooling and Everyday Life,* 79.

22. Lusted, "Why Pedagogy?," 4.

23. V. N. Volosinov, *Marxism and the Philosophy of Language* (Cambridge: Harvard University Press, 1986), 36. Many scholars believe that Volosinov and Bakhtin are the same author. I have maintained Volosinov's authorship because of the edition of the text.

24. Greene, *The Dialectic of Freedom,* 16.

Chapter Six

1. Parts of this section are a revision of my original article, "Cultural Myths in the Making of a Teacher: Biography and Social Structure in Teacher Education," *Harvard Educational Review* 56 (November 1986): 442–56.

2. Walter Benjamin, "The Work of Art in the Age of Mechanical Reproduction," in *Illuminations*, 263.

3. My introduction of the term "interpellation" glosses over its problems and potentials. For a discussion of this term, see Louis Althusser, "Ideology and Ideological State Apparatus (Notes towards an Investigation)," in *Lenin and Philosophy and Other Essays*, (New York: Monthly Review Press, 1971), 127–86. Also see Weedon, *Feminist Practice and Poststructural Theory*.

4. Stuart Hall, "Signification, Representation, Ideology: Althusser and Post-Structuralist Debates," *Critical Studies in Mass Communication* 2 (June 1985): 102.

5. Descombe, "The Hidden Pedagogy and Its Implications," 249–65.

6. Waller, *Sociology of Teaching*, 410.

7. For an insightful discussion of how a particular pedagogy can work against itself, see Elizabeth Ellsworth, "Why Doesn't This Feel Empowering? Working Through the Repressive Myths of Critical Pedagogy," *Harvard Educational Review* 59 (August 1989): 297–324.

8. Belsey, *Critical Practice*, 4.

9. See Corrigan, "Punk, Pedagogy, and Popular Cultural Forms," in *Popular Culture: Schooling and Everyday Life*, 79.

10. Hall, "Signification, Representation, Ideology," 105.

11. Descombe, "Hidden Pedagogy."

12. Ward Churchill, "White Studies: The Intellectual Imperialism of Contemporary Imperialism of Contemporary U.S. Education," *Integrated Education* 19 (January 1982): 52–57. For a discussion of white teachers' understanding of race, see Meyer Weinberg, *The Search for Quality Integrated Education: Policy and Research on Minority Students in Schools and Colleges* (Westport, Conn.: Greenwood Press, 1983).

13. For discussions that critique the ways race has been understood in the curriculum and in pedagogical practice, see, for example, Paul Gilroy, *There Ain't No Black in the Union Jack: The Cultural Politics of Race and Nation* (London: Hutchinson, 1987); Beverly Gordon, "Toward Emancipation in Citizenship Education: The Case of African-American Cultural Knowledge," *Theory and Research in Social Education* 12 (1985): 33–45; Stuart Hall, "Teaching About Race," in *The School in the Multicultural Society*, Alan James and Robert Jeffcoate, eds. (London: Harper and Row, 1981), 58–69; Special Issue, "Race, Racism, and American Education: Perspectives of Asian Americans, Blacks, Latinos, and Native Americans," *Harvard Educational Review* 58 (August 1988); Charles Payne, *Getting What We Ask For: The Ambiguity of Success and Failure in Urban Education* (Westport, Conn.: Greenwood Press, 1984); Madan Sarup, *The Politics of Multiracial Education* (Boston: Routledge and Kegan Paul, 1986); and

Catherine Walsh, *Pedagogy and the Struggle for Voice: Issues of Language, Power, and Schooling for Puerto Ricans* (Westport, Conn.: Greenwood Press, 1991).

14. Richard Sennet and Jonathan Cobb, *The Hidden Injuries of Class* (New York: Vintage Books, 1972).

15. For a thoughtful analysis of the teacher's exclusion of social difference, see Linda Brodkey, "On the Subjects of Class and Gender in 'The Literacy Letters,'" *College English* 51 (February 1989): 125–41.

16. William Ryan, *Blaming the Victim* (New York: Vintage Books, 1971). For an insightful critique of Ryan's category, see Charles Payne, *Getting What We Asked For.*

17. For an interesting discussion of the unknowable in teaching, see Shoshana Felman, "Psychoanalysis and Education: Teaching Terminable and Interminable," *Yale French Studies* 63 (1982): 21–44. For a discussion on the unknowable in research, see Patti Lather, "Postmodernism and the Politics of Enlightenment," *Educational Studies* 3 (1989): 7–28.

18. M. M. Bakhtin, *The Dialogic Imagination.* Also see Tzvetan Todorov, *Mikhail Bakhtin: The Dialogical Principle.* (Minneapolis: University of Minnesota Press, 1984).

19. Greene, *The Dialectic of Freedom,* xi.

20. For exemplary examples of the research produced by teachers as researchers, see Connelly and Clandinin, *Teachers as Curriculum Planners;* Goswami and Stillman, eds., *Reclaiming the Classroom* ; Miller, *Creating Spaces;* Nelson, *Theory in the Classroom;* Margo Okazawa-Rey, James Anderson, and Rob Traver, eds., *Teachers, Teaching, and Teacher Education* (Cambridge: Harvard Educational Review, 1987); and Smyth, ed., *Educating Teachers.*

21. For discussions of the politics of youth, see Giroux and Simon, eds., *Popular Culture: Schooling and Everyday Life;* and Roman, Christian-Smith, and Ellsworth, eds., *Becoming Feminine.*

22. Brodkey, "On the Subjects of Class and Gender," 140.

23. Greene, *Dialectic of Freedom,* 17.

CHAPTER SEVEN

1. Edward Said, *Orientalism* (New York: Vantage, 1978), 21.

2. James Clifford, "Introduction: Partial Truths," in *Writing Culture: the Poetics and Politics in Ethnography,* James Clifford and George Marcus, eds., 1–27 (Berkeley: University of California Press, 1986), 5.

3. Paul Smith, *Discerning the Subject* (Minneapolis: University of Minnesota Press 1988), 86.

4. T.Minh-Ha Trinh, *Woman, Native, Other: Writing Postcoloniality and Feminism* (Bloomington: Indiana University Press, 1989), 79.

5. Ellen Rooney, *Seductive Reasoning: Pluralism as the Problematic of Contemporary Literary Theory* (Ithaca: Cornell University Press, 1989), 37.

6. Paul Atkinson, *The Ethnographic Imagination: Textual Constructions of Reality* (New York: Routledge, 1990), 2.

7. Peggy Phelan, *Unmarked: the Politics of Performance* (New York: Routledge, 1993), 1.

8. See Linda Brodkey, *Academic Writing as Social Practice* (Philadelphia: Temple University Press, 1987), Donald Dippo, "Tantalizing Textuality," *The Review of Education*, 15 (1993): 29–40, M. Fine, *Framing Dropouts: Notes on the Politics of an Urban Public High School* (Albany: State University of New York Press, 1991), Patti Lather, *Getting Smart: Feminist Research and Pedagogy with/in the Postmodern* (New York: Routledge, 1991), and Daniel Yon, *Elusive Culture: Schooling, Race, and Identity in Global Times* (Albany: State University of New York Press, 2000).

9. See Toni Morrison, *Playing in the Dark: Whiteness and the Literacy Imagination* (Cambridge, MA: Harvard University Press, 1992), and Phelan, *Unmarked: the Politics of Performance.*

10. See M.M. Bakhtin, *Art and Answerability: Early Philosophical Essays*, Michael Holquist and Vadim Liapunov, eds., trans. Vadim Liapunov (Austin: University of Texas Press, 1990), Judith Butler, *Gender Trouble: Feminism and the Subversion of Identity* (New York: Routledge, Chapman, and Hall, 1990), and Clifford Owens, *Beyond Recognition: Representation, Power and Culture*, S. Bryson, Barbara Kruger, Lynn Tillman, and Jane Weinstock, eds. (Berkeley: University of California Press, 1992).

11. See, for example, Judith Butler, *Bodies that Matter: on the Discursive Limits of "Sex"* (New York: Routledge, 1993), James Clifford and V. Dhareshwar, eds.,"Travelling Theories, Travelling Theorists," *Inscriptions* 5 (1989), A. Feldman, *Formations of Violence: the Narrative of the Body and Political Terror in Northern Ireland* (Chicago: University of Chicago Press, 1991), Michel Foucault, *The History of Sexuality: an Introduction* (Vol. 1) (New York: Pantheon, 1978), A. Ong, "Colonialism and Modernity: Feminist Re-presentations of Women in Non-Western Societies," *Inscriptions* 314 (1988): 79–93, Mary Louise Pratt, *Imperial Eyes: Travel Writing and Transculturation* (New York: Routledge, 1992), and M. Wolfe, *A Thrice-Told Tale: Feminism, Postmoderism, and Ethnographic Responsibility* (Stanford: Stanford University Press, 1992).

12. Phelan, *Unmarked: the Politics of Performance*, 1.

13. Brodkey, *Academic Writing as Social Practice.*

14. Walter Benjamin, "The Work of Art in an Age of Mechanical Reproduction," in *Illuminations*, ed. Hannah Arendt, 217–252 (New York: Schocken 1969), 263.

15. E. L. Kennedy and M. D. Davis, *Boots of Leather, Slippers of Gold: the History of a Lesbian Community* (New York: Routledge, 1993).

16. See Butler, *Gender Trouble: Feminism and the Subversion of Identity*, and *Bodies that Matter: on the Discursive Limits of "Sex,"* Teresa deLauretis, *Technologies of Gender:*

Essays on Theory, Film, and Fiction (Bloomington: Indiana University Press, 1987) and Diana Fuss, *Essentially Speaking: Feminism, Nature, and Difference* (New York: Routledge, 1989).

17. Samuel Delany, "Street Talk/Straight Talk," *Differences: A Journal of Feminist Cultural Studies* 5 (1991), 28.

Bibliography

Adorno, Theodor. *Critical Models: Interventions and Catchwords*. Trans. Henry Pickford. New York: Columbia University Press, 1998.

Alcoff, Linda. "Cultural Feminism Versus Poststructuralism: The Identity Crisis in Feminist Theory." *Signs* 13 (1988): 405–36.

Althusser, Louis. "Ideology and Ideological State Apparatus (Notes towards an Investigation)," in *Lenin and Philosophy and Other Studies*. New York: Monthly Review Press, 1971.

Alvarado, Manuel, and Bob Ferguson. "The Curriculum, Media Studies and Discursivity: A Reconsideration of Educational Theory." *Screen* 24 (May–June 1983): 20–34.

Anyon, Jean. "Social Class and School Knowledge." *Curriculum Inquiry* 11 (Spring 1981): 3–42.

Apple, Michael. "Redefining Equity: Authoritarian Populism and the Conservative Restoration." *Teacher's College Record* 90 (Winter 1988): 167–84.

———. *Teachers and Texts: A Political Economy of Class and Gender Relations in Education*. New York: Routledge and Kegan Paul, 1986.

———. *Ideology and Curriculum*. Boston: Routledge and Kegan Paul, 1979.

Arendt, Hannah. "The Crisis in Education," in *Between Past and Future: Eight Exercises in Political Thought*, 173–196. New York: Penguin, 1993.

———. *The Human Condition*. Chicago: University of Chicago Press, 1958.

Aronowitz, Stanley, and Henry Giroux. *Education Under Siege: The Conservative, Liberal and Radical Debate Over Schooling*. S. Hadley, Mass.: Bergin and Garvey, 1985.

Atkinson, Paul. *The Ethnographic Imagination: Textual Constructions of Reality*. New York: Routledge, 1990.

Bakhtin, M. M. *Art and Answerability: Early Philosophical Essays*, Michael Holquist and Vadim Liapunov, eds. Trans. Vadim Liapunov. Austin: University of Texas Press, 1990.

———. *The Dialogical Imagination*. Michael Holquist, ed. Austin: University of Texas Press, 1981.

Barthes, Roland. *Mythologies*. New York: Hill and Wang, 1985.

Belsey, Catherine. *Critical Practice*. New York: Methuen, 1980.

Benjamin, Walter. "The Work of Art in an Age of Mechanical Reproduction," in *Illuminations*, Hannah Arendt, ed., 217–252. New York: Schocken, 1969.

Berlack, Ann. "Teaching for Outrage and Empathy in the Liberal Arts." *Educational Foundations* 3 (Summer 1989): 69–93.

Bernfeld, Siegfried. *Sisyphus or the Limits of Education*. Trans. Frederic Lilge. Berkeley: University of California Press, 1973.

Beyer, Landon. *Knowing and Acting: Inquiry, Ideology and Educational Studies*. New York: Falmer Press, 1988.

———. "Aesthetic Experience for Teacher Preparation and Social Change." *Educational Theory* 35 (Fall 1985): 385–87.

Bisseret, Noelle. *Education, Class, Language and Ideology*. London: Routledge and Kegan Paul, 1979.

Boggs, Carl. *Gramsci's Marxism*. London: Pluto Press, 1978.

Borrowman, Merle. *The Liberal and the Technical in Teacher Education*. Westport, Conn.: Greenwood Press, 1956.

Britzman, Deborah P. *Lost Subjects, Contested Objects: Toward a Psychoanalytic Inquiry of Learning*. Albany: State University of New York Press, 1998.

———. "The Terrible Problem of Knowing Thyself: Toward a Poststructuralist Account of Teacher Identity." *Journal of Curriculum Theorizing* 9 (Fall 1990).

———. "Who Has the Floor?: Curriculum, Teaching, and the Student Teacher's Struggle for Voice." *Curriculum Inquiry* 19 (Summer 1989): 143–62.

———. "Cultural Myths in the Making of a Teacher: Biography and Social Structure in Teacher Education." *Harvard Educational Review* 56 (Nov. 1986): 442–56.

Brodkey, Linda. "On the Subjects of Class and Gender in 'The Literacy Letters.'" *College English* 51 (Feb. 1989): 125–41.

———. *Academic Writing as Social Practice*. Philadelphia: Temple University Press, 1987.

Buchmann, Margaret, and J. Schwille. "Education: The Overcoming of Experience." *American Journal of Education* 92 (Nov. 1983): 30–51.

Butler, Judith. *Bodies that Matter: on the Discursive Limits of "Sex."* New York: Routledge, 1993.

———. *Gender Trouble: Feminism and the Subversion of Identity*. New York: Routledge, Chapman, and Hall, 1990.

Butt, Richard. "Arguments for Using Biography in Understanding Teacher Thinking," in *Teacher Thinking: A New Perspective on Persistent Problems in Education*, R. Halkaes and J. K. Olsen, eds. 95–102. Heirewig, Holland: Swets Publishing Service, 1984.

Cazden, Courteny. "Four Comments," in *Children In and Out of School*, Alan Glatthorn, ed. Washington, D.C.: Center for Applied Linguistics, 1982.

Cherryholmes, Cleo. *Power and Criticism: Poststructural Investigations in Education*. New York: Teachers College Press, 1988.

Churchill, Ward. "White Studies: The Intellectual Imperialism of Contemporary U.S. Education." *Integrated Education* 19 (Jan. 1982): 52–57.

Clandinin, D. Jean. *Classroom Practices: Teacher Images in Action*. Philadelphia: Falmer Press, 1986.

———. "Personal Practical Knowledge: A Study of Teachers' Classroom Images." *Curriculum Inquiry* 15 (Winter 1985): 361–85.

Clifford, James, and V. Dhareshwar, eds. "Travelling Theories, Travelling Theorists." *Inscriptions* 5 (1989).

Clifford, James. "Introduction: Partial Truths," in *Writing Culture: The Poetics and Politics of Ethnography*, James Clifford and George Marcus, eds. Berkeley: University of California Press, 1986.

College Board. *Academic Preparation for College: What Students Need to Know and Be Able to Do*. New York: College Entrance Examination Board, 1983.

College Linked to Vietnam War. *New York Times* (2 September 1984): 24.

Collins, Randall. *The Credential Society: An Historical Sociology of Education and Stratification*. New York: Academic Press, 1979.

Connell, R. W. *Teachers' Work*. Sidney, Australia: George Allen & Unwin, 1985.

Connelly, E. Michael, and D. Jean Clandinin. *Teachers as Curriculum Planners: Narratives of Experience*. New York: Teachers College Press, 1988.

———. "Personal Practical Knowledge and the Modes of Knowing: Relevence for Teaching and Learning," in *Learning and Teaching the Ways of Knowing*, Elliot Eisner, ed., 174–98. 84th Yearbook of the National Society for the Study of Education. Chicago: University of Chicago Press, 1985.

———. "Personal Practical Knowledge at Bay Street School: Ritual Personal Philosophy and Image," in *Teacher Thinking: A New Perspective on Persistent Problems in Education*, R. Halkaes and J. K. Olsen, eds., 134–48. Heirewig, Holland: Swets Publishing Service, 1984.

Cornbleth, Catherine, and Esther Gottlieb. "Reform Discourse and Curriculum Reform." *Educational Foundations* 3 (Fall 1989): 63–78.

Corrigan, Philip. "Playing . . . Contra/dictions, Empowerment, and Embodiment: Punk, Pedagogy, and Popular Cultural Forms (on Ethnography and Education)," in *Popular Culture: Schooling and Everyday Life*, Henry Giroux and Roger Simon, eds. 67–90. S. Hadley, Mass.: Bergin and Garvey, 1989.

Counts, George S. "Break the Teacher Training Lockstep." *Social Frontier*, 1 (June 1935): 6–7. Reprinted in *Teacher Education in America*, Merle L. Borrowman, ed., 218–23. New York: Teachers College Press, 1965.

Davies, Bronwyn. *Frogs, Snails, and Feminist Tales: Preschool Children and Gender*. Sydney: Allen and Unwin, 1989.

Delany, Samuel. "Street Talk/Straight Talk." *Differences: A Journal of Feminist Cultural Studies* 5 (1991): 21–38.

DeLauretis, Teresa. *Technologies of Gender: Essays on Theory, Film, and Fiction*. Bloomington: Indiana University Press, 1987.

———, ed. *Feminist Studies/Critical Studies*. Bloomington: Indiana University Press, 1986.

Descombe, Martyn. "The Hidden Pedagogy and Its Implications for Teacher Training." *British Journal of Sociology of Education* 3 (1982): 249–65.

Dewey, John. *Experience and Education*. New York: Collier Books, 1972.

Dippo, Donald. "Tantalizing Textuality." *The Review of Education*, 15 (1993): 29–40.

Donald, James. "Language, Literacy, and Schooling," in *The State and Popular Culture*. Milton Keynes, England: Open University Press, 1987.

———. "Green Paper: Noise of Crises." *Screen Education* 30 (Spring 1979): 13–49.

Dorfman, Ariel. *The Emperor's Old Clothes: What the Lone Ranger, Babar, and Other Innocent Heroes Do to Our Minds*. New York: Pantheon Books, 1983.

Elbaz, Freema, and Robert Elbaz. "Curriculum and Textuality." *Journal of Curriculum Theorizing* 8:2 (Summer 1988): 107–131.

Elbaz, Freema. *Teacher Thinking: A Study of Practical Knowledge*. New York: Nichols Publishing, 1983.

Ellsworth, Elizabeth. "Why Doesn't This Feel Empowering? Working Through the Repressive Myths of Critical Pedagogy." *Harvard Educational Review* 59 (1989): 297–324.

Evans, Kate. *Negotiating the Self: Identity, Sexuality, and Emotion in Learning to Teach*. New York: Routledge, 2002.

Everhart, Robert. *Reading, Writing and Resistance*. New York: Routledge and Kegan Paul, 1983.

Feldman, A. *Formations of Violence: the Narrative of the Body and Political Terror in Northern Ireland*. Chicago: University of Chicago Press, 1991.

Felman, Shoshana. "Education and Crisis, Or the Vicissitudes of Teaching." In *Testimony: Crises of Witnessing in Literature, Psychoanalysis, and History*, Shoshana Felman and Dori Laub, 1–56. New York: Routledge, 1992.

———. "Psychoanalysis and Education: Teaching Terminable and Interminable." *Yale French Studies* 63 (1982): 21–44.

Fine, M. *Framing Dropouts: Notes on the Politics of an Urban Public High School*. Albany: State University of New York Press, 1991.

Finkelstein, Barbara. "Education and the Retreat from Democracy in the United States, 1979–198?" *Teachers College Record* 86 (Winter 1984): 275–82.

Flax, Jane. "Postmodernism and Gender Relations in Feminist Theory." *Signs: Journal of Woman in Culture and Society* 12 (Summer 1987): 621–43.

Foucault, Michel. *The History of Sexuality: Volume I.* New York: Vintage, 1980.

Franklin, Barry. *Building the American Community: The School Curriculum and the Search for Social Control.* London: Falmer Press, 1986.

Freedman, Sara, Jane Jackson, and Katherine Boles. "The Other End of the Corridor: The Effect of Teaching on Teachers." *Radical Teacher* 23 (1982): 2–23.

Freire, Paulo. *Pedagogy of the Oppressed.* New York: Herder and Herder, 1971.

Freud, Anna. "Four Lectures on Psychoanalysis for Teachers and Parents (1930)," in *The Writings of Anna Freud, Volume 1 1922–1935,* 73–136. New York: International Universities Press, 1974.

Freud, Sigmund. "The Dynamics of Transference (1912)," in *Standard Edition* (Vol. 12), 97–108. London: Hogarth Press, 1968.

Fuss, Diana. *Essentially Speaking: Feminism, Nature and Difference.* New York: Routledge, 1989.

Gallup, George. "The 15th Annual Gallup Poll of the Public's Attitudes Toward the Public Schools." *Phi Delta Kappan* 65 (Sept. 1983): 33–47.

Geertz, Clifford. *Local Knowledge: Further Essays in Interpretive Anthropology.* New York: Basic Books, 1983.

Giddens, Anthony. *Central Problems in Social Theory: Action, Structure and Contradictions in Social Analysis.* Berkeley: University of California Press, 1986.

Gilligan, Carol. *In a Different Voice: Psychology and Women's Development.* Cambridge: Harvard University Press, 1982.

Gilroy, Paul. *There Ain't No Black in the Union Jack: The Cultural Politics of Race and Nation.* London: Hutchinson, 1987.

Ginsburg, Mark. *Contradictions in Teacher Education and Society: A Critical Analysis.* New York: Falmer Press, 1988.

———. "Reproduction, Contradiction, and Conceptions of Professionalism: The Case of Pre-Service Teachers," in *Critical Studies in Teacher Education: Its Folklore, Theory and Practice,* Thomas Popkewitz, ed., 86–129. Philadelphia: Falmer Press, 1987.

———. "Reproduction, Contradictions and Conceptions of Curriculum in Preservice Teacher Education." *Curriculum Inquiry* 16 (Fall 1986): 283–309.

Giroux, Henry. *Schooling and the Struggle for Public Life: Critical Pedagogy in the Modern Age.* Minneapolis: University of Minnesota Press, 1988.

———. *Theory and Resistance in Education: A Pedagogy for the Opposition.* S. Hadley, Mass.: Bergin and Garvey, 1983.

Giroux, Henry, and Peter McLaren, eds. *Critical Pedagogy, the State and Cultural Struggle.* Albany: State University of New York Press, 1989.

Giroux, Henry, and Roger Simon. eds. *Popular Culture: Schooling and Everyday Life.* S. Hadley, Mass.: Bergin and Garvey, 1989.

———. "Curriculum Study and Cultural Politics." *Journal of Education* 166 (Fall 1984): 226–53.

Gitlin, Todd. *Inside Prime Time.* New York: Pantheon Books, 1983.

Gordon, Beverly. "Toward Emancipation in Citizenship Education: The Case of African-American Cultural Knowledge." *Theory and Research in Social Education* 12 (Winter 1985): 1–23.

———. "Teaching Teachers: 'A Nation at Risk' and the Issue of Knowledge in Teacher Education." *Urban Review* 17 (1985): 33–46.

Gramsci, Antonio. *Selections from the Prison Notebooks.* Quintin Hoare and Geoffrey Nowell Smith, eds. New York: International Publishers, 1976.

Greene, Maxine. *The Dialectic of Freedom.* New York: Teachers College Press, 1988.

———. "Excellence, Meanings and Multiplicity." *Teachers College Record* 86 (1984): 283–97.

———. "The Matter of Mystification: Teacher Education in Unquiet Times," in *Landscapes of Learning,* 53–73. New York: Teachers College Press, 1978.

———. *The Public School and the Private Vision: A Search for America in Education and Literature.* New York: Random, 1965.

Griffith, Peter. *Literary Theory and English Teaching.* Philadelphia: Open University Press, 1987.

Grossberg, Lawrence. "Rockin' with Reagan, or the Mainstreaming of Postmodernity." *Cultural Critique* 10 (Fall 1988): 123–50.

Grumet, Madeleine. *Bitter Milk: Women and Teaching.* Amherst: University of Massachusetts Press, 1988.

———. "Pedagogy for the Patriarchy: The Feminization of Teaching." *Interchange* 12 (1981): 165–84.

———. "Supervision and Situation: A Methodology of Self Report for Teacher Education." *Journal of Curriculum Theorizing* 1 (1979): 191–257.

Hall, Stuart. "Signification, Representation, Ideology: Althusser and Post-Structuralist Debates." *Critical Studies in Mass Communication* 2 (June 1985): 91–114.

———. "Teaching about Race," in *The School in Multicultural Society,* Alan James and Robert Jeffcoate, eds., 58–69. London: Harper and Row, 1981.

Heath, Shirley B. *Way with Words: Language, Life and Work in Communities and Classrooms.* Cambridge: Cambridge University Press, 1983.

Henriques, Jules, Wendy Hollway, Cathy Urwin, Couze Venn, and Valerie Walkerdine, eds. *Changing the Subject: Psychology, Social Regulation and Subjectivity.* London: Methuen, 1984.

James, William. *Talks to Teachers on Psychology: and to Students on Some of Life's Ideals.* Cambridge: Harvard University Press, 1983.

Kelly, Gail. "Setting the Boundaries of Debate about Education," in *Excellence in Education: Perspectives on Policy and Practice,* Philip Altbach, Gail Kelly and Lois Weiss, eds., 31–42. Buffalo: Prometheus Books, 1985.

Kennedy, E. L., and M. D. Davis. *Boots of Leather, Slippers of Gold: the History of a Lesbian Community.* New York: Routledge, 1993.

Kliebard, Herbert. *The Struggle for the American Curriculum, 1893–1958.* Boston: Routledge and Kegan Paul, 1986.

Kristeva, Julia. *Hannah Arendt.* Trans. Ross Guberman. New York: Columbia, 2001.

Lather, Patti. *Getting Smart: Feminist Research and Pedagogy with/in the Postmodern.* New York: Routledge, 1991.

———. "Postmodernism and the Politics of Enlightenment." *Educational Foundations* 3 (1989): 7–28.

———. "Research as Praxis." *Harvard Educational Review* 46 (1986): 257–77.

———. "Critical Theory, Curricular Transformation and Feminist Mainstreaming." *Journal of Education* 166 (March 1984): 49–62.

Lortie, Dan. *Schoolteacher: A Sociological Study.* Chicago: University of Chicago Press, 1975.

Lusted, David. "Why Pedagogy?" *Screen* 27 (Sept.–Oct. 1986): 2–14.

Marx, Karl. *The Eighteenth Brumaire of Louis Bonaparte.* New York: International Publishers, 1981.

Mathieson, Margaret. *Preachers of Culture: A Study of English and its Teachers.* Totowa, New Jersey: Rowman and Littlefield, 1975.

McCarthy, Cameron, and Michael Apple. "Race, Class, and Gender in American Research: Toward a Nonsynchronous Parallelist Position," in *Class, Race, and Gender in American Education,* Lois Weis, ed., 9–42. Albany: State University of New York Press, 1988.

McLaren, Peter. *Schooling as Ritual Performance.* Boston: Routledge and Kegan Paul, 1986.

McNeill, Linda. *Contradictions of Control: School Structure and School Knowledge.* New York: Routledge and Kegan Paul, 1986.

Miller, Janet. *Creating Spaces and Finding Voices: Teachers Collaborating for Empowerment.* Albany: State University of New York Press, 1990.

Mills, C. Wright. *The Sociological Imagination.* New York: Oxford University Press, 1968.

Minh-ha, Trinh T. *Woman, Native, Other: Writing Postcoloniality and Feminism.* Bloomington: Indiana University Press, 1989.

Morris, Adeline. "Dick, Jane and American Literature: Fighting with Canons." *College English* 47 (Sept. 1985): 467–81.

Morrison, Toni. *Playing in the Dark: Whiteness and the Literacy Imagination.* Cambridge, MA: Harvard University Press, 1992.

Morton, Donald, and Mas'ud Zavazadeh. "Cultural Politics of the Fiction Workshop." *Cultural Critique* (Winter 1988–89): 155–73.

Narayan, Uma. "Working Together Across Difference: Some Considerations on Emotions and Political Practice." *Hypatia* 3 (Summer 1988): 31–47.

National Commission on Excellence in Education. *A Nation at Risk: The Imperative for Educational Reform.* Washington, D.C.: Government Printing Office, 1983.

Nelson, Cary, ed. *Theory in the Classroom.* Chicago: University of Illinois Press, 1986.

Okazawa-Rey, Margo, James Anderson, and Rob Traver, eds. *Teachers, Teaching and Teacher Education.* Cambridge: Harvard Educational Review, 1987.

Olsen, Tilly. *Silences.* New York: Dell, 1979.

Ong, A. "Colonialism and Modernity: Feminist Re-presentations of Women in Non-Western Societies." *Inscriptions* 314 (1988): 79–93.

Owens, Clifford. *Beyond Recognition: Representation, Power and Culture.* S. Bryson, Barbara Kruger, Lynn Tillman, and Jane Weinstock, eds. Berkeley: University of California Press, 1992.

Payne, Charles. *Getting What We Ask For: The Ambiguity of Success and Failure in Urban Education.* Westport, Conn.: Greenwood Press, 1984.

Phelan, Peggy. *Unmarked: the Politics of Performance.* New York: Routledge, 1993.

Pinar, William, William Reynolds, Patrick Slatter and Peter Taubman. *Understanding Curriculum: An Introduction to the Study of Historical and Contemporary Curriculum Discourses.* New York: Peter Lang, 1995.

Pinar, William. "The Voyage Out: Curriculum as the Relation Between the Knower and the Known." *Journal of Curriculum Theorizing* 2 (Winter 1980): 71–92.

Pinar, William, and Madeleine Grumet. *Toward a Poor Curriculum.* Dubuque, Iowa: Kendall/Hunt, 1974.

Popkewitz, Thomas, ed. *The Formation of School Subjects: The Struggle for Creating an American Institution.* New York: Falmer Press, 1987.

Pratt, Mary Louise. *Imperial Eyes: Travel Writing and Transculturation.* New York: Routledge, 1992.

——. "Scratches on the Face of the Country; or, What Mr. Barrow Saw in the Land of the Bushman," in *"Race," Writing and Difference,* Henry Louis Gates, ed., 138–62. Chicago: University of Chicago Press, 1986.

"Race, Racism and American Education: Perspectives of Asian Americans, Blacks, Latinos, and Native Americans." *Harvard Educational Review* 58 (August 1988).

Rich, Adrienne. *On Lies, Secrets, and Silences: Selected Prose 1966–1978*. New York: Norton, 1979.

Roman, Leslie, Linda Christian-Smith, and Elizabeth Ellsworth, eds. *Becoming Feminine: The Politics of Popular Culture*. New York: Falmer Press, 1988.

Rooney, Ellen. *Seductive Reasoning: Pluralism as the Problematic of Contemporary Literary Theory*. Ithaca: Cornell University, 1989.

Rosen, Harold. "The Autobiographical Impulse," in *Linguistics in Context: Connecting Observation with Understanding*, Deborah Tannen, ed., 69–88. Norwood, New Jersey: Ablex Publishing, 1988.

Rousseau, Jean-Jacques. *Emile or On Education*. Trans. Allan Bloom. New York: Basic Books, 1979.

Rugg, Harold. *The Teacher of Teachers: Frontiers of Theory and Practice in Teacher Education*. Westport, Conn.: Greenwood Press, 1970.

Ryan, William. *Blaming the Victim*. New York: Vintage Books, 1971.

Said, Edward. "Opponents, Audiences, Constituencies, and Community," in *The Anti-Aesthetic: Essays on Postmodern Culture*, Hal Foster, ed., 135–59. Port Townsend, Wash.: Bay Press, 1983.

———. *Orientalism*. New York: Vantage, 1978.

Sarason, Seymour, K. Davidson, and B. Blatt. *The Preparation of Teachers*. New York: John Wiley, 1962.

Sarup, Madan. *The Politics of Multiracial Education*. Boston: Routledge and Kegan Paul, 1986.

Savage, Mary. "Can Ethnographic Narrative Be A Neighborly Act?" *Anthropology and Education Quarterly* 19 (1988): 3–19.

Schneider, Barbara. "Tracing the Provenance of Teacher Education," in *Critical Studies in Teacher Education*, Thomas Popkewitz, ed., 211–41. New York: Falmer Press, 1987.

Seager, Joni, and Ann Olsen. *Women in the World: An International Atlas*. New York: Simon and Schuster, 1986.

Searle, Chris. *Words Unchained: Language and Revolution in Grenada*. London: Zed Books, 1984.

Segal, Avner. *Disturbing Practice: Reading Teacher Education as Text*. New York: Peter Lang, 2002.

Sennet, Richard, and Jonathan Cobb. *The Hidden Injuries of Class*. New York: Vintage Books, 1972.

Shapiro, H. Svi. "Capitalism at Risk: The Political Economy of the Educational Reports of 1983." *Educational Theory* 35 (Winter 1985): 57–85.

Shaughnessy, Mina. "Diving In: An Introduction to Writing," in *Reclaiming the Classroom: Teacher Research as an Agency for Change*, Dixie Goswami and Peter Stillman, eds. Montclair, New Jersey: Boynton/Cook Publishers, 1987.

Shor, Ira. *Cultural Wars: School and Society in the Conservative Restoration, 1969–1984*. Boston: Routledge and Kegan Paul, 1986.

Simon, Roger. "Work Experience," in *Critical Pedagogy and Cultural Power*, David A. Livingstone, ed., 155–78. S. Hadley, Mass.: Bergin and Garvey, 1987.

Simon, Roger, and Donald Dippo. "On Critical Ethnographic Work." *Anthropology and Education Quarterly* 17 (1986): 195–202.

Smith, Barbara Herrnstein. *Contingencies of Value: Alternative Perspectives of Critical Theory*. Cambridge: Harvard University Press, 1988.

———. "Contingincies of Value." *Critical Inquiry* 10 (1983): 1–35.

Smith, Paul. *Discerning the Subject*. Minneapolis: University of Minnesota Press, 1988.

Smith, Richard, and Anna Zantiotis. "Practical Teacher Education and the Avant-Garde," in *Critical Pedagogy, the State, and Cultural Struggle*, Henry Giroux and Peter McLaren, eds. Albany: State University of New York Press, 1989.

Steedman, Carolyn. *The Tidy House: Little Girls' Writing*. London: Virago Press, 1982.

Tabachnick, Robert. "Intern-Teacher Roles: Illusion, Disillusion and Reality." *Journal of Education* 162 (1980): 122–37.

Task Force on Education for Economic Growth. *Action for Excellence: A Comprehensive Plan to Improve Our Nation's Schools*. Denver: Education Committee of the States, 1983.

Todorov, Tzetan. *Mikhail Bakhtin: The Dialogical Principle*. Minneappolis: University of Minnesota Press, 1984.

Tolstoy, Leo. *Anna Karenina*. Trans. Richard Pevear and Larissa Volokhonsky. New York: Viking, 2001.

Treichler, Paula. "AIDS, Homophobia, and Biomedical Discourse: An Epidemic of Signification," in *AIDS: Cultural Analysis, Cultural Activism*, ed. Douglas Crimp, 31–71. Boston: MIT Press, 1988.

Trinh, T.Minh-Ha. *Woman, Native, Other: Writing Postcoloniality and Feminism*. Bloomington: Indiana University Press, 1989.

Turkle, Sherry. *Psychoanalytic Politics: Freud's French Revolution*. New York: Basic Books, 1978.

Twentieth-Century Fund Task Force on Federal Elementary and Secondary School Policy. *Making the Grade*. New York: Twentieth-Century Fund, 1983.

Volosinov, V. N. *Marxism and the Philosophy of Language*. Cambridge: Harvard University Press, 1986.

Waller, Willard. *The Sociology of Teaching*. New York: Russell and Russell, 1961.

Walsh, Catherine. *Pedagogy and the Struggle for Voice: Issues of Language, Power and Schooling for Puerto Ricans*. Westport, Conn.: Greenwood Press, 1991.

Weedon, Chris. *Feminist Practice and Poststructuralist Theory.* New York: Basil Blackwell, 1987.

Weiler, Kathleen. *Women Teaching for Change: Gender, Class and Power.* S. Hadley, Mass.: Bergin and Garvey, 1988.

Weinberg, Meyer. *The Search for Quality Integrated Education: Policy and Research on Minority Students in Schools and Colleges.* Westport, Conn.: Greenwood Press, 1983.

Wexler, Philip. "Structure, Text and Subject: A Critical Sociology of School Knowledge," in *Cultural and Economic Reproduction in Education: Essays on Class, Ideology and the State,* Michael Apple, ed. Boston: Routledge and Kegan Paul, 1982.

Whitty, Geoff. *Sociology and School Knowledge: Curriculum Theory, Research and Politics.* London: Methuen, 1985.

Williams, Raymond. *The Long Revolution: An Analysis of the Democratic, Industrial, and Cultural Changes Transforming Our Society.* New York: Columbia University Press, 1961.

Willinsky, John. *Learning to Divide the World: Education at Empire's End.* Minneapolis: University of Minnesota Press, 1998.

———. "Getting Personal and Practical with Personal Practical Knowledge." *Curriculum Inquiry* 19:3 (1989): 247–64.

Willis, Paul. *Learning to Labour: How Working Class Kids Get Working Class Jobs.* Westmead, England: Saxon House, 1977.

Wolfe, M. *A Thrice-Told Tale: Feminism, Postmoderism, and Ethnographic Responsibility.* Stanford: Stanford University Press, 1992.

Woods, Peter. "Life Histories and Teacher Knowledge," in *Educating Teachers: Changing the Nature of Pedagogical Knowledge,* John Smyth, ed. London: Falmer Press, 1987.

———. "Conversation with Teachers: Some Aspects of Life History Method." *British Educational Research Journal* 11 (1985): 13–26.

Yon, Daniel. *Elusive Culture: Schooling, Race, and Identity in Global Times.* Albany: State University of New York Press, 2000.

Index

Printed in the United States
42052LVS00005B/100-204